FOUNDATIONS OF MODERN ANTHROPOLOGY SERIES

Marshall D. Sahlins, *Editor*

FOUNDATIONS OF MODERN ANTHROPOLOGY SERIES

P R E N T I C E - H A L L , I N C . , *Englewood Cliffs, New Jersey*

David Kaplan

Robert A. Manners, Brandeis University

Culture Theory

Library of Congress Cataloging in Publication Data

KAPLAN, DAVID.
  Culture theory.

  (Foundations of modern anthropology series)
  Includes bibliographical references.
  1. Ethnology. I. Manners, Robert Alan, 1913–
joint author. II. Title.
GN315.K3   301.2'01   72–90
ISBN 0–13–195529–2
ISBN 0–13–195511–X (pbk.)

To our teachers, Julian H. Steward and Leslie A. White,
who were the first to impress upon us the possibilities
of a theoretical anthropology.

PRENTICE-HALL
FOUNDATIONS OF MODERN ANTHROPOLOGY SERIES

Marshall D. Sahlins, *Editor*

10   9   8   7   6   5   4   3   2   1

PRENTICE-HALL INTERNATIONAL, INC., *London*
PRENTICE-HALL OF AUSTRALIA, PTY., LTD., *Sydney*
PRENTICE-HALL OF CANADA, LTD., *Toronto*
PRENTICE-HALL OF INDIA PRIVATE LIMITED, *New Delhi*
PRENTICE-HALL OF JAPAN, INC., *Tokyo*

Acknowledgments

The authors wish to thank the following publishers and individuals for permission to reprint copyrighted materials in this book:

BLAKE, JUDITH AND KINGSLEY DAVIS, "Norms, Values, and Sanctions," in Robert E. L. Faris (ed.), *Handbook of Modern Sociology*, © 1964 by Rand McNally & Company, Chicago, pp. 460–61. Reprinted by permission of the publisher.

BURLING, ROBBINS, "Cognition and Componential Analysis: God's Truth or Hocus-Pocus?" *American Anthropologist*, 66 (1964), pp. 25–26. Reprinted by permission of the author and the publisher.

FRANKEL, CHARLES, "Philosophy and the Social Sciences," in Charles E. Boewe and Roy F. Nichols (eds.), *Both Human and Humane: The Humanities and Social Sciences in Graduate Education* (Philadelphia: University of Pennsylvania Press, 1960), pp. 95–96. Reprinted by permission of the publisher.

HARSANYI, JOHN C., "Explanation and Comparative Dynamics in Social Science," in Robert A. Manners and David Kaplan (eds.), *Theory in Anthropology* (Chicago: Aldine-Atherton, Inc., 1968), p. 96. Reprinted by permission of the publisher.

LÉVI-STRAUSS, CLAUDE, *The Savage Mind* (Chicago: The University of Chicago Press, 1962), pp. 118–19. Reprinted by permission of the publisher.

LÉVI-STRAUSS, CLAUDE, *Structural Anthropology*, trans. Claire Jacobson and Brooke Grundfest Schoepf (New York: Basic Books, Inc., 1963), pp. 50–51. Reprinted by permission of the publisher.

MEEHAN, EUGENE J., *Contemporary Political Thought: A Critical Survey* (Homewood, Ill.: The Dorsey Press, 1967), pp. 164–65. Reprinted by permission of the publisher.

MERTON, ROBERT K., "The Bearing of Sociological Theory on Empirical Research," in *On Theoretical Sociology* (New York: The Free Press, 1967), pp. 141–42. Reprinted by permission of the publisher.

NISBET, ROBERT A., "The Irreducibility of Social Change: A Comment on Professor Stebbins' Paper," *Pacific Sociological Review*, 8, No. 1 (Spring 1965), 12–15. Reprinted by permission of the publisher, Sage Publications, Inc.

PITT-RIVERS, JULIAN, "Contextual Analysis and the Locus of the Model," *Archives Européennes De Sociologie (European Journal of Sociology)*, 8 (1967), 30–32. Reprinted by permission of the author and the publisher.

SAHLINS, MARSHALL D., "The Segmentary Lineage: An Organization of Predatory Expansion," in *The Evolution of Life*, Vol. 1 (Chicago: The University of Chicago Press, 1960), p. 554. Reprinted by permission of the publisher.

STOCKING, GEORGE W. JR., "Franz Boas and the Culture Concept in Historical Perspective," in *Race, Culture and Evolution: Essays in the History of Anthropology* (New York: The Free Press, 1968), p. 210. Reprinted by permission of the publisher.

TYLER, STEPHEN, "Introduction," in S. A. Tyler (ed.), *Cognitive Anthropology* (New York: Holt, Rinehart & Winston, Inc., 1969), p. 3. Reprinted by permission of the publisher.

WOLF, ERIC R., "Closed Corporate Peasant Communities in Mesoamerica and Central Java," *Southwestern Journal of Anthropology*, 13 (1957), 8–9, 12. Reprinted by permission of the author and the publisher.

Foundations
of Modern Anthropology
Series

The Foundations of Modern Anthropology Series is a documentation of the human condition, past and present. It is concerned mainly with exotic peoples, prehistoric times, unwritten languages, and unlikely customs. But this is merely the anthropologist's way of expressing his concern for the here and now, and his way makes a unique contribution to our knowledge of what's going on in the world. We cannot understand ourselves apart from an understanding of *man*, nor our culture apart from an understanding of *culture*. Inevitably we are impelled toward an intellectual encounter with man in all his varieties, no matter how primitive, how ancient, or how seemingly insignificant. Ever since their discovery by an expanding European civilization, primitive peoples have continued to hover over thoughtful men like ancestral ghosts, ever provoking this anthropological curiosity. To "return to the primitive" just for what it is would be foolish; the savage is not nature's nobleman and his existence is no halcyon idyll. For anthropology, the romance of the primitive has been something else: a search for the roots and meaning of ourselves—in the context of all mankind.

The series, then, is designed to display the varieties of man and culture and the evolution of man and culture. All fields of anthropology are relevant to the grand design and all of them—prehistoric archaeology, physical anthropology, linguistics, and ethnology (cultural anthropology)—are represented among the authors of the several books in the series. In the area of physical anthropology are books describing the early condition of humanity and the subhuman primate antecedents. The later development of man on the biological side is set out in the volume on races, while the archaeological accounts of the Old World and the New document development on the historical side. Then there are the studies of contemporary culture, including a book on how to understand it all—i.e., on ethnological theory—and one on language, the peculiar human gift responsible for it all. Main types of culture are laid out in "The Hunters," "Tribesmen," "Formation of the State," and "Peasants." Initiating a dialogue between contemplation of the primitive and the present, the volume on "The Present as Anthropology" keeps faith with the promise of anthropological study stated long ago by E. B. Tylor, who saw in it "the means of understanding our own lives and our place in the world, vaguely and imperfectly it is true, but at any rate more clearly than any former generation."

Preface

Like Alfred Kroeber, and others before and since, we have felt obliged in this book at least to raise the issue whether anthropology should be considered a branch of the humanities, a kind of natural history, or a science. Well, if anthropology is what anthropologists do, then it is clearly all of these. But since we were writing a book about *theory*, we, of course, focused on one of these components or emphases and have treated the discipline as a science, a struggling science to be sure, but a science nonetheless.

Theory is a term that appears with great frequency in the anthropological literature. Yet, as anyone who has made the effort knows, it is difficult to get a clear notion of what various anthropologists mean when they use the term. We believe it would be impossible at present to reach a consensus among anthropologists about what is and what is not theory; indeed, few even see consensus as an important issue. But obviously one could hardly write a book on theory without making an effort to define the central subject matter of the work. In the following pages, therefore, we have tried to indicate what we think distinguishes theory from nontheory. We make no claims for originality, nor do we maintain that what we have offered is the only way to think about or to define theory. However, it does seem to us that what we have presented is at least a *useful* way of thinking about theory. If the reader finds our treatment of the matter unacceptable, we hope at least that he will be stimulated by our discussion to try to improve upon it.

In an effort to clarify some of the difficulties of the subject we thought it would be helpful also to make a distinction between what we call *theoretical orientations* and *theory*, properly so-called. We did so because we hoped that such a distinction would help to illuminate some of the problems encountered by anthropologists when they engage in that mysterious process called theorizing, and because we felt strongly that there are some important differences between the framing or application of methodologies and the creation of theories.

Surveying and bringing together the kinds of things anthropologists have called theory yielded a very varied product. Thus, for example, there is considerable material about what we may call *conceptual* matters, about the definition and use of critical terms (e.g., what is caste? what ought we to mean by patrilineal?). Then there is a large body of *generalizations* and these vary in the degree of their abstractness and in their scope.

Throughout the writing of this book we have tried to steer a middle course. On the one hand, while we have dealt with conceptual matters, we have tried to provide enough concrete examples to insure that the book would not consist entirely of abstractions and disembodied concepts. And, on the other hand, we have discussed some of the examples and generalizations employed by anthropologists without making the book a simple catalogue of empirical generalizations. In short, we have attempted a critical survey of what seems to us to be the present range of theoretical interests in anthropology. We have not tried to frame or advance new theories of our own. This does not mean, as will be apparent, that we have been timid about taking a stand on issues when it seemed to us that such a stand was warranted.

In the course of writing this book, we were impressed repeatedly by the relative lack in anthropology, as compared with some of the more developed scientific disciplines, of an accepted or common theoretical language or corpus of theoretical terms that would enable anthropologists to communicate with each other about empirical matters without becoming continually bogged down at the definitional level.

We were struck, also by the lack of consensus about clear standards for deciding when a proposition has evidential support and when it does not. Until and unless we achieve greater consensus on such matters than we now have, anthropology will continue to be what some critics have called it, a quasi-science. Yet one thing remains quite clear. And that is that anthropologists cannot even describe and analyze cultural phenomena without employing theory and some degree of generalization, however tentative these may be.

Many people aided in the preparation of this book. We wish especially to acknowledge the help of the general editor of this series, Marshall Sahlins, who read an earlier draft of the manuscript and made a number of very valuable suggestions. To Ann Levine of Prentice-Hall we are most grateful for her patience and perceptive editorial assistance. And, finally, for typing the manuscript in its several versions we owe a special debt to Carol Kaplan and Doris Rabinowitz.

Contents

One Anthropology:
Methods and Issues
in Theory Formation

The Scope
of Anthropology

Anyone who has thumbed, even casually, through an introductory text on anthropology can hardly have failed to notice the discipline's enormous scope. Whatever else anthropology may be, it is surely the most presumptuous of all the social sciences. For not only does it take man's cultures at all times and places as its legitimate province, but it ranges topically over kinship and social organization, politics, technology, economics, religion, language, art, and mythology—to mention only a few of those concerns of anthropology that come quickly to mind. What is more, it is the only one of the social sciences that attempts to speak to both sides of man's nature—i.e., to his biological (physical anthropology) as well as his cultural side (cultural anthropology).

Given the great diversity of interest and the seeming amorphousness of subject matter that characterizes anthropology, is there nevertheless something that gives the discipline a kind of unity? What, in short, do anthropologists of all persuasions (e.g., those who take a more humanistic or natural

1

history approach as well as those who take a more abstract, generalizing, or scientific approach) have in common other than the fact that they belong to the same department in a university? The answer, we believe, is that since the emergence of anthropology as a systematic field of inquiry in the late nineteenth century, the issues that anthropologists have been concerned with can be subsumed under two broad and interrelated questions: (1) How do different cultural systems work? and (2) How have these cultural systems, in their considerable variety, come to be as they are? Note that these questions are addressed to the *differences*—in space as well as over time—among cultures. If all cultures were identical, there would probably be no need for the discipline of anthropology. Human biology viewed broadly would be the discipline through which we would seek explanations of human behavior. This is not to say, however, that anthropologists have not been concerned with the *similarities* among cultures. They have, but cultural similarities arise as issues to be explored when they are seen against the contrasting background of other human, or in some cases infrahuman, differences.

If, as all anthropologists assume, it is true that the various populations of the world belong to a single species, *Homo sapiens,* and if it is also true— following this—that the psychobiological nature of each of these populations is roughly the same, we should expect to find that all human societies would look pretty much alike or, at least, that they would exhibit certain broad similarities. And indeed in certain respects they do. To put it somewhat more concretely: if it is the case—and nobody has been able to demonstrate the contrary—that the psychobiological makeup of, let us say, the Trobriand Islanders and the Europeans is not significantly different, then it would be logical to assume that since both "groups" have occupied the planet as *Homo sapiens* for the same length of time, their cultures or lifeways should be much more alike in structure and content than they are. However, having noted the *differences* between the Trobrianders and the Europeans, we generally tend to be more impressed by these than by the apparent similarities evidenced by their cultures. Not only are we impressed, but we are likely to ask why the differences exist. If the psychobiological infrastructure is indeed a constant, it is obvious that we cannot look to it to provide us with an answer to our question. For while psychobiology may account for many of the broad cultural resemblances that we observe, it cannot at the same time explain the differences.

In addition to the cultural similarities that may be attributed to the psychobiological "unity" of man, there are other similarities which cannot be explained by this unity. We refer to those resemblances in cultural form and pattern that arise from convergent processes of growth, change, or development—for example, the similarities, despite certain persisting dissimilarities in culture content, between industrial Japan and industrial Germany. They interest us in this connection because we know that the sociocultural systems of these two countries differed profoundly in the era immediately preceding the launching of their respective industrial revolutions. Thus, parallel processes of industrialization clearly led to increasing similarities in ideology and social structure. And, although it may be more difficult to demonstrate, it seems fairly clear that the personality type implied by the term *industrial man* signifies some convergence of "social personality" as well.

Throughout this entire period of intense change, the psychobiological features of these two populations, so far as one can tell, remained constant.

Anthropology's central problems, then, are the explanation of cultural similarities and differences, of cultural maintenance as well as cultural change over time. As change may be seen only against the background of cultural stability or maintenance, so stability may be understood only against a background of change. If cultures did not differ from each other, and if they did not change, questions about the mechanisms of change or stability would never arise. But we observe that cultures do differ from each other and—at varying rates—do change over time. We cannot fall back on intraspecific variation to account for the cultural differences found so often among populations in the past as well as in the present.

Only in examining those mechanisms, structures, and devices lying outside of man—the means by which he achieves his own transformation—can we learn why some groups differ in their beliefs, values, behavior, and social forms from others. And in this search the view of "differences over time" provides the best evidence for a sociocultural, as opposed to psychobiological, explanation of man's dissimilarities.

Those collective mechanisms, structures, and devices lying outside of man (*outside* in an analytic rather than in some metaphysical sense) are what anthropologists have called culture. To most anthropologists—at least in the United States—culture has been the discipline's core concept. Yet if one consults the exhaustive review of the concept conducted by Kroeber and Kluckhohn some years ago,[1] one will find well over one hundred different definitions of *culture*. However, the situation is not nearly so depressing as this bewildering array of definitions might suggest. Anthropologists involved in empirical research have no trouble locating their subject matter, and they do, most of the time, manage to communicate with each other. We are not going to attempt another definition of *culture* here. Let us just say that *culture* is a class of phenomena conceptualized by anthropologists in order to deal with questions they are trying to answer. In other words, anthropologists are concerned not simply with human behavior, but rather with *traditional* or *institutionalized* human behavior. The nineteenth-century anthropologists felt a need for some such concept as culture because they had to have some way of "explaining" variations in patterns of behavior and societal institutions that could not be explained biologically. Or, to put it another way, *culture* refers to those phenomena which account for patterns of behaving that cannot be *fully* explained by psychobiological concepts.

Culture is admittedly an omnibus term. Many investigators have suggested that it is too omnibus to be useful as an analytic tool. If it is to be used at all, they would urge us to confine the concept to content, or the symbolic dimensions of society, and to concentrate our attention on some other more "viable" and "analytically useful" concept like social structure or social system.

In most instances we can probably evade the issue by referring to the

---

[1] A. L. Kroeber and C. Kluckhohn, "Culture: A Critical Review of Concepts and Definitions," Harvard University *Papers of the Peabody Museum of American Archaeology and Ethnology* (1952), vol. 47.

phenomena we study as "sociocultural" and let it go at that. But we believe there are several good reasons for anthropologists to retain the concept of culture and to keep it analytically distinct from social structure. First of all, social organization is not unique to man; other, infrahuman animals do have social systems. But there is a profound difference between human social systems and infrahuman ones. For infrahuman social systems are biosocial— that is, they reflect to a very large degree the biological nature of the species. Human social systems, on the other hand, are highly variable and thus seem clearly to reflect the impact of a great variety of "inherited traditions"; they are, in short, truly *sociocultural* systems.

Secondly, anthropologists have been concerned with the interaction between subsystems or institutions such as the social structural, ideological, and technoeconomic. Indeed, theories in anthropology are generally concerned with the causal weighting of these various subsystems. We need to give some name to the larger system of which these various institutional orders or subsystems are a part. *Culture* seems to be as good as any.

Marshall Sahlins makes this point:

> The "concrete reality" after all includes as coordinate and influential elements such things as tools, techniques, tenure arrangements and the like. They are *in* the system. They enter into functional relations with social structure; in these relations, they, and not social elements alone, may be forces of constraint. It is a system of things, social relations, and ideas, a complex mechanism by which people exist and persist. It is organized not merely to order relations, but to sustain human existence. An understanding of the design of such mechanisms, then, would probably have to consider still wider nets of relation, would consider the influential context, natural and superorganic, in which societies are enclaved. Our vision is magnified several powers. Most important, it is extended to that complex mechanism—including the set of social relations—the name of which in American anthropology is "culture." [2]

Anthropologists have reacted to the diversity of cultural arrangements in two ways. On the one hand, they have taken these differences as *simply there*, as phenomena to be charted, as variations on the grand theme of cultural relativism. In this view, they note that all peoples of the world, both past and present, have had to wrestle with many of the same problems (making a living, providing shelter, maintaining social order, dealing with the unknown), for which they have evolved different solutions. One solution is not necessarily better or worse than another, just different. Out of this anthropological perspective has come a rich and varied literature depicting the lifeways of a great number of peoples of the world. In addition to its inherent interest, this literature has orchestrated the great lesson of anthropology: Man is one, cultures vary. Every social scientist who has sought to generalize about "man's nature" has had to confront the vast range of human adaptations as these are revealed in the "literature of cultural differences."

---

[2] Marshall Sahlins, "Remarks on Social Structure in Southeast Asia," *Journal of the Polynesian Society* 72 (1963): 49.

There is, however, another way in which anthropologists have reacted to the evidence of cultural variation. Rather than taking these varied forms as phenomena simply to be recorded, they have asked how the differences can be explained. They have, in other words, asked for theories. Paradoxically, however, much of the literature emphasizing cultural distinctions has often acted as a deterrent to the formation of more general propositions. Part natural history, part literary and humanistic in character, the literature has so emphasized the concrete and unique features of each cultural system that it has served often to intimidate those anthropologists—and other social scientists—who have tried to move toward more abstract theoretical formulations of such cultural differences.

Relativism
vs Comparison

Anthropology's theoretical-methodological stance has been both relativistic and comparative. Since the two positions appear to be diametrically opposed, it might seem that trying to straddle them could only result in a kind of methodological schizophrenia (and, in truth, anthropology does sometimes seem to present a split personality in this regard). We believe, however, that as one looks more closely at the relativist-comparativist issue in anthropology, one sees that relativism implies comparison. This may require some explanation.

To begin with, it is useful to distinguish what might be called the ideological thesis of relativism from the methodological. Although these may be closely and perhaps even inseparably linked in the minds of anthropologists, they can be distinguished analytically.

Relativism as an ideological thesis states that each culture is a unique configuration with its own special flavor, its own style and genius. More often than not this "uniqueness" is expressed as an article of faith, and little attempt is made to account for or explain it. Now, it is certainly true that in some sense each culture is unique—just as each individual, each blade of grass, and each atom in the universe is unique. But how can one ever know this unless one has first compared a given culture with other cultures? What is more, there are degrees of distinctiveness. If a phenomenon were *wholly* unique, we could not possibly comprehend it. We are able to understand any phenomenon only because it bears *some* similarities to things we already know.

The relativist tells us that a culture must be examined as a totality and only in terms of itself; while the comparativist says that an institution, process, complex, or item must be removed from its larger cultural matrix *so that* it can be compared with institutions, processes, complexes, or items in other sociocultural contexts. The extreme relativist begins with the assumption that no two cultures are alike; that pattern, order, and meaning are violated if elements are abstracted for purposes of comparison; and, therefore, that comparison of parts abstracted from wholes is analytically indefensible. The cultural circle is self-contained. And the entire theoretical-methodological stance of the relativists may thus, from their point of view, be justified because, in *fact*, no two sociocultural wholes *are* alike. Hence the functionally related features of each cannot be compared with features embedded in other sociocultural wholes.

But since the very apprehension of unlikeness has resulted from comparison, it cannot be said that the relativistic and comparative approaches are incompatible. Where the two positions *do* part company is on the issue of inviolability. And this is largely an ideological issue, a matter of interest and emphasis, which in its turn gives rise to different methodological approaches. The comparativist knows just as well as the relativist that no two cultures are exactly alike. But he departs from the committed and the practicing relativist in at least two important respects: (1) while he accepts, at least in general, the dictum that all parts of a culture are somehow functionally interrelated (see pp. 55–67), he adds the Orwellian modifier that some parts are more interrelated than others; and (2) he believes that comparison following abstraction is not only nonrapacious but is methodologically legitimate, heuristically suggestive, and scientifically fruitful. The comparativist, having accepted more seriously than the relativist the premise of the psychic unity of mankind, is therefore more prepared also to accept the similarities revealed by observation and comparative empirical research. The relativist is concerned overwhelmingly with the differences. The comparativist is interested in the similarities as well as the differences. For the relativist each culture is demonstrably unique. For the comparativist each culture's demonstrable uniqueness as a whole may be overshadowed by the demonstrable similarity of many of its parts to those of other cultures. The narrow relativist tends to be esthetically offended by comparison, for comparison must inevitably play down or blur some of the distinctions that give each culture its pure flavor. The comparativist, on the other hand, tends to be "scientifically" offended at the relativist's insistence on the differences. For while he knows that no two objects or events in nature are exactly alike, taxonomies, typologies, and processes are defined and ordered through selection and abstraction, by a process in which the relevant is separated from the less relevant and the irrelevant.

To investigate anything in this universe requires to some extent that it be "removed" from its context. The real problem confronting the social scientist (or any scientist, for that matter) is to know how much of the phenomenon's context one must take with it when one isolates it conceptually for purposes of analysis or study.

Clearly, relativism is a useful reminder that in studying cultures other than our own we must try not to be swayed by our cultural preconceptions. Looked at in this way, relativism is a methodological precept, not an ideological position. If there are differences among anthropologists with regard to the ideological version of relativity, all anthropologists accept the methodological version. But, like Einstein (who actually was an antirelativist), we must take a relativist stand only to enable us to surmount it. To hold consistently and implacably to a relativist stance would undermine the whole anthropological enterprise. It would automatically destroy the cross-cultural relevance of all accumulated anthropological knowledge. That is, all such knowledge—including the doctrine of cultural relativism itself—would be relative to the culture in which it originated or developed. And we would thus end up with an

Eskimo anthropology, a Trobriand anthropology, a Nuer anthropology, and so on—with a series of cultural configurations, each of which is defined as unique and therefore not comparable.

Anthropology must surmount the excesses of relativism precisely because such excesses make comparison and, hence, scientific inquiry, difficult if not impossible. As Durkheim put it: "Comparative sociology is not a particular branch of sociology; it is sociology itself, insofar as it ceases to be purely descriptive and aspires to account for facts." [3]

Since comparison obtains in either explicit or implied form at all levels of anthropological inquiry, we are not here suggesting a revolutionary method-ological overhaul of the discipline. Moreover, since the trend in recent years has been in the direction of more self-conscious and systematic comparison and less pure relativistic research and writing, we are only attempting now to applaud and to encourage that tendency. For without comparison made ex-plicit there can be no theory in anthropology. Thus, the comparative method is essential to theory formation in at least a few ways. Even the single ethnographic monograph involves comparison, since the ethnographer can hardly help comparing the culture he is studying with those of a similar type that he has either read about or experienced. To describe *any* society one must use categories, terms, and concepts which transcend the individual case.

Not only does comparison provide a means of suggesting more general statements about cultural phenomena, but, more importantly, in the absence of the opportunity to experiment it is the only means we have of testing such general propositions. The logic of the comparative method is not difficult to comprehend. If we hypothesize that conditions A, B, C, and D are necessary before phenomenon E can occur, our object is to find phenomenon E in some other cultural setting and to see whether the necessary conditions A, B, C, and D are indeed essential to its occurrence. Thus, only through com-parison are we enabled to sift out the general from the particular or to posit "reasonable" cause-and-effect relationships.

One of the problems one runs into in comparing anything with anything else is that of making certain that the phenomena being compared are close enough in form, structure, or process to warrant the comparison. As Edmund Leach points out, this is "the heart of the whole matter." Along with a num-ber of other anthropologists, Leach continues to express some skepticism about the validity of cross-cultural comparisons and generalizations. He argues that cultural phenomena, unlike those of the natural sciences, are not amenable to precise taxonomic discrimination and description. "Natural law regularities are summaries of events which actually occur; customs are mere mental configurations." He goes on to say:

> The units of ordinary anthropological description—expressions like "patrilineal descent," "uxorilocal residence," "matrilateral cross-cousin marriage," "ancestor worship," "bride price," "shifting cultivation," etc. —which are still used as the discriminating traits in even the most sophisticated forms of cross-cultural analysis—are not in any way com-

---

[3] Emile Durkheim, *The Rules of Sociological Method* (New York: The Free Press, 1964), p. 139.

parable to the precisely defined diagnostic elements which form the units of discourse in natural science. . . . Those who claim to formulate "scientific" generalizations on the basis of cross-cultural comparison are asserting that they can recognize by inspection that a characteristic *x* found in culture A belongs or does not belong to the same subclass of social facts as a characteristic *y* found in culture B. The following is a case in point. The inhabitants of the tiny Polynesian island of Tikopia recognize that their social system is composed of social groups called *paito*; the Nuer of the Sudan recognize groups called *thok dwiel*; the Kachin of northern Burma recognize groups called *amyu*; the Chinese recognize groups *tsung-tsu*; and so on. In the jargon of contemporary social anthropology all these entities are to be classed as patrilineal descent groups; they are examples of "the same thing." Such propositions clearly leave room for plenty of skepticism. To assert of even one particular that the Tikopia and the Chinese have "the same kind of social structure" must invite caution. What could such a proposition really mean?[4]

What Leach's argument fails to recognize, or at least fails to mention, is that when we classify two or more cultural phenomena as being of the "same kind" we are making what is essentially a theoretical judgment. That is, we focus on what we consider to be the critical features of the phenomena involved; and then we decide whether these features are enough alike for the phenomena to be called the "same kind." Thus the patrilineal descent groups of the Tikopia and the Chinese may be said to be *either* the same "kind" of social unit or not. The judgment depends both upon one's purposes in making such a comparison and what one identifies as the crucial features. Comparison is not, as Leach indicates, a matter of simple inspection but one of *selection* guided by theoretical presuppositions. In any event, whatever the difficulties in arriving at these theoretical judgments may be, the anthropologist cannot avoid making cross-cultural comparisons, whether he does so consciously or otherwise. And despite his skepticism about arriving at "scientific" generalizations through comparison, Leach concedes the pervasiveness of the method ("in practice . . . all anthropologists have resorted to cross-cultural comparison") as well as its fruitfulness ("such comparison . . . gives insight" and may also "generate ideas").

Structural Types and Comparison

It is in making decisions about the comparability or noncomparability of cultural phenomena that the notion of structural types, for example, is of particular importance. By a *structural type* we mean a classification of the phenomenon under consideration in terms of its critical features as we define these features. Here we must pause to make two important points about structural types: first, such a construct, as we have just stressed, implies a kind of theory, since in the very act of selecting those features of a phe-

---

[4] Edmund Leach, "The Comparative Method in Anthropology," *International Encyclopedia of the Social Sciences* (New York: The Free Press, 1968), 1, 340–41. See also E. E. Evans-Pritchard, *The Comparative Method in Social Anthropology*, L. T. Hobhouse Memorial Trust Lecture no. 33. (London: The Athlone Press, 1963).

nomenon which one labels critical, one moves toward construction of a theory; and secondly, since there are no absolute classifications of phenomena, structural types will vary with the problems being posed. It should also be noted that like the character in the Molière play who discovered, much to his amazement, that he had been speaking prose all his life, anthropologists always think in terms of "structural types" whether they know it or not. Every time we use such phrases as "industrial society," "band society," "oriental state," "segmentary lineage system," "peasant community," "matrifocal family," etc., we are referring to structural types. We are merely suggesting here that we accept the reality and spell out our type constructs for everyone to see.

As we noted previously, much of the comparative work in anthropology has been informal and often implied rather than expressed. When anthropologists have been more self-conscious and systematic about their comparisons, they have generally engaged in two types of studies: small-scale comparisons within a geographical region, and large-scale cross-cultural surveys involving a number of historically unrelated cultures. The twin advantages of small-scale studies, over large-scale cross-cultural ones are that in the first place they lend themselves more readily to traditional field research techniques, and in the second place, technologically simple societies within a given geographic region are more likely to be similiar in their structural type. By the same token, however, cultures in a single region are more likely to be historically related and therefore to present us with the problem of deciding whether we are dealing with a single, fragmented case or with several cases that have arisen independently. Of course, if one is interested in exploring the differences among a set of historically related cases, this kind of small-scale regional analysis would be entirely appropriate.

Large-scale studies, on the other hand, enable one to include a greater number of independent cases. But the major weakness of some of these studies has been their failure to clearly delineate types so that comparisons can be made within these types as well as between these and other types.

Both kinds of comparativists—those who focus on small scales comparison within a region and those who are concerned with larger-scale cross-cultural surveys—have emphasized the importance of utilizing structural types for purposes of comparison. Isaac Schapera, for example, who has been interested in the "intensive study of a given region," argues for the utility of typologies as follows:

> By carefully comparing the forms taken among those peoples by the particular social phenomena with which we are concerned—as, in this instance, kinship and marriage—we try to establish, by a process of generalization, one or more basic types into which the various forms can be classified. . . . Then, by establishing "types" or "species" of kinship system, government, age organization, or whatever else may be our topic, we shall obtain units of the kind that could be used in wider comparative studies of a continental or even universal scope: instead of comparing individual "societies," we could compare larger groups each characterized by a uniform type of kinship, etc. The units would be not only far fewer than the total number of "societies," and therefore easier to handle, but

would also be constant in character, and therefore strictly comparable. This should meet the difficulty of defining "unit entities" for purposes of comparison.[5]

Yehudi Cohen, whose research has dealt with large-scale comparisons, has also emphasized the methodological and heuristic importance of structural types. Working with a developmental typology borrowed from Steward's concept of "levels of sociocultural integration," Cohen suggests that cross-cultural comparisons will be fruitful only when they issue from a taxonomy which has in turn been informed by a theoretical position:

> If the notion of levels of sociocultural integration in any way reflects cultural reality, and I do not think that there can be much question about this, we are forced to question and re-evaluate some of the fundamental tenets of large-scale comparisons in anthropology. Can we select a given variable and compare 60 or 120 societies randomly with respect to it, disregarding the different levels of development achieved by them? Can we compare modes of impulse control, for example, among a randomly selected sample of societies and disregard the fact that cultures at different stages of development require different controls as aspects of their adaptations? Can we, to cite one more instance, compare political organization among the Shoshoneans of western Nevada, the Tikopia of Polynesia, and the ancient Mesopotamians?

> Or must we, instead, adopt the following two-fold procedure? First, establish a taxonomic scheme based on levels of sociocultural integration. This, of course, must include a statement explaining why the particular taxonomy has been established. Different problems require different classificatory schemes. . . . Once this taxonomy has been established, a comparison of societies within each level of integration is undertaken. . . .

> The second step in this two-fold procedure is a comparison of the levels of sociocultural integration. An important point to bear in mind in this connection is that not all levels are equally comparable, just as not all societal or cultural units are equally comparable. Instead, what is necessary is to compare stages sequentially, that is, to compare those stages that are closest to each other in developmental terms. Thus, for example, one would not compare people who subsist almost entirely by foraging with those who live in complex states with large-scale irrigation networks.[6]

Thus, while Schapera deals with comparison on a small scale and in a non-developmental framework, and Cohen is concerned with large-scale comparison and development, they agree on the need for the creation of structural types as indispensable prerequisites to meaningful cross-cultural comparison. It is apparent, therefore, that there is no conflict between small- and large-scale researches. Indeed, as Stanislav Andreski points out, they complement each other:

---

[5] I. Schapera, "Some Comments on Comparative Method in Social Anthropology," *American Anthropologist* 55 (1953): 359–60.

[6] Yehudi A. Cohen, "Macroethnology: Large Scale Comparative Studies," in *Introduction to Cultural Anthropology*, ed. James A. Clifton (Boston: Houghton Mifflin, 1968), pp. 443–44.

Some people have questioned the wisdom of having recourse to a wide range of data, instead of concentrating on a more detailed study of two or three cases. The answer to this is simple: in order to ascertain the limits within which a connection between two factors holds, we must vary the other circumstances as widely as possible. Fortunately, however, there need be no "either or" in this matter: various combinations are possible, and here as elsewhere science can proceed by successive approximations. On the basis of an analysis of a fairly narrow range of data, a hypothesis can be formulated which may be later modified in the light of wider (or at least different) evidence; and this process can go on being repeated. Ideally, comparative analyses should be carried out within all accessible ranges of data—narrow as well as wide.[7]

The Problem
of Defining Theory

Survival in any culture demands some knowledge of the way things work in the world around one. In part, this knowledge may be experiential and "nonexplanatory." In part, it is theoretical knowledge—i.e., knowledge that attempts to explain empirical phenomena. Theories, then, are more than merely abbreviated summaries of data, since they not only tell us *what* happens but *why* it happens as it does. Any worthwhile theory should thus perform the double function of explaining facts already known as well as opening up new vistas which can lead us to new *facts*. In an especially apt passage, which follows, Idus Murphree shows us that when the same event is interpreted in different theoretical contexts, it will yield very different kinds of facts. (Murphree is describing pre- and post-Darwinian interpretations of fossil materials and Paleolithic implements.)

> Everything was accountable in one way or another—as a freak of nature, as a result of violent upheaval and flood, as the work of elves, or even as tests to try men's faith. Facts took their place under the accepted premises, and the prevailing beliefs were maintained. In 1690 nobody paid much attention when a crudely shaped tool was uncovered near the skeleton of an "elephant" in London, but there was little reason to. When the same discovery is reported in the vocabulary of modern science, however, a new import emerges: "The first Paleolithic flint implement ever recognized and preserved as a relic of ancient man was a Chellean tool of the cleaver type discovered in Pleistocene gravels at Gray's Inn Lane, London." Expressed in this way the "facts" are radically different.[8]

Since a theory is a kind of generalization, it is appropriate that we begin by discussing briefly the nature of a generalization itself. In its simplest terms, a *generalization* is a proposition that relates two or more classes of phenomena

[7] Stanislav Andreski, *The Uses of Comparative Sociology* (Berkeley: University of California Press, 1965), pp. 66–67.

[8] Idus L. Murphree, "The Evolutionary Anthropologists: The Concepts of Progress and Culture in the Thought of John Lubbock, Edward B. Tylor, and Lewis H. Morgan," *Proceedings of the American Philosophical Society* 105 (1961): 271.

to each other. An important logical property of generalizations is that they make claims which go beyond what has been observed or recorded. Thus, the statement, "All human societies *of which we have any anthropological record* exhibit incest taboos," is a *descriptive statement*, not a generalization. But the statement, "*All* human societies have incest taboos," is a generalization. The crucial difference is that the latter statement refers to *all* human societies: past, present, and future, recorded or not. On the basis of observing a limited number of societies we have made an inductive leap and generalized to all human societies.

Theories are also generalizations, but generalizations of a special kind. And it is useful to distinguish them from *empirical* (or *inductive*) *generalizations*, since they differ from these in several very important respects. Empirical generalizations label regularities of nature, but theories tell us *why* such regularities hold. Empirical generalizations, to be sure, go beyond observation, but their explanatory fertility is limited. They tell us about the same kinds of relationships among the same kinds of phenomena that we have already observed in a restricted number of cases. *Theoretical generalizations*, on the other hand, lead us to new facts and open up new lines of research.[9] Thus, for example, Darwin's theories about natural selection and evolution led to a variety of new researches and new theoretical formulations in the fields of embryology, paleontology, comparative anatomy, etc. Theories suggest explanations not only for the phenomena that invoked them in the first place, but for other phenomena as well. For example, the statement, "All human societies have incest taboos," is an empirical generalization, for, as we noted above, it extends an observed relationship in a sample of cases to all members of the class. Now suppose we wish to go further and ask *why* all human societies have incest taboos. One might frame a functionalist theory that goes something like this: In early human societies incest taboos had enormous adaptive and evolutionary value. (Whether this was the reason for their genesis and initial spread cannot, of course, be demonstrated by a functional argument alone.) In any case, it seems quite likely that the taboos should have minimized conflict within the family by deflecting the competition for sexual partners outside of a critical circle of cooperating kin. And second, by forcing individuals to seek sexual partners outside this circle of kinsmen, the taboo extended the network of cooperation by enlarging the network of kinsmen. Incest taboos persist in all human societies because they continue to perform, at least in part, some of these same crucial functions.[10]

---

[9] A precise definition of theory has so far eluded even those scientists and philosophers of science who are directly concerned with the clarification of such matters. But while there may be some disagreement about what theory *is*, there seems to be considerable agreement about what theories may *do*. In general, if a proposition or a body of propositions explains, predicts, retrodicts or leads us to "new" facts or "new" avenues of research it is likely to be called a theory. In short, theories are defined pragmatically rather than strictly in terms of their formal properties.

[10] Whether this theory holds up under empirical investigation is not our concern here. Also, we have oversimplified somewhat for illustrative purposes. If we were to state the matter more precisely, we would distinguish between incest taboos and what anthropologists call "rules of exogamy." Actually, incest taboos prohibit *sexual relations* within a prescribed circle of kin or quasi kin. Thus, although they are related, the two kinds of cultural regulations are not precisely congruent.

As we have expressed the above theory, it refers only to the universality of incest taboos and may, therefore, be considered somewhat restricted in its scope. But we can expand this theory by making it more abstract, by suggesting other practices and institutional arrangements which, like incest taboos, appear also to have adaptive value through "extending the network of cooperation." Thus a theory of the exchange of women (or men) may be broadened to include gift exchange, ceremonial trade, communal ritual, redistribution, or any other kind of exchange or relationship that serves to extend and cement the network of cooperation, thereby promoting the adaptation and, ultimately, the survival of the society.

In the foregoing paragraphs we have discussed *descriptive statement, empirical generalization,* and *theoretical generalization,* each of which represents an increasingly higher level of generality and abstraction. Descriptive statements refer to events occurring in a specific space-time context. Empirical generalizations, on the other hand, refer to relationships which hold under specified conditions irrespective of time and place. Finally, theoretical generalizations refer to highly abstract relationships under which empirical generalizations and descriptive statements can be subsumed as special instances.

There are other terms in common usage that are often used in place of those just mentioned. But it is possible to overemphasize the significance of terminological precision in these matters. What counts is that while the words one uses to refer to the phenomena we have called descriptive statements, empirical generalizations, and theoretical generalizations may vary, there is common agreement among scientists and philosophers of science that one must recognize the important conceptual distinctions that obtain with regard to their level of generality, degree of abstractness, and explanatory power. John Hospers, for example, writes that "after we have observed certain invariant relations in nature, we are led to construct theories to explain them. The distinction between a theory and a law [an empirical generalization] is somewhat vague, but it is very important: in general, we *construct* or devise theories, but we *discover* laws of nature." [11] What Hospers seems to be emphasizing here is that "laws of nature" are nothing more or less than inductive extensions of observation. Consequently, they are usually couched in terms closely linked to empirical data, and are generally confirmable or disconfirmable in terms of direct observation. For example, it is not difficult to ascertain whether a human society does or does not have incest taboos. Submitted to such relatively simple observational tests, the empirical generalizations may "hold up" or "fail to hold up."

Theories, on the other hand, always involve abstract terms which refer to

---

For summaries of the theories concerning the origins and universality of incest taboos see the following: L. A. White, "The Definition and Prohibition of Incest," *American Anthropologist* 50 (1948): 1042–59; D. F. Aberle et al., "The Incest Taboo and the Mating Patterns of Animals," *American Anthropologist* 65 (1963): 253–65; Frank B. Livingstone, "Genetics, Ecology and the Origins of Incest and Exogamy," *Current Anthropology* 10 (1969): 45–61, R. Fox, *Kinship and Marriage* (London: Penguin, 1967), pp. 54–76.

11 John Hospers, *An Introduction to Philosophical Analysis,* 2d ed. (London: Routledge and Kegan Paul, 1967), p. 236.

nonobservables, especially if their explanatory power is to transcend a particular relationship or set of relationships. Thus, in the social sciences, theories characteristically include such abstract terms as *social cohesion, anomie, class, caste, values, norms, symbols, themes, ego, unconscious mind, segmentary lineage,* etc. (In the incest taboo example above, we find terms like *conflict, cooperation, adaptation.*) Now, all of these terms denote highly complex processes, arrangements, patterns, emotional states, "states of the system," or entities—none of which are open to simple and direct observation. Nor are any of these the product of simple induction from observational data. Rather, they are constructs *created* by the social scientist to help him explain various items of behavior and institutional arrangements that may have provoked his interest and perhaps even wonder.

The implication, then, is that theories, because they are more abstract constructions than empirical generalizations or laws of nature, are only *indirectly* confirmable or disconfirmable. Before we can verify or refute a theory, we must provide the key terms of the theory with an empirical interpretation or, in the language of certain philosophers, we must *operationalize* the key theoretical terms. For example, Robert Murphy has argued that warfare among the Mundurucú (a savannah-dwelling trible in the interior of Brazil) serves to displace in-group hostility and aggression and therefore contributes to intratribal social cohesion.[12] However, he does not provide us with a clear empirical measure of in-group hostility or social cohesion. Moreover, the relationship between aggression and displacement and stability remains to be proved. While Murphy apparently sees the hostility arising from internal contradictions in Mundurucú society, other writers posit a fund of aggression in all human societies. Proponents of this latter theory argue that the society's peaceful functioning—if not, indeed, its very survival—depends upon the existence of socially approved channels for displacement of the inevitable fund of aggression. Sometimes the aggression is displaced outside the group, as in the case of warfare, headhunting, counting coups, etc.; sometimes by means of sanctioned intragroup activities like moiety lacrosse contests, Eskimo song duels, bullfights, the World Series, etc.

What kind of empirical data would one need to verify that intratribal hostility is being displaced in a manner that promotes or maintains cultural stability? Murphy has not provided us with any empirical measures for "hostility," "displacement," and "cohesion," all of which are needed to test the theory. And until and unless he does so, it is impossible to evaluate the theory, to prove or disprove it, and to analyze the relationship among the the factors upon which it rests.

The logical relationship between general theoretical propositions (i.e., those propositions which attempt to tell not simply what happens but *why* it happens as it does) and the generalizations and facts they purport to explain is variable. The ideal relationship as enunciated by philosophers of science (who clearly have physics in mind) is a *deductive* one. Indeed, to most philosophers of science a theory is something that explains a phenomenon or a set of phenomena by means of a formal deductive system. In

---

[12] Robert F. Murphy, "Intergroup Hostility and Social Cohesion," *American Anthropologist* 59 (1957): 1018–35.

this view, given one or more empirical generalizations or laws and a series of singular statements of fact (the initial and boundary conditions of the situation), one can logically deduce (or predict, since in a truly deductive system prediction and explanation are symmetrical) the phenomena to be explained. For in a deductive system, the conclusion is logically entailed by the premises. For example, it may be stated as an empirical law that a class of metals will rust under certain given conditions. From this law, together with a statement of certain factual conditions—namely, that a particular metal is one of that class and that these conditions exist—one can deduce or predict that the metal will rust. Conversely, given the fact that the metal has rusted, we can explain why it has—that it belongs to a certain class and that certain conditions must have existed. This low-level law can, in turn, be deduced from more general and abstract laws such as those having to do with oxidation.

Thus, a deductive system requires universal laws (e.g., all A's are B's). Now, if we were to insist on this kind of theoretical purity, maintaining that there can be no exception to the universal proposition that all A's are B's, we would wind up with few or no theories in the social sciences. So we must modify our desire for theoretical perfection and settle for something less than 100% certainty even while we assert the validity of the deductive principle in theory formation. But, then, even the explanations of the more "exact" sciences must reckon with the possibility of exceptions.

What we refer to here are explanations characterized by one or more statistical generalizations. Such explanations are generally called *probabilistic*. Unlike a deductive explanation in which the premises (the universal propositions and statements of the initial and boundary conditions) entail the conclusion, in a probabilistic explanation the premises can only make the conclusion more or less probable.

There is, however, an important difference between the statistical generalizations of the "exact" sciences and those of the social sciences, particularly anthropology. In the former, one frequently finds statistical generalizations of the form, "Given condition A, phenomenon B will occur in 95% of all cases." In anthropology, on the other hand, the kinds of statistical generalizations we are able to make are of a much weaker form. Rarely, if ever, can we state the precise frequency with which B will occur. Ordinarily the statistical generalizations of anthropology take the form, "Given condition A, there is a 'strong tendency' or 'low probability' that phenomenon B will occur." When we make such predictions, we are simply stating that the generalizations involved are weakly statistical in nature, and/or we are confessing that we are in no position to enumerate all the relevant initial and boundary conditions of the situation to which the theory is being applied. In anthropology we can rarely state *all* the necessary and sufficient conditions for the occurrence of an event. Thus, it looks as if anthropologists (and other social scientists) must decide either to accept a relatively high degree of uncertainty in their explanations and theoretical formulations or abandon themselves completely to relativism, antiscience, or gross error.

In addition to the deductive and probabilistic forms of explanation, a third type of explanation, one said to be particularly prominent in anthropology and the other social sciences, employs what have been called *concatenated* (or *factor*) theories and *pattern* theories. There are certain differences between these, but for our purposes here they are enough alike to be included under the same general type.

Abraham Kaplan characterizes a concatenated theory as

> one whose component laws enter into a network of relations so as to constitute an identifiable configuration or pattern. Most typically, they converge on some central point, each specifying one of the factors which plays a part in the phenomenon which the theory is to explain. (It has therefore been called a theory of the factor type, as contrasted with the law type.) This is especially likely to be true of a theory consisting of tendency statements, which attain closure only in their joint application. A law or fact is explained by a concatenated theory when its place in the pattern is made manifest.[13]

For example, one might explain the origins of capitalism by adducing various technoeconomic, social structural, ideological, and personality factors—all of which may have had a part in giving rise to capitalism. However, having determined the relevance of these factors to capitalism, we might then be able to go on to explore the relationships among the factors themselves, We might find that these factors, together with capitalism, form a configuration or pattern. We might find also that certain elements of the pattern are more central, crucial, or strategic than others in determining the overall configuration. Moreover, since we mean by *patterning* the way the various cultural elements relate to each other to form a larger system, we can see no reason why these relationships cannot be expressed in propositional form, either statistical or universal in nature.

Thus concatenated theories may frequently be converted into pattern explanations. And what has been called pattern explanation may simply be a variant of probabilistic or deductive theory.

It should be apparent from the foregoing discussion that much of the material referred to in anthropology as theory might more accurately be called quasitheory. In making this distinction we are not posing a semantic quibble but are seeking rather to underline an existential problem of definition. For in the social sciences definitions often create or compound theoretical problems. Physical scientists sometimes complain that social scientists seem to spend all their time arguing about definitions. It seems so to them because the physical scientists no longer argue about such terms as temperature, or mass, or length or time. But in anthropology, terms like *segmentary lineage system, caste,* or *capitalist economy* have uncertain theoretical implications because different ways of defining these very complex entities may focus attention on very different aspects of each. For example, some years ago Paul Kirchhoff made an important conceptual distinction between what he called "egalitarian clans" and "stratified or conical clans."[14] He emphasized

---

[13] Abraham Kaplan, *The Conduct of Inquiry* (San Francisco: Chandler, 1964), p. 298. See also Quentin Gibson, *The Logic of Social Inquiry* (New York: Humanities Press), pp. 144–54.

[14] See Paul Kirchhoff, "The Principles of Clanship in Human Society," in *Readings in Anthropology,* ed. Morton H. Fried (New York: Thomas Y. Crowell, 1959), 2, 259–70.

that the political significance and potential of each of these two kinds of social units are very different. Now, if one wanted to be rigid about the use of the term *theory*, one would have to say that Kirchhoff's formulation is not a theory because he did not specify the conditions which yielded each of these social forms. But the distinction Kirchhoff did make is the first important step toward the formulation of a theory. For what he in effect did was to reveal that the term *clan* had been loosely applied to two very different types of structure—and, furthermore, that these two structural types have vastly different potentials for economic and political development.

Writing about the theoretical problem of recognition and definition in the sciences, Anatol Rapoport notes that there are important differences between the natural and the social sciences with regard to these issues:

> For the natural, especially the physical scientist, theory . . . is a collection of derived theorems tested in the process of predicting events from observed conditions. The physical scientist is able to address himself to problems of this sort, because for him the problems of recognition, of definition and of meaningful classification either do not exist or have been largely solved. For the social scientist, all too often the latter kinds of problems are central. The social scientist's aim, therefore, must be lower than that of the physicist.[15]

Rapoport illustrates the above points:

> In the mechanics of motion . . . position and time were fundamental. Actually there are three fundamental kinds of quantities in mechanics, from which all others are derived: length, time and mass. Nor is there any question (in classical mechanics) how these quantities are to be measured. . . . In pursuing the question to what extent a quantitative variable can be sharply defined, a most important problem looms: the problem of recognition.

> Note that the problem is trivial in mechanics. To determine the position of an object, we must, of course, recognize the object in all positions, but this is ordinarily so easy as to present no problem. As we pass from physics to chemistry, the problem of recognition becomes more important.[16]

And as we pass from the physical to the social sciences the problem of recognition takes on even greater theoretical importance. The social scientist, for example, may ask,

> "What sort of thing shall we *call* a social action?"
> Consensus is not easy to reach because the various definitions will presumably have different consequences. *Social action*, once defined, will presumably be a key term in some social science disciplines. It will (hopefully) appear in the theorems of the future theory. Therefore, its par-

---

[15] Anatol Rapoport, "Various Meanings of Theory," in *Politics and Social Life*, ed. Nelson W. Polsby, Robert A. Dentler, and Paul A. Smith (Boston: Houghton Mifflin, 1963), p. 79.

[16] Ibid., p. 77.

ticular definition serves to focus attention on the component events from which the definition is compounded. It may or may not be fruitful to focus attention on this or that combination of events. Hence, the problem of definition becomes a "theoretical" problem, something which is often difficult for the natural scientist to recognize.[17]

One final note about definitions and theory. In the preceding paragraphs we have said that the goal of theory formation is explanation rather than prediction. But in a very real sense the two are inseparable. For when we have utilized a theory to explain, we have paved the way for prediction and, hence, for the test of explanation. It has sometimes been maintained, however, that not all scientific explanations have predictive implications—that it is possible to explain a phenomenon without predicting it. The natural-selection theory of biological evolution, because it is concerned largely with events of the past, may be cited as a case in point. But to the extent that this theory explains the events of the past it can be said to "retrodict" them. And a theory that can "retrodict" past phenomena should be capable *in principle* of predicting these same phenomena *if* the conditions that obtained in the past were to be repeated in the future, however unlikely such a repetition may be.

If all satisfactory explanation has some predictive (or "retrodictive") import, not all prediction stems from satisfactory explanation. There are many events that one might be able to predict even though one could not explain them. For example, one might predict the rise and fall of the tides without knowing either how the table of tides is constructed or what it is that accounts for their ebb and flow.

There is a difference, in other words, between a *correct* prediction and a *warranted* prediction. A warranted prediction is not only accurate, but it is supported by an acceptable theoretical *justification*. Thus, a warranted prediction can only issue from a theory for which there is some degree of scientific confirmation, a theory in which we have some confidence. In the case of a correct prediction, we may have no idea why the prediction is correct (as in the example of the tides above), or the theoretical justification for the prediction may be scientifically unacceptable. Astrologers, for example, may sometimes make correct predictions about human affairs. But we have no confidence in the theories which support astrological predictions because they contradict such a large portion of well-confirmed scientific knowledge. There is simply nothing in the corpus of this knowledge that would lead us to expect a direct causal relationship between the configuration of the planets and stars and human events.

At the beginning of this section we asserted that coping with the world involves theorizing about it. In other words, theory-building and the framing of explanations have important pragmatic implications. Being able to predict correctly allows us to anticipate events and thus to prepare for them. But if we know why we are able to predict correctly, we are provided with a mechanism by which we may also be able to intervene in events and exert some control over them.

---

[17] Ibid., p. 79.

In the preceding pages we have discussed theoretical and empirical generalizations and their role in explanation. And we have suggested that anthropology has produced a variety of lawlike empirical generalizations of some interest and significance as well as certain more abstract formulations which might properly be called theoretical generalizations.

By and large we have avoided using the term *law* because it implies a degree of consensus and verification which ordinarily does not hold when applied to the higher level theoretical generalizations of anthropology. Thus, how one answers the question, "Are there cultural laws?" will depend upon what one means by a *law*. If by *laws* one has in mind the sort of verified hypotheses of universal scope that sometimes turn up in the natural sciences, then quite clearly there are no such laws in anthropology. If, however, one is willing to settle for generalizations of more modest scope—that is, generalizations whose range might be restricted to a given class of structures—then it is likely that such lawlike statements may be found in anthropology. However, it should be reemphasized that these lawlike propositions will prove to be highly probabilistic in nature. For example, the postulated relationship between the construction and maintenance of large-scale irrigation works and the rise of centralized despotic states (Wittfogel); the relationship between segmentary lineage organization and societal expansion of a certain kind (Sahlins); the relationship between patrilocality, patrilineal band organization, and ecological factors (Steward); the relationship between revitalization movements and certain patterns of acculturation (Worsley, Wallace); the relationship between forms of family organization and social and economic factors (Lévi-Strauss); the relationship between "rituals of rebellion" and political stability (Gluckman)—all such relationships may be stated in the form of lawlike propositions.[18] To be sure, none of these relationships commands the consensus that one finds attached to lawlike propositions in the physical sciences. In varying degree, all remain controversial. Yet, despite the uncertain status of lawlike propositions in anthropology, we find that we cannot work without them. What Andreski says of sociology can be applied with equal force to anthropology or any of the social sciences:

> A sociologist can formulate his hypothesis, try to show with the aid of data which happen to exist that it seems to be valid, and hope that it will not be entirely discarded by later investigators. If his successors find after many years that there is "something in it" he achieves the status

---

[18] See Karl A. Wittfogel, *Oriental Despotism* (New Haven: Yale University Press, 1957); Julian H. Steward et al., *Irrigation Civilizations: A Comparative Study* (Washington, D.C.: Pan American Union, 1955); Marshall D. Sahlins, "The Segmentary Lineage: An Organization of Predatory Expansion," *American Anthropologist* 63 (1961): 321–43; Julian H. Steward, "The Economic Basis of Primitive Bands," in *Essays in Anthropology in Honor of Alfred Louis Kroeber* (Berkeley: University of California Press, 1936), pp. 311–50; Peter Worsley, *The Trumpet Shall Sound*, 2d ed. (New York: Schocken Books, 1968); Anthony C. Wallace, "Revitalization Movements," *American Anthropologist* 58 (1956): 264–81; Claude Lévi-Strauss, "The Family," in *Studies in Social and Cultural Anthropology*, ed. John Middleton (New York: Thomas Y. Crowell), pp. 128–55; Max Gluckman, *Custom and Conflict in Africa* (Glencoe, Ill.: Free Press, 1955). See also Gluckman, introductory essay in *Order and Rebellion in Tribal Africa* (Glencoe, Ill.: Free Press, 1963).

of a great thinker, for more often than not "there is nothing in it." Thus steps of successive approximation and modification which may take place in a laboratory during one series of experiments, are here spread over generations. The very important practical lesson which emerges from this argument is that if, unintelligently aping physicists and chemists, we demand that no thesis must be put forth unless it is fully substantiated by factual data, we condemn sociology to sterility. Intuition and surmisal play . . . , of course, an indispensable role in the process of discovery in any field; the peculiarity of sociology and related sciences lies in the greater need for publishing unproven products of speculation. Naturally, in order to be fruitful, a contribution to sociological theory must take into account available data, but it must outrun them.[19]

Steward also chides anthropologists for being overly cautious about advancing lawlike propositions: "It is obvious that the minutiae of culture history will never be completely known and that there is no need to defer formulations until all archeologists have laid down their shovels and all ethnologists have put away their notebooks." [20]

Finally, even an anthropologist like Evans-Pritchard, who is skeptical about the possibility of discovering cultural laws, recognizes that the effort itself may produce beneficial results: "My skepticism does not mean that I think we should cease to look for such regularities as can be established by various forms of the comparative method. It would be a great convenience were we to succeed in finding them. If we do not, we shall at least in the search have achieved a deeper understanding of human society." [21]

We would also point out that typologies of cultural forms frequently imply one or more lawlike generalizations, since the more fruitful typologies with which we are concerned are based upon a critical relationship alleged to exist among certain sociocultural phenomena. And, of course, typologies in anthropology are legion. Virtually all anthropologists would agree that cultural phenomena are patterned and do exhibit certain regularities. This being the case, then, there is no reason why this patterning or these regularities cannot be formulated as general statements. And perhaps we ought also to bear in mind that the so-called laws of the natural sciences—despite the claim that they are universal in scope—frequently refer to highly "idealized" limiting conditions such as bodies falling in a perfect vacuum, and, what is more, are only applicable under certain specified circumstances. Galileo's law of falling bodies, for example, only applies to free fall near the surface of the earth, and Boyle's law in chemistry only applies to gases of low density, etc.

Some humanistically oriented anthropologists object to the search for cultural laws. We believe that their objections may stem, at least in part, from a misunderstanding about the logical status of such laws. They seem sometimes to feel, or act as if they feel, that the formulation of lawlike generalizations about sociocultural phenomena assails human dignity and diminishes human freedom. Such a view could only arise from looking at

---

[19] Andreski, *Comparative Sociology*, pp. 43–44.

[20] Julian Steward, "Cultural Causality and Law: A Trial Formation of the Development of Early Civilizations," *American Anthropologist* 51 (1949): 24–25.

[21] Evans-Pritchard, *The Comparative Method*, p. 28.

scientific laws as though they were prescriptive in the way that traffic laws are. But scientific laws are descriptive, not prescriptive—they do not compel events to happen in the world, they do not prescribe patterns of human behavior; they merely enable us to understand, and thus help us, perhaps, to deal more effectively with our total environment.

The Relation between Ethnological Theory and Ethnographic Fact

It is a widely held notion that any science consists of two kinds of statements: on the one hand empirical statements of *fact*, gained by observation, which are solid and indisputable; and on the other, *theoretical* statements, which are thought to be speculative and subject to the vagaries of shifting opinion. In this view, once one has gleaned all the relevant facts, theories may be formulated and tailored to explain or fit the facts. This distinction between fact and theory has become enshrined in anthropology in the distinction between ethnography (the description of cultures) and ethnology (the theorizing about these descriptions)—a dichotomy that may be misleading. What *are* the relevant facts that underpin a theory, and how do we go about observing them? The notion that we may record all the facts is an obvious absurdity. We observe and filter the facts through a screen of interest, predisposition, and prior experience. And all of our descriptions are inevitably interpenetrated by theoretical considerations. Thus, the notion that there is such a thing as pure description is a mistaken notion. In the closing paragraph of his justly famous essay, "Cultural Causality and Law," Julian Steward makes these same points most tellingly when he says, "Fact collecting of itself is insufficient scientific procedure; facts exist only as they are related to theories, and theories are not destroyed by facts—they are replaced by new theories which better explain the facts." [22]

Social psychologists and philosophers of science have also stressed, over and over again, that *all* of our observations are selective in terms of some point of view, some theoretical stance, some bias (this problem is discussed in more detail below). Even if we *were* able to describe everything about an event or an institution, such a description could hardly serve any scientific function. For fruitful description is always description with a purpose; and in evaluating descriptions it is important to know the purposes that motivated them. We know that if we confront a biologist, psychologist, and anthropologist with the same event, each of them will come up with a different description of the event. Because they are asking different questions of the event, they will conceptualize it in different ways; they will *observe* it in different ways. What they consider phenomena to be noted and explained and what they consider background will in each case be different. Thus, the same event may be described in a number of different ways, each of them potentially valid but each prepared from a different perspective and for different theoretical purposes.

---

[22] Steward, "Cultural Causality and Law," p. 25.

The point we are making here is that descriptions vary with the conceptual or theoretical framework within which they are couched. To evaluate a description properly one must know something about the theoretical framework that brought it into being. Indeed, a more logical way of classifying social scientists, rather than in terms of the departments that employ them, would be in terms of the kinds of conceptual frameworks within which they operate.

Special Problems
in Anthropological Theorizing

The Inside vs. the Outside View of a Culture

Social scientists, unlike physical scientists, are confronted by a special data problem. Not only does the anthropologist operate within his own conceptual framework, but the people he studies operate within *their* own conceptual framework or frameworks. This poses a particular problem for the anthropologist, because more often than not the concepts of the people he studies are very different from his own. It raises a perennial methodological problem in anthropology, namely, in describing another culture, do we describe it in terms of the way it looks to those within the culture—in terms of the native's conceptual categories (the emic approach)—or do we describe it in terms of the conceptual categories of anthropology—how it looks from the outside (the etic approach). (This discussion is amplified in Chapter 4.) Actually, most ethnographies alternate between these two points of view. A significant number of anthropologists, going back to Malinowski, have argued that the aim of ethnography should be to discover what one would have to know in order to get around in a particular culture. This may be *one* aim of ethnography, but is it *the* aim? That will depend upon what one conceives to be the purpose of ethnographic description. If one wishes to produce accounts which convey what the culture is like from the viewpoint of someone inside the culture, then one ought to strive to produce an account in terms of native concepts, categories, and interpretations. But if one sees ethnographic description as contributing to a body of theory which explains how cultures come into being, how they are maintained, and how they change, then one cannot be content with just an inside view of the system.

Indeed, an inside view may be very misleading. There are several reasons for this. For one thing, most persons have a very limited and often distorted view of how their system works; they tend to see it from the vantage point of their own structural position within it. Moreover, a native's interpretation of his culture is heavily loaded with rationalizations and "things as they ought to be." In an interesting—and, we think, accurate—statement of the relation between the native's model and the anthropologist's model, Julian Pitt-Rivers has had this to say:

The models of the native differ from those of the anthropologist in that they are centered on his own place in society, inevitably, since they are models-for-action rather than models-for-comparison. They partake of his knowledge of his society, but they also represent his aspirations. They are not only the world as he knows it, they are also the world as he would like it to be.[23]

Elsewhere in the same essay, Pitt-Rivers notes:

> The natives classify according to the categories of their culture by which they explain the world and determine how they should act, but the investigator reclassifies with quite a different aim in mind: that of establishing equivalence from one culture to another in accordance with the criteria he regards as significant for that purpose. He regards them as significant on account of the theories he entertains of how societies or cultures or human relations "work." He therefore sees implications and consistencies or inconsistencies which they do not see and what appears reasonable to them may not seem so to him, and vice versa. His categories surpass those of the culture he studies in their comparative range and therefore the assumptions on which they are based are of quite another order. Not concerned with knowing how he *should* act, but only how *they do*, he includes their conceptual system as part of what requires to be explained, placing their own explanations as it were "in quotes"; he constructs models out of the models of those he preys on which he breaks down and re-orders for another purpose. *Their* reasoning succeeds or fails according to whether it attains a desired social response in a particular context; *his* aims to escape from its servitude to context by making context explicit and thereby achieve a universal validity at a higher level of generalization.[24]

Interestingly enough, the position expressed by Pitt-Rivers in the preceding quotation was also enunciated by Bronislaw Malinowski. Thus it is ironic to note that Malinowski, who is most often cited as advocating the view that the main mission of ethnography is "to grasp the native's point of view, his relation to life, to realize *his* vision of *his* world," has elsewhere in the very same volume from which this quotation is taken, said:

> Yet, it must be remembered that what appears to us an extensive, complicated, and yet well ordered institution is the outcome of ever so many doings and pursuits, carried on by savages, who have no laws or aims or charter definitely laid down. They have no knowledge of the *total outline* of any of their social structure. They know their own motives, know the purpose of individual actions and the rules which apply to them, but how, out of these, the whole collective institution shapes, this is beyond their mental range. Not even the most intelligent native has any clear idea of the Kula [25] as a big organized social construction, still less of its sociological function and implications. If you were to ask him what the Kula is, he would answer by giving a few details, most likely by giving his personal experiences and subjective views on the Kula, but nothing approaching the definition just given here. Not even a partial coherent

---

[23] Julian Pitt-Rivers, "Contextual Analysis and the Locus of the Model," Archives Européennes de Sociologie, *European Journal of Sociology* 8 (1967): 31–32.

[24] Ibid., 30–31.

[25] A ceremonial trade cycle involving a group of islands northeast of New Guinea.

account could be obtained. For the integral picture does not exist in his mind; he is in it and cannot see the whole from the outside.[26]

Thus it appears that we may confirm an ancient ethnographic virtue—namely, that proper anthropological research involves not only the attempt to discover the native's point of view, the way he perceives and orders his universe, his ideal and subjective observations of the social world in which he lives, but the way all of these relate to the less context-bound constructs, understandings, and theories of the anthropologist. For, as Malinowski points out, even the most intelligent native may be unaware of the way in which system and structure impinge upon his day-to-day behavior.

The Objectivity of Anthropological Reporting

A perennial problem in the social sciences is that of investigator bias. How can we hope to achieve objective knowledge of sociocultural phenomena when the practitioners of social science are at the same time ideologues? This has been an especially nagging problem in anthropology because of the way its basic data are gathered. Traditionally, a single anthropologist has gone off for a year or more to an exotic culture where he has lived among the people he is studying, observing their institutions and lifeways. He then returns and writes up his report on "the way it is among the. . . ." But to what extent is his account a reflection of his own personal biases, his own likes and dislikes?

This problem has been brought home to anthropologists on several occasions with particular poignancy. Perhaps the classic case is that of Tepoztlan, a village in southern Mexico. The original ethnography of Tepoztlan was done by Robert Redfield in the late 1920s. The picture which emerges from his account is that of a generally harmonious, egalitarian, halcyon folk community. Oscar Lewis studied Tepoztlan some twenty years later.[27] His portrayal of Tepoztlan is vastly different from that of Redfield. It is described as a community characterized by sharp differences in wealth and riven by a high degree of interpersonal conflict. In part the differences in the two accounts may be attributed to the changes that had taken place in the intervening decades—but only in small part. How do we decide which account is closer to the "truth," and what does this mean as far as the objectivity of anthropological knowledge is concerned?

To begin with, let us admit that *all* human beings, not only anthropologists, are biased. It is a mistake to try to locate objectivity in the minds and attitudes of individual anthropologists. Rather, as Karl Popper has noted, objectivity should be sought in the institutions and critical traditions of a discipline.[28] It is only through the give and take of open criticism and the ongoing interplay of many different kinds of biases that anything approach-

---

[26] Bronislaw Malinowski, *Argonauts of the Western Pacific* (New York: E. P. Dutton, 1961), pp. 25, 83.

[27] See Robert Redfield, *Tepoztlan—A Mexican Village* (Chicago: University of Chicago Press, 1930), and Oscar Lewis, *Life in a Mexican Village: Tepoztlan Restudied* (Urbana: University of Illinois Press, 1951).

[28] Karl R. Popper, *The Poverty of Historicism* (New York: Harper Torch Books, 1964), pp. 155–59.

ing objectivity will emerge. In other words, the essential objectivity of a discipline is promoted cumulatively over time. The accounts of the work of Redfield and Lewis have stimulated such a critical exchange and review based upon a comparison of these accounts with those of other peasant communities, in particular with those of other peasant communities in Mexico.[29] Out of this, we believe, has come a closer approximation to an "objective" picture of peasant life.

Field work in anthropology has tended to be in part a salvage operation, in part an enterprise determined by "political" concerns, and in part an activity motivated by interest in specific problems. But sometimes the "salvage" and/or the "politically attractive" aspects of work in a particular place have deflected research away from the areas of greater potential theoretical significance. Moreover, each anthropologist who sets out to do his first field research normally looks for a people or group that has not been "done" before. The aim, of course, has been to broaden the arena of comparison as well as to record cultures before they disappear. Unfortunately, what we may have gained in breadth of coverage from this practice, we may have lost in depth of analysis. Perhaps if anthropology had followed more systematically a policy of restudies (especially by different researchers), the cumulative individual biases would have tended to cancel each other out and to yield understandings that more closely approximate what we conceive to be objectivity.

If all persons, including anthropologists, look at the world through a screen of their individual values, biases, and points of view, what then is the possibility of a value-free social science? A significant body of social scientists would indeed deny any such possibility. Since all knowledge of sociocultural phenomena inevitably reflects the investigator's personal values and biases, they would argue, the search for objectivity and neutrality is chimerical.

One of the weaknesses of such an argument, as we have already indicated, is that it seeks to locate objectivity in the minds and attitudes of the investigators, rather than where it should more properly be sought—in the critical traditions of a discipline. But there is another flaw in such a relativist position: It fails to distinguish what philosophers of science have called the "context of discovery" from the "context of justification." Thus, biases and individual values play a role in the former, but they need not and indeed should not play a significant role in the latter. As one of us has commented elsewhere, while "inquiries into the sources of a scholar's knowledge may cast light on the motivations which led him to espouse certain ideas, they are logically irrelevant to a critical appraisal of the validity of those ideas." [30] Thus, for example, certain critics have been tempted to dismiss Marx's formulations by pointing out that Marx was a Jew who suffered from carbuncles. But this sort of argument is patently absurd and illogical: his ideas must stand or fall on their own logical merits. Whatever the source of one's ideas and theories

---

[29] See, for example, George M. Foster, "Interpersonal Relations in Peasant Society," and comments and rejoinder by Oscar Lewis, Julian Pitt-Rivers, and George M. Foster, *Human Organization* 19 (1960–61): 174–84.

[30] David Kaplan, "The Formal-Substantive Controversy in Economic Anthropology: Reflections on its Wider Implications," *Southwestern Journal of Anthropology* 24 (1968): 232. See also R. A. Manners, "Comments on Opler," *Current Anthropology* 6 (1965): 1–2, 319–20.

may be, if we are unwilling to concede that there are nonpersonal standards for assessing evidence and argumentation, then anthropology and all the social sciences become nothing more than a collection of ideologies; the adherence to one or another becomes a matter of personal aesthetics, prejudice, or politics rather than adherence based upon the logical consistency of the argument itself and upon the way evidence is used to support the position.

Theory Formation

Is anthropology one of the humanities, a science, or some "third culture" with one foot in each camp? A great deal of ink has been spilled in trying to answer this question. Like the discussion about the possibility of "social laws," many of the discussions having to do with this issue strike one as being, at bottom, ideologically motivated; that is, they seem very much to hinge upon conceptions about human freedom, moral responsibility and the like.

Those who have argued that it is a mistake to view anthropology as a science akin to the natural sciences seem to be taking too narrow a view of what science is. Definitions of science are of course legion. The view that seems to us to come closest to capturing the spirit of the scientific enterprise is the one which sees science as an intellectual method or, in Ernest Nagel's words, "a set of logical canons for testing claims to knowledge." [31] In Karl Popper's rather apt phrase, science is a process of "conjectures and refutations" [32]—advancing bold conjectures about the state of the world and then trying to refute them.

Some "disciplines," such as music, poetry, or art, are concerned with conveying experiences which may enrich our emotional life or heighten our sensibilities. But they are generally *not* concerned with conveying cognitive knowledge. Any discipline which purports to advance knowledge-claims about the empirical world and seeks to explain this world in terms of general underlying principles is subject to the canons of testing and evidence that go by the name of science—and this is so whether the discipline considers itself a science or not. To the extent that anthropology wishes to discern general patterns and regularities within cultural phenomena and to make some sort of general statements about such patterns and regularities, there is no reason for denying it scientific status.

Verstehen. It is true, of course, that neither in scope, explanatory power, or degree of agreement has anthropology (or, for that matter, any other social science) produced anything that even approaches the theories of a natural science like physics. Often this is attributed to the immaturity of the social sciences, and it is asserted that eventually the social sciences will develop theories of the sort that have been produced by the more sophisticated natural sciences. At other times, however, it has been argued that the data of the social sciences are so radically different, in an ontological sense, from those

---

[31] E. Nagel, "The Place of Science in a Liberal Education," *Daedalus* (Winter 1959): 59–60.

[32] Karl R. Popper, *Conjectures and Refutations.* (New York: Basic Books, 1962).

of the natural sciences that we may never hope to produce the kinds of general theories propounded by the so-called hard sciences. In this view, the social sciences are said to be *ideographic* (particularistic) in their nature rather than *nomothetic* (generalizing). For those who subscribe to this position, the aim of social science is not the formulation of general explanatory systems, but rather the organization and presentation of the data in such a way as to make them intelligible through a process of individual understanding, empathy, or *verstehen*. There seems to be something misleading about this position. For while the process of empathy or *verstehen* may generate fruitful concepts and hypotheses, by itself it cannot function to validate such hypotheses publicly. One man's *verstehen* differs from the next man's. The heuristic advantages as well as the practical limitations involved in the use of empathetic understanding or *verstehen* as a technique of investigation in the social sciences has been most cogently summarized by Charles Frankel:

> It is fairly obvious that the ability to identify with what is being studied is frequently a major aid in forming significant hypotheses, and that the difference between the capacities of different observers for sympathetic projection is in many fields the difference between a first-rate and second-rate mind. It is also fairly plain that human studies offer a more promising field for the exercise of empathy and what has come to be known as "verstehen" then, say, astronomy or geology. Does this mean that the method we employ to understand the behavior of unconscious objects must be radically different from the method we employ to understand conscious beings? In contrast with the former, which we can understand "from the outside," can we explain the latter only "from the inside?" The answer to these questions, it seems to me is No. Quite apart from the fact that sympathetic imagination has its uses in many fields in the natural sciences such as zoology, the possibility of exercising sympathetic imagination in the humanistic disciplines is a mixed blessing. It can make the creation of hypotheses easier; but it can also make the creation of false hypotheses easier. Most important of all, we cannot tell whether sympathetic imagination has in a specific case led us to error or to truth by using the method of sympathetic imagination as our test.[33]

Frankel then goes on to say:

> But an "objectivist" approach to human affairs does not require the denial of either the significance or the poignancy of human feelings and aspirations; and no method of disciplined inquiry can dispense with the necessity of selecting certain salient features in a gross complex of events and dealing with them in abstract terms. If "understanding" a subject-matter were the same thing as identifying with that subject matter, knowledge would be an idle reduplication of experience and not a clarification of it. Sympathetic identification, in short, is neither sufficient nor essential to guarantee the discovery of truth in the human studies. It is not sufficient because the mistakes that people make when they think they have identified with others are notorious; it is not essential because it is possi-

---

[33] Charles Frankel, "Philosophy and The Social Sciences," in *Both Human and Humane; The Humanities and Social Sciences in Graduate Education*, ed. Charles E. Boewe and Roy F. Nichols (Philadelphia: University of Pennslyvania, 1960), pp. 95–96.

ble to explain another person's behavior without identifying with him. It would be something of a nuisance if we tried to be schizophrenic while we studied schizophrenia. . . . It is false to say that we understand the actions of other human beings "only because they are known to us from the working of our own minds." Indeed such a special use of the word "understanding" invites the erection of personal and parochial intuition into criteria of truth.[34]

Science is not a method for *generating* theories. Theories are the creative act of an informed and disciplined mind. Science, as we have already noted, is an intellectual method for reducing error. As Frankel has emphasized, understanding and intelligibility are essentially psychological processes and will vary from person to person. What we are or should be seeking in anthropology is *public* reliable knowledge about sociocultural affairs.

Without in any way implying that there is some sort of *inherent* difference between the data of anthropology and those of the natural sciences, we believe that there *are* significant differences which help to explain the relatively uncertain character of anthropological theory as well as the paucity of what the logicians would probably refer to as "genuine" theory.

Among the many differences which might help us to account for this uncertainty and paucity, four seem to be especially cogent.

(1) *Historicity.* In the first place, the natural sciences—and let us take physics as an example—have not had to contend, as has anthropology, with the historicity of the systems they investigate. It is true, of course, that all natural phenomena have a temporal dimension. But overwhelmingly the processes studied by physicists have been recurrent over enormous periods of time. In those cases where physicists have dealt with systems that are not truly repetitive over long periods of time—that is, where they have dealt with phenomena that have undergone systematic change—their theories have the same uncertain character as those of the social sciences. Using an example from the field of astrophysics, Wilbert Moore makes this point with respect to static theories (i.e., those concerned with recurring cycles within a system) versus dynamic theories (i.e., those concerned with changing systems).

> Some of the nuances with respect to "static" and "dynamic" principles can be illustrated from the study of astronomy. Many carefully recorded observations, plus the integrated capacity of several brilliant theoretical minds, went into the theory that explains the orderly interdependence and movement of planets of our solar system. Yet that system is essentially "functional," the cycles neatly recurrent and the longest one requiring only a few earth-years to run its course. The impressive manner in which scientists predicted the position of unseen planets was, however, a static prediction based on the characteristics of the visible system and "necessary" in order to complete an orderly picture of its operation. A truly dynamic theory of the solar system, to say nothing of the universe, is very much lacking. That is to say, there is no commonly accepted and

---

[34] Ibid., pp. 99–100.

moderately verifiable formulation that is concerned with changes in the system itself, its history, and its destiny.[35]

Even in the case of the biological sciences, where the time spans dealt with are more limited, the investigator can assume relative stability of structure and process over periods of thousands and sometimes millions of years. But for the investigator of sociocultural phenomena the situation is quite different. Here a structure, process, or event can change, often quite dramatically, almost overnight. Evans-Pritchard has made this point somewhat picturesquely:

> Just as we can understand the anatomy and physiology of a horse without requiring to know anything about its descent from its five-toed ancestor, so we can understand the structure of a society and the functioning of its institutions without knowing anything about its history. But a society, however defined, in no way resembles a horse, and, mercifully, horses remain horses—or at least they have done so in historic times— and do not turn into elephants or pigs, whereas a society may change from one type to another, sometimes with great suddenness and violence.[36]

The implication here is that theories in anthropology are likely to be more limited in scope and narrower in application than those of the physical and/or biological sciences.

The theories themselves will, of course, be valid for a particular place, time and set of social conditions, but the social conditions themselves are subject to change over time. Hence, new theories will have to be generated to account for or to explain the new structures and the new social arrangements. For example, it is possible that a theory which illuminates the social nature of religious phenomena in hunting and gathering societies may be of limited value in illuminating the social nature of religious phenomena in an industrial society.

Open Systems. Second, the kinds of systems that anthropologists deal with are highly open systems. It is true that in nature all systems are open. But physical scientists, perhaps because of the kinds of variables they deal with and perhaps because they are able to exert greater control over these variables in the experimental situation, seem to have had greater success in stating the conditions of closure of the systems they investigate. Anthropologists, on the other hand, dealing with many more and different kinds of variables, are unable to exert control over all of the possibly relevant variables —thus, once more, the highly probabilistic nature of our explanations.

John Hospers comments:

> Physics is in an advantageous position in that its laws are *simpler*—not in the sense of "easier to understand," for physics is more difficult for most

---

[35] Wilbert Moore, *Social Change*. (Englewood Cliffs, N.J.: Prentice-Hall, 1963), p. 4.

[36] E. E. Evans-Pritchard, "Anthropology and History," in *Essays in Social Anthropology* (London: Faber and Faber, 1962), p. 55.

students than any of the other empirical sciences, but in the sense that
a law of physics can be stated in the smallest number of conditions.
In stating the velocity at which objects fall, one can ignore most of
the universe. One can ignore the color of the object, its smell or taste, the
temperature of the environment, the number of people watching the
event and so on for thousands of factors. By contrast, in dealing with
human behavior it would be difficult to say what might *not* turn out to
be relevant. . . . The best we can do, usually, is to state certain general
tendencies of human behavior, allowing for many exceptions.[37]

Social Issues. Third, physicists and other natural scientists, while not
completely immune to influences from the wider society, seem to be freer
to respond to the problems generated by the internal development of their
disciplines. In other words, at any given period of its development, the
problems that largely occupied a field like physics were more or less com-
mensurate with the level of theoretical sophistication reached by the discipline at that time. Physicists tackle problems they have a reasonable chance
of solving.

Anthropology and the other social sciences, however, often had problems
thrust upon them by the concerns of the larger society; and this despite the
fact that the conceptual and analytic tools available to these disciplines have
been inadequate to the task of resolving the problems. Moreover, many social
scientists are themselves highly sensitive to the social issues of their times
and often feel it their "duty" to address themselves to these issues. A number
of physical anthropologists, for example, have noted that the enormous time
and effort that has gone into the study of race as a biological phenomenon is
far out of proportion to the significance of the problem in the evolution of
man. Quite clearly this expenditure of energy reflects the significance of race
as a *social* problem. Indeed, the social sciences are often looked to for solutions
to a great variety of social ills whose sources may lie in complex sets of circumstances. For the social scientist this means that he is inevitably drawn into
a research situation in which he must attempt to cope with a large number of
variables. Society expects explanations and expects them in detail. Consequently, anthropologists come to demand of themselves the same kind of
detailed explanations. As May Brodbeck observes:

> The physicist may know all the principles involved yet be quite at a loss
> to predict, say, how many leaves will blow off a tree in the next storm.
> The poignant difference is, of course, that in social matters we desperately
> want explanation in detail; while in physical sciences we are frequently
> indifferent. Laws in social science, if we had them, would contain many
> more variables than those of physics. Yet we berate the social sciences
> for not being able to do what even the model sciences cannot do.[38]

Ideology. Finally, one reacts to general propositions in the social sciences
in a dual context: both as theories and as ideologies. This has made it difficult

---

[37] Hospers, *An Introduction to Philosophical Analysis*, p. 232.

[38] May Brodbeck, "On the Philosophy of the Social Sciences," *Philosophy of Science* 21 (1954): 146–47.

to sort out theories, keeping the more fruitful and discarding the less fruitful or the erroneous. Often theories are advanced, and reacted to, in terms of wholly extrascientific factors such as their moral implications (or what one thinks are their moral implications). Thus many theories may be rejected not on logical or empirical grounds, but simply because they are too deterministic and are seen as dehumanizing. Indeed, sometimes the logical and empirical merits of the theory are not even considered. Long before anthropologists become anthropologists they have absorbed the folk social science of their culture—some of it probably accurate and insightful but much of it rationalization and even plain nonsense.

It is true, of course, that anthropology is not unique in this regard. Even a cursory reading of the history of science reveals that all sorts of extrascientific factors have played a part in the acceptance or rejection of theories. But we do not believe they have intruded themselves so prominently into the physical sciences as they have into the social sciences. What is more, ideological factors have been most conspicuous in the reaction to physical science theories where there are clear moral implications in the theory or where its implications for man have been directly perceived.

Anthropology, like all other fields of systematic inquiry, seeks to generate public, reliable knowledge about its subject matter. As we have noted above, anthropology's outstanding achievement thus far has been the production of a rich and varied literature, depicting, often in vivid fashion, the lifeways of an enormous range of human societies, both past and present. But this literature is largely natural history, not theoretical science. Theory is knowledge organized so that facts are subsumed under general principles. Not only is theoretical knowledge therefore more easily comprehended and transmitted than knowledge organized in any other form, it also has a potentiality for development that the mere accumulation of facts does not have. Indeed, one could question whether accumulated facts by themselves ought to be termed knowledge at all.

Anthropologists, we believe, can learn a great deal from philosophers of science, logicians, and philosophically minded scientists concerning the canons of satisfactory theoretical explanation. But while these canons may provide us with the "ideal" at which we should be aiming, we ought not to become intimidated by the failure of anthropology to achieve these high standards. We may take heart from the knowledge that while our theories rarely, if ever, achieve such "perfection," those of the natural sciences often fall short as well.

Two Theoretical Orientations

In this chapter we deal with four *approaches* or *theoretical orientations:* evolutionism, functionalism, history, and cultural ecology. These four theoretical orientations, we believe, have in the main characterized anthropology since its beginnings as a separate field of inquiry. We refer here to these four approaches as *theoretical orientations* rather than as *methodologies* or *theories* quite purposefully, because they seem to us to be something more than strictly formal methodologies and at the same time something less than full-fledged theories. *Methodology,* in its most precise sense—i.e., as it is used by philosophers of science—is concerned with the form or logic of scientific inquiry. Thus, methodological issues and problems are usually not confined to a single discipline, but may be seen in the context of groups of related disciplines, or, at their most general level, in terms of all scientific inquiry. If methodologies are formal, theories are substantive. Theories concern themselves with entities that have specific empirical implications and with the relationships among such entities.[1]

---

[1] Anthropologists commonly use terms like *methodology, theoretical approach,* and *methodological approach* in their discussions. Sometimes these terms are used inter-

In the social sciences, what are often referred to as methodologies may be concerned with *more* than the strictly formal procedures of inquiry. They may serve to orient the social scientist toward the substantive issues which concern him, and are therefore likely to have definite theoretical implications. Purely formal methodologies—as these are defined by philosophers of science —do not have such implications. It is because we wish to distinguish the purely formal meaning of *methodology* from the way in which it is frequently used by the social scientist that we call the latter a *theoretical orientation.* Instead, we might have employed the term *general anthropological orientation,* paralleling sociologist Robert Merton's use of "general sociological orientation." The term *theoretical orientation,* however, seems to us more pointed and slightly less awkward than *general anthropological orientation,* although we are trying to clarify the same set of issues to which Merton addresses himself in his attempt to distinguish theories per se from "general sociological orientations" (our "theoretical orientations"). According to Merton, "general sociological orientations" consist of

> general orientations toward substantive materials. Such orientations involve broad postulates which indicate *types* of variables which are somehow to be taken into account rather than specifying determinate relationships between particular variables. Indispensable though orientations are, they provide only the broadest framework for empirical inquiry. This is the case with Durkheim's generic hypothesis, which holds that the "determining cause of a social fact should be sought among the social facts preceding it" and identifies the "social" factor as institutional norms toward which behavior is oriented. Or, again, it is said that "to a certain approximation it is useful to regard society as an integrated system of mutually interrelated and functionally interdependent parts." . . . Such general orientations may be paraphrased as saying in effect that the investigator ignores this *order of fact* at his peril. They do not set forth specific hypotheses. . . .
>
> The chief function of these orientations is to provide a general context for inquiry; they facilitate the process of arriving at determinate hypotheses. To take a case in point: Malinowski was led to re-examine the Freudian notion of the Oedipus complex on the basis of a general sociological orientation, which viewed sentiment formation as patterned by social structure. The generic view clearly underlay his exploration of a specific "psychological" complex in its relation to a system of status relationships in a society differing in structure from that of western

changeably. However, it is usually clear from context when such terms may be equated with what we call a *theoretical orientation* rather than a purely formal methodology. We wish to emphasize that we are not suggesting these phrases be dropped and *theoretical orientation* substituted in their place. They have a well-established usage in anthropological writings. And, indeed, throughout this book, as the reader will note, we have ourselves used them on occasion to refer to "theoretical orientations." Context should make clear when we mean a purely formal methodology or a methodology that orients us toward certain kinds of variables. All we have tried to do by introducing the term *theoretical orientation* into our discussion is to point up some of the differences (from the usage and meaning of *methodology* as the term is employed by philosophers of science) which already exist in the theoretical writings of anthropologists and other social scientists.

Europe. The *specific* hypotheses which he utilized in this inquiry were all congruent with the generic orientation but were not prescribed by it. Otherwise put, the general orientation indicated the relevance of *some* structural variables, but there still remained the task of ferreting out the particular variables to be included.[2]

In sum, then, we look upon the four approaches which form the topic of this chapter as ways of selecting, conceptualizing, and ordering data in response to certain kinds of questioning. These approaches may help to generate theories; they are not in themselves theories.

The four approaches do not, of course, exhaust the theoretical orientations utilized by anthropologists. To be sure, there are others. For example, within recent years a number of anthropologists have been concerned with exploring the nature of "native conceptual models." This concern manifests itself in somewhat different forms, such as structuralism, ethnoscience, ethnosemantics, componential analysis, etc. Would it be proper to refer to these various types of "formal analysis" (individually *or* collectively) as a special kind or kinds of theoretical orientation? Or should they be subsumed under the more traditional rubrics—evolutionism, functionalism, history, and cultural ecology—as in the present chapter? On the one hand, is not ethnoscience, since it is concerned with the way persons classify and categorize their environment, a variant of cultural ecology? And do not certain aspects of, let us say, Claude Lévi-Strauss's "structural analyses" in fact ultimately comprise a special version of "functional" analysis—for example, his argument that incest taboos serve to augment solidarity among potentially competing groups? In this respect, of course, Lévi-Strauss offers us the same kind of functional explanation for the incest taboo as was suggested by Tylor more than half a century earlier.

Yet at the same time it does strike us that the varieties of contemporary formal analysis do have a somewhat special character which would justify treating them as yet another kind of theoretical orientation. Although the issues or problems that concern contemporary anthropologists engaged in formal analysis are not entirely new—for example, the interest in the "native's conceptual models" is itself an old issue in anthropology—the contemporary approach to "native models" incorporates a number of new formal methodological devices drawn from linguistics, communication science, cybernetics, symbolic logic, etc. Although our decision may seem somewhat arbitrary, we believe, therefore, that the special methodological character of contemporary formal analysis merits separate treatment, and we have thus reserved such a discussion for Chapter 4.

In this chapter, we have also departed somewhat from tradition by including cultural ecology among the major theoretical orientations in anthropology along with functionalism, evolutionism, and history. Broadly conceived, cultural ecology is concerned with problems of cultural and group adaptation. Yet, it seems to us that all anthropologists, whether self-styled ecologists or

---

[2] Robert K. Merton, "The Bearing of Sociological Theory on Empirical Research," in *On Theoretical Sociology* (New York: Free Press Paperback, 1967), pp. 141–42.

not, are concerned either explicitly or implicitly with questions of adaptation at some level: individual, group, institutional, or the total cultural system. In short, the concept of "adaptation" so permeates anthropological thinking that we believe cultural ecology properly belongs among the major theoretical orientations in anthropology.

Finally, some preliminary remarks about our approach toward functionalism, evolutionism, and history. As we have tried to indicate in Chapter 1, whatever other aims and interests anthropology may be said to have, certainly the primary goal of a scientifically conceived anthropology is to provide the best possible explanations for a broad range of problems which can be subsumed under two general questions: How do cultural systems work? and How have they come to be as they are?

Throughout much of the history of anthropology, these questions have been viewed as closely related, if not indeed inseparable. During the early decades of the twentieth century, in the aftermath of the great functionalist assault on both evolutionism and "conjectural" history (is there any other kind?), anthropological inquiry tended to separate questions of development from those of function more sharply than ever before. This trend is reflected, for example, in the sharp distinction drawn between synchronic studies (studies at a given point in time) and diachronic studies (those over time). The distinction has had a very real impact on the kind of research and theorizing that has gone on in anthropology since the 1920s and 1930s. Writers with theoretical positions seemingly as diverse as the functionalist Radcliffe-Brown and the evolutionist Leslie White are in agreement that each kind of study merits its own appropriate methodology and mode of explanation: some variant of functional analysis for synchronic studies, and an evolutionary or historical approach for diachronic studies.

In this chapter we wish to suggest, first, that the two questions—How do cultural systems work? and How have they come to be as they are?—in some sense mutually presuppose one another; that is to say, wherever we begin our inquiry, an answer to one implies an answer to the other. And second, we would argue that insofar as we are engaged in furnishing explanations for the way cultural systems work (or how they come to be what they are) we will, at some point—consciously or not—employ functional, evolutionary, *and* historical ways of looking at the data. In other words, we are not simply asserting—as has been said before—that these approaches are merely different and equally valid, but rather that, like the questions from which they issue, they logically entail one another. Or, as Linton Freeman has phrased it:

> All of these schools, the evolutionists, the structural-functionalists, and the culture historians are expressing the same hypotheses in different linguistic guises. Their methodological assumptions differ, but when we look to their hypotheses their conflict disappears—they become congruent—a single theory of socio-cultural form and process.[3]

---

[3] Linton C. Freeman, "Conflict and Congruence in Anthropological Theory," in *Selected Papers of the Fifth International Congress of Anthropological and Ethnological Sciences,* ed. Anthony F. C. Wallace (Philadelphia: University of Pennsylvania Press, 1960), p. 96.

General Historical Framework

During the nineteenth century most fields of social inquiry were clearly dominated by evolutionary or developmental orientations. The discovery of distant lands, exotic peoples, and extraordinary new animal species all had greatly widened the intellectual purview of European scholars and enormously expanded the time scale within which man had formerly been considered. The fixed and static categories of medieval thought were gradually discarded (not without a soul-searching wrench, of course), to be replaced by notions of change and evolution, in the developing biological sciences as well as the inchoate social disciplines.[4]

In anthropology, pioneers like Edward B. Tylor (*Primitive Culture*, 1871), Lewis Henry Morgan (*Ancient Society*, 1877), and Sir Henry Maine (*Ancient Law*, 1861) were exponents of the evolutionary position. Even in sociology, which had not yet become sharply distinquished from anthropology, such outstanding figures as Herbert Spencer (*Principles of Sociology*, 1876) and Emile Durkheim (*Division of Labor in Society*, 1893) either argued for the evolutionary point of view with passion (Spencer) or accepted and operated within its basic assumptions (Durkheim).[5]

Around the turn of the twentieth century a reaction against evolutionary modes of thought in the foundling social sciences set in. In part, this shift seems to have been a result of a humanistic revulsion against what many took to be the "social Darwinist" or racist implications of nineteenth-century evolutionist writings. In part—and this, of course, applies most particularly to anthropology—the reaction stemmed from the increasing depreciation of "armchair speculation" and a growing emphasis upon empirical field research. Largely as a result of the early field work of Franz Boas in the New World and A. R. Radcliffe-Brown and Bronislaw Malinowski in the Old, it became clear that some of the data upon which the nineteenth-century evolutionists had drawn were inaccurate, biased, and fragmentary. Boas, Radcliffe-Brown, Malinowski, and their followers argued that if anthropology was to become a responsible empirical discipline, it could not continue to rely on

---

[4] See Harry L. Shapiro, "Anthropology and the Age of Discovery," in *Process and Pattern in Culture*, ed. Robert A. Manners. (Chicago: Aldine, 1964), pp. 337–48.

[5] It is often said that the social and cultural evolutionists received their main inspiration from the writings of Charles Darwin. But to keep the historical records straight, it should be pointed out that all of the major works contributing to the social evolutionary viewpoint (those of Comte, Hegel, Marx, and Spencer) either appeared before *The Origin of Species* or, as Robert A. Nisbet indicates, "clearly involved work that had begun much earlier, the works of such men as Sir Henry Maine, Edward Tylor, and Lewis Morgan. None of these classics in social evolution refer to, or show any objective evidence of relation to, the line of study in biological speciation that came out of the eighteenth century and culminated in Darwin's great book" [*Social Change and History* (New York: Oxford University Press, 1969), p. 161].

It is true, of course, that Darwin's writings lent great impetus to the interest in cultural evolutionism, but the nineteenth-century evolutionists owe more to the French Enlightenment writers such as Condorcet, Turgot, and Voltaire and to the Scottish social philosophers like Adam Ferguson, David Hume, and Adam Smith than they do to Charles Darwin. Clearly, development and evolution were in the air.

the impressionistic accounts of missionaries, travelers, and traders. A discipline of anthropology demanded a systematic approach to the observation, collecting, and recording of cultural data at first hand. Boas, in particular, stressed the urgency of conducting widespread ethnographic research among the simpler cultures of the world before they should disappear.

The "humanistic revulsion" to which we have referred provided an additional rationale for the increasing emphasis on field work. It was assumed that through intensive first-hand contact with non-Western cultures anthropologists could effectively expose the social Darwinist fallacies which were seen by them to be a part of the evolutionists' writings. Direct confrontation would, in this view, reveal the essential worth of all cultures no matter how simple; it would document the skill and inventiveness with which each people had resolved common human problems of existence. In short, field work would provide the empirical evidence for the humanistic premise that cultures were not to be evaluated as higher or lower, superior or inferior, better or worse—but simply as *different*. Thus, cultural relativism and historical particularism were offered as an antidote to evolutionism, and as the intellectual complement to at least one prominent version of functionalism—namely, the doctrine asserting that each culture is a distinctive configuration made up of uniquely interrelated parts, and that these parts are to be understood only in terms of their relationship to the wider configurational context. Idus Murphree has remarked upon this connection:

> This more modern frame of mind is best expressed as one centering around the concept of cultural relativity; its concurrent appearance with "functionalism" in anthropology and sociology speaks of more than a tenuous connection, for the notion of cultural context undergirds cultural relativity.[6]

It is easy to see why this relativistic-functionalist methodology should have proved so congenial to a discipline increasingly concerned with empirical field research among small-scale societies; and why, in turn, the field research should have served to solidify and deepen the anthropologists' commitment to the relativist-functionalist position. As Hopkins and Wallerstein have noted:

> Functionalism, then as now a research directive as well as a theoretical orientation, was securely tied to empirical inquiry on the scale of the single field worker, which at most is not a very broad scale. If at this time anthropology lost its evolutionary focus to an ahistorical perspective, that was as much because of assumptions about what one person, directly observing events in the course of a two-year stint, could reliably see and infer, as it was because of a theoretical concern with how a particular society hung together.[7]

---

[6] Idus L. Murphree, "The Evolutionary Anthropologists: The Concepts of Progress and Culture in the Thought of John Lubbock, Edward B. Tylor, and Lewis H. Morgan," *Proceedings of The American Philosophical Society* 105 (1961): 284.

[7] Terence K. Hopkins and Immanuel Wallerstein, "The Comparative Study of National Societies," *Social Science Information* 6 (1967): 36.

For a number of years the emphasis on cultural configuration that characterized the writings of the relativists and functionalists in anthropology dominated the discipline and thrust a concern for problems of development into the background. Since the end of World War II, however, there has been a sharply revived interest in developmental and evolutionary issues. This renewed interest is not hard to understand, for what were formerly "backward areas," the almost exclusive preserve of anthropology among the social sciences, became almost overnight "developing areas." Societies that had been bastions of relativist "differences" now rejected their differences and opted for changes that would make them more like the "developed" societies. Lévi-Strauss noted the irony when he observed that the very people in whose name the doctrine of cultural relativity was proclaimed have come to reject it.[8] We might add a further irony: in accounting for certain kinds of cultural differences, the nineteenth-century evolutionists referred to the simpler societies as cases of arrested development. They explained the condition of these societies as owing to a combination of cultural or physical isolation, along with certain historical and/or special geographical factors. Although anthropologists do not now use precisely the same terminology, they have always distinguished between technologically advanced and technologically backward societies. Today, instead of employing nineteenth-century terminology, anthropologists generally refer to the former as developed and the latter as underdeveloped or developing societies.

But even when antievolutionist sentiment was at its peak, anthropologists —including the aggressive ultrarelativists—could not escape a terminology that reflected their recognition of developmentalism. Whether they used terms like *higher* and *lower levels, simple* and *advanced,* or *"primitive," preliterate,* or even *nonliterate* in place of the ostensibly more pejorative *savage* or *barbarian,* it is fairly clear that they were dealing with a ranking system based on development.[9] Nor is it necessary to emphasize the heuristic advantage and the scientific respectability of employing a nomenclature that looks at social change from a developmental or evolutionary point of view.

Nineteenth-Century Evolutionism: A Historical Perspective

Before turning to a consideration of contemporary evolutionary approaches in anthropology, we shall briefly review some of the main features of the earlier nineteenth-century evolutionary writings. There are at least two good reasons for a summary of this kind: first, because we believe the theoretical formulations of the nineteenth-century writers have often been treated either cavalierly or inaccurately by latter-day anthropologists; and, second, because we believe that at least some of the nineteenth-century formulations have relevance for contemporary conceptions of development.

---

[8] See Claude Lévi-Strauss "Anthropology: Its Achievement and Future," *Current Anthropology* 7 (1966): 125.

[9] See Leslie A. White, "Evolutionary Stages, Progress, and the Evaluation of Cultures," *Southwestern Journal of Anthropology* 3 (1947): 165–92.

One of the more common criticisms leveled at the nineteenth-century evolutionists is that they were highly ethnocentric—i.e., that they assumed that Victorian England, or its equivalent, represented the highest achievement of mankind. Another is the charge that they engaged in unwarranted armchair speculation—i.e., that they built their logical reconstructions on questionable data. And finally they are faulted for having postulated a unilineal scheme of cultural development associated with the inevitability of progress—i.e., they are said to have argued that all cultures must pass through the same, or roughly the same, succession of stages in their ultimate march toward the heights achieved by nineteenth-century Victorian England.

While these criticisms are not without considerable justification, they appear to overstate the case against the concepts and methodology of the nineteenth-century evolutionists. The latter-day critics to whom we have referred may not have given enough weight to the special historical circumstances under which the evolutionists' writings were produced. There are two aspects of these circumstances that are especially noteworthy. First, it must be recalled that the nineteenth-century evolutionists were struggling to establish a naturalistic study of cultural phenomena, or what Tylor called "the science of culture." The main way in which they hoped to establish such a science was to demonstrate that culture had developed in a natural step-by-step fashion. As Idus Murphree has so cogently expressed it:

> In judging the Victorian ethnologists, we should not forget that they were embattled men straining to take the curse of Adam from their primeval ancestors. They recognized that progress was a human creation due to man's natural capacity as a social animal. As much as anything else, their contention of human progress was a note of confidence for the species against those who insisted that if evolutionary man was a wayward ape, he would have been doomed to brutishness. In all the loose talk about progress, the evolutionary anthropologists worked their way toward the view that a sequence of development imposed its own logic on the ordering of events, and that later stages presupposed earlier ones without which the later were impossible. If they misconstrued the logic they held soundly to the evolutionary principle that the chain of events ushered the new from the old. . . .
>
> The decorous and grammatical pronouncements of these Victorian spokesmen for science should not obscure their deep partisanship. They were engaged in a serious business. Their commitment to the evolutionary method stems from their prepossessing task, the creation of what Tylor called, without embarrassment, "The Science of Culture." They looked to the secular, mundane, and ordinary to relieve human behavior of causeless spontaneity and supernatural influence. Their excesses in speculation and logic, finding connections where there weren't any, had a basis in the conviction that the connections must be there if they could be found. Tylor maintained that the only proper antidote to "arbitrary impulses, causeless freaks, chance and nonsense, and indefinite accountability" was "to see the line of connexion in events." [10]

---

[10] Murphree, "The Evolutionary Anthropologists," pp. 267, 276.

The problem of natural versus supernatural explanations of cultural events is no longer an issue in anthropology. The nineteenth-century evolutionists won that battle. But from the vantage point of the mid-twentieth century we sometimes forget how crucial and how difficult the conflict was.

Not only were these early efforts to establish a scientific discipline of anthropology hampered by the climate of supernatural explanations, but the nineteenth-century evolutionists had to cope as well with a paucity of reliable empirical materials. Faced with this shortage of data, they attempted to bridge the gaps in their evolutionary schema with logical and frequently imaginative reconstructions, i.e., by engaging in "armchair speculation." Of course, this kind of speculation is perfectly acceptable scientific procedure. The mistake the speculators often made was to assume that the empirical world was under some obligation to conform to their logical reconstructions. In a discussion of Tylor's evolutionism, George Stocking reflects on this very issue when he makes the point that Tylor's central problem was, in effect, to

> fill the gap between Brixham Cave and European Civilization without introducing the hand of God. To this end Tylor was primarily concerned —in the absence of specifically historical data—with showing how one *might* get from one to the other in strictly *uniformitarian* manner. He used the comparative method and the doctrine of survivals to trace civilization backwards in order to recreate a forward movement which showed no sharp breaks, and in which the governance of natural law was manifest in a series of regularly recurring stages and in the regularity of human reason reacting to similar environmental conditions. But beyond this, process in any specific terms was no great concern to Tylor. It is precisely for this reason that modern anthropologists whose problems are quite different ones, and who have long since taken for granted the point which Tylor was laboring to prove, are ill-advised to look for a dynamic either of "technological determinism" or of "cultural Darwinism." Evidence can, of course, be found for either view—but only by reading specific passages out of their proper place in the overall context of Tylor's work and the controversies of his day.[11]

The charge that the nineteenth-century writers held simplistically unilineal views of cultural development also requires some qualification. It is true that one can interpret certain of their statements as implying that *all* societies had to pass through the same developmental stages. On the other hand, one may find ample evidence in their writings that they were not bound by such a naïve unilineal assumption. They were fully aware of the facts of cultural diffusion and the way in which diffusion had enabled societies to "skip" certain developmental stages. But they were less concerned with the development of specific cultures *in situ* than with the evolution of "Culture" taken as a global phenomenon—culture conceived as a great stream of tradition coming down from the past and imprinting itself on the present. Their stages apply to the history of man and not to the development of specific societies and cultures. As Robert A. Nisbet has observed:

---

[11] George W. Stocking, " 'Cultural Darwinism' and 'Philosophical Idealism' in E. B. Tylor: A Special Plea for Historicism in the History of Anthropology," *Southwestern Journal of Anthropology* 21 (1965): 141.

Had any of the classical social evolutionists been around to defend themselves, they would have had no difficulty, I think, in making plain two very important facts: the first in defense and clarification of their own work; the second, and to me more interesting, in counter-attack upon their critics.

They would have been able to say, first, that they were well aware indeed of the inapplicability of their evolutionary sequences to all the areas and peoples on the earth's surface, and would have been able to point chapter and verse to their knowledge of differences and divergences of history in these areas and peoples. What they could have said—Comte, Spencer, Morgan, Tylor and the others—was that they were not pretending to deal with these concrete areas and peoples; that the sole object of their labors, for better or worse, was to identify the natural line of development of, first, civilization as a whole, as civilization reaches from the remote past down to the present, and, second, of one or more of the generalized institutions which in their aggregate form human society. Criticisms based upon the concrete histories of the Crow Indians, the Melanesians, the modern Europeans, and other peoples were therefore irrelevant to the expressed purpose of their labors.[12]

Because writers like Morgan and Tylor were primarily interested in reconstructing the stages through which mankind as a whole had passed in arriving at the present, they were more or less indifferent to probing for the actual mechanisms by which man had advanced from one stage to another. At one time, they seem to favor ideological causations, at another, technological causations or determinism. This is another reason why recent anthropological literature includes controversies about what Morgan and Tylor "really meant." [13]

Finally, the criticism that the nineteenth-century evolutionists were both ethnocentric and naïvely optimistic about man's inevitable progress also requires some comment. In the first place, one can be ethnocentric in several ways. For example, at one extreme a person may be ignorant of the great diversity of cultural arrangements and believe that his own lifeways are not only right and proper but that they reveal human nature. Quite clearly, the evolutionists were not ethnocentric in this sense. Another form of ethnocentricism is one in which a person assumes the moral and intellectual superiority of his own culture over all others. In this respect, there is ample evidence that the nineteenth-century evolutionists attributed this kind of superiority to their own culture. While the question of the moral superiority of one culture over another is virtually impossible to measure, intellectual superiority (societal but not individual), as reflected by the accumulated body of knowledge extant in a culture, does have a kind of measurability. It enables us to compare one society with another, to evaluate the overall effectiveness of each in deal-

---

[12] Nisbet, *Social Change and History*, pp. 224–25. See also Leslie A. White, "Diffusion vs. Evolution: An Anti-Evolutionist Fallacy," *American Anthropologist* 47 (1945): 339–56.

[13] See, for example, Thomas G. Harding, "Morgan and Materialism: A Reply to Professor Opler," *Current Anthropology* 5 (1964): 109; and comments by Eleanor Leacock and Morris E. Opler in same issue, 109–14.

ing with its total environment. Looking back over the course of cultural evolution as they perceived it, it was evident to these nineteenth-century scholars that there had been a steady and progressive accumulation of knowledge. And this accumulation of knowledge involved an increasingly efficient means of adapting to and controlling the environment. As they looked around them, it seemed self-evident that in terms of accumulated knowledge and control over the environment, Victorian England represented the peak of this progressive development up to that time. But they did not, as it is sometimes charged, believe that the cultural achievements of Victorian England would not be surpassed at some future time. Indeed, such a view is entirely inconsistent with their assumptions about the cumulative nature of the cultural tradition. (On the other hand, they did not discount the possibility of individual instances of cultural regression under special historical circumstances.) To quote from Murphree's excellent discussion once again:

> For all their concern with progress, the evolutionists never subscribed to a theory of "guaranteed," "automatic," or "necessary" progress. They were prepared to recognize degeneration, although they thought it more likely to be true of individuals than of cultures and true of culture only under limited circumstances, neither occurrence invalidating the general tendency toward progress. A set of qualifying, environing circumstances was always accessory to cultural advancement, and the essential conviction of the evolutionary school was, not that progress was inevitable and uniform, but that the condition of progress was indissociable from the nature of cultural evolution.[14]

Some contemporary relativists have assailed evolutionary formulations by cataloguing the virtues of simpler societies and contrasting these with the vices and shortcomings of modern industrial societies. Such critics claim to be avoiding the crude ethnocentric biases of the developmentarians. In point of fact, what they appear to be doing is engaging in a kind of ethnocentricism-in-reverse, an other-ethnocentricism in which the societies to which they belong are denigrated and the simpler societies are treated with a Rousseauean admiration.

A curious double standard seems to be operating here. When the members of tribe X exhibit cruel and sadistic behavior toward others—for example, head-hunting—their behavior is not to be condemned but understood, the relativist would say, in terms of the way in which the act fits into the broader cultural pattern of that society. But let a Northern or Southern racist in our own society act out his fears by barring the school entrance to a Negro child and his behavior is sure to be condemned by the same relativist. This latter behavior may indeed be worthy of condemnation. But what seems to be operating in these hypothetical cases is a detached, objective, relativistic (paternalistic?) approach to tribe X on the one hand and, on the other, a highly evaluative, nonrelativistic set of standards applied to a pattern of behavior in our own society.

To return to the nineteenth-century evolutionists: whatever the deficiencies of their analyses may have been—and we would agree with their critics that

---

14 Murphree, "The Evolutionary Anthropologists," p. 279.

their work does (especially from the vantage point of our present information and knowledge) reveal serious shortcomings—they laid the foundations for an organized discipline where none had existed before. And they left us a legacy of at least three basic assumptions which have become an integral part of anthropological thought and research methodology: (1) the dictum that cultural phenomena are to be studied in naturalistic fashion; (2) the premise of "the psychic unity of mankind," i.e., that cultural differences between groups are not due to differences in psychobiological equipment but to differences in sociocultural experience; and (3) the use of the comparative method as a surrogate for the experimental and laboratory techniques of the physical sciences.

Contemporary Evolutionism

Childe, White, and Steward

During the long period of some forty years in which cultural evolutionism was in almost total eclipse, a few anthropologists continued to work within the evolutionary tradition. Perhaps the best known of them are the American anthropologists Leslie A. White and Julian H. Steward and, in England, the celebrated archeologist V. Gordon Childe.

In a series of technical archeological works, as well as several more popular treatments (*Man Makes Himself*, 1941, and *What Happened in History*, 1946), Childe used the archeological record to demonstrate that certain dramatic technical advances in the history of man (the domestication of plants and animals, irrigation agriculture, the invention of metallurgy, etc.) had produced revolutionary changes in the entire fabric of man's cultural life. Social and political structures, as well as the organization and content of knowledge by which man apprehended reality became transformed. In the main, Childe argued, the archeological record indicates that the overall pattern of these changes was evolutionary and progressive in nature: from a simple, nomadic Paleolithic hunter and gatherer, man had advanced to assume the life of a sedentary horticulturalist in compact Neolithic communities. And out of this Neolithic base in certain favorable areas came the classical urban civilizations of the ancient world—Egypt, Mesopotamia, Greece, and Rome. While in certain of his writings Childe seems to retreat into what Julian Steward has referred to as "a combination of Morganism with historical particularism, diffusionism and relativism," [15] the total corpus of his work is clearly evolutionary in its impact.

If Childe sometimes wavered in his devotion to evolutionary assumptions and principles, White and Steward have always been consistent in their espousal of an evolutionary orientation.[16] To appreciate fully White's view of

---

[15] Julian Steward, "Review of V. Gordon Childe's *Social Evolution*," *American Anthropologist* 55 (1953): 240–41.

[16] For Leslie White's views on culture and cultural evolution, see *The Evolution of Culture* (New York: McGraw-Hill, 1959), and *The Science of Culture* (New York: Farrar, Straus, 1949). For Julian Steward's views on culture and cultural evolution, see *Theory of Culture Change* (Urbana: University of Illinois Press, 1955).

cultural evolution, it is necessary first to understand something about his conception of culture. Basic to this conception is a distinction between sign behavior and symboling behavior. Signs, White maintains, are things or events whose meaning is inherent in their physical form, or so closely identified with their form as to seem inherent. Symbols, on the other hand, are things or events whose meaning is arbitrarily bestowed upon them by their collective users. The significance of this distinction, White asserts, is that while the behavior of all higher animals other than man is typically sign behavior, man is the only animal capable of performing both sign and symboling behavior.

The most prominent form of symboling behavior, of course, is human language. It is when we consciously consider the connection between a word-sound and its referent (as when we are learning a foreign language) that we realize most clearly the arbitrary nature of this relationship, and thus the symbolic nature of human communication. However, once the connection between a word and its referent becomes fixed in our nervous system through conditioning, we react to the word as though its meaning were inherent in the sound. Sounds that functioned as symbols when meaning was originally bestowed upon them may come subsequently to function as signs. Or, to give an example outside of language, an experienced driver coming upon a red traffic light will stop automatically, without consciously thinking about it. In other words, he reacts to the light as a sign, as though the meaning "stop" were inherent in the color red in the way that, for example, the meaning "rain" is inherent in a thundercloud. Of course there is no such inherent reason why red should mean "stop" or why green should mean "go." It could be the other way around if we all agreed upon the convention. The important point to remember is that the meaning of symbols is assigned to them by their users. Your dog, for example, will understand certain words or phrases directed to him; but it is *you* who determine what the words or the sounds that you utter will mean. They can only function as signs to the dog. And no matter how hard you may try you will never get him to apprehend the meaning of the cross or the American flag, or to know what distinguishes Sunday from Wednesday, or to understand the differences between a parallel cousin and a cross-cousin. So White argues.

The implication of all this for White's view of culture is that since the behavior of the higher infrahuman animal species is nonsymbolic in nature, they are limited to a world of their own sensory experiences. To be sure, such species may be capable of a high degree of learning, and may even exhibit certain behavior patterns which are clearly not biogenetic and are nevertheless passed on from generation to generation. (Such behavior has been referred to as *protoculture* by some investigators. White would reject this term: a species either exhibits culture or it does not; there is no middle ground.) But over time these learned and transmitted behavior patterns among infrahumans seem to be nonprogressive and noncumulative in nature —like tool-using among the higher primates.

Man, on the other hand, because he can symbolically represent (and, of course, misrepresent) the world to himself, is capable of transcending his own sensory experiences. He can talk about places he has never seen, events in which he has not participated; he can speculate about the past, dream about the future, and even invent entities that do not exist, like unicorns and witches. Symboling enables man to husband and to represent his experiences in such a form that they become part of a cumulative and progressive tradition. It is primarily through this extrasomatic stream of tradition embracing technoeconomics, social organization, and ideology—or simply culture—that man adapts to and exploits the world around him.

Thus, when White uses the term *culture*, he does so in much the same way as did his nineteenth-century predecessors. Both he and they used the word to refer to the cumulative, collective experiences of mankind, rather than to the history of this or that particular group culture. And when he speaks of stages of development, he is referring to universal stages which can be said to characterize these collective experiences. The charge of unilineality is therefore as irrelevant to his evolutionary schema as it was to that of most of the nineteenth-century evolutionists.

It is because White in his evolutionary formulations is more concerned with culture writ large rather than its local manifestations that he can ignore geographical factors as well as psychobiological variations in the species. Culture, to be sure, has its origin in the processes of biological evolution. But once it appears it comes to have a life and momentum of its own, which is why, says White, culture is explainable only in terms of culture. Neither changes in this total superorganic tradition (culture) nor local variations over time within it are explainable by an appeal to geographical or psychobiological factors, for these have probably not changed appreciably since the end of the Pleistocene, around 20–25,000 years ago.

There is another and very important dimension to White's conception of cultural evolution. While culture is the adaptive device by which man accommodates himself to nature and nature to him, basically man-in-culture performs these functions by harnessing free energy and putting it to work for the species. Thus, White, unlike his nineteenth-century predecessors, has been quite explicit about the basic mechanisms of evolutionary change. He has proposed the following formula for explaining cultural development: culture advances as the amount of energy harnessed per capita per year increases or as the efficiency with which energy is utilized increases ($E \times T \to C$, where E is energy, T is the efficiency of the tools or technology, and C is culture). In this energy-harnessing process, White sees all the major institutional orders of culture—technology, social and political organization, and ideology—as contributing to the effectiveness with which the system appropriates and utilizes the energy available to it. But "the primary role is played by the technological system." Because of this stance White has often been accused of a mechanical technological determinism—and this despite his assertion that all parts of culture are interrelated; each reacts upon the others and is affected by them in turn. White defends his stance with regard to the primacy of technology by emphasizing that it is through his technology that man most closely articulates with the surface of the planet. He feels, therefore, that it is this component that exerts the greater causal weight in accounting for cultural evolution.

In general, Julian Steward does not dispute White's evolutionary schema. Along with White, Steward has been critical of the cultural relativists for their emphasis on the distinctiveness of each culture and their virtual neglect of the impressive cross-cultural similarities revealed by cultural processes. Like White, he feels that the wave of antievolutionism which dominated the discipline for so many years has been counterproductive to the development of a genuine science of sociocultural phenomena. For, again like White, he believes that the central aim of anthropology should be the discovery of cultural regularities through time and their explanation in cause-and-effect terms.

Where Steward departs from White and, in effect, from the nineteenth-century evolutionists is in the level of generality with which he conceptualizes cultural evolution. His main criticism of White is not that White's evolutionary formulations are wrong, but that they are so broad and general as not to be very helpful in understanding particular sequences of development. Thus, while Steward deplores historical particularism, he is also critical of theoretical formulations which seem too abstract and remote from empirical materials. Steward appears in most of his work to be searching for general propositions analogous to what Merton calls "theories of the middle range." In short, Steward is far more interested in *cultures* (or groups of cultures) than in *culture* conceived in White's broad terms.

Steward labels White's brand of evolutionism universal (because it applies to all culture and not to cultures), contrasting it with the unilineal approach (in which all cultures are alleged to have passed through the same or similar stages) attributed to the nineteenth-century writers and with his own approach, which he has called multilinear evolution.

Steward defines the multilinear approach as a methodology for dealing with cultural differences and similarities through a comparison of parallel sequences of development, generally in widely separated geographic areas. Underlying this methodology are certain basic assumptions about the nature of cultural processes. These assumptions arise out of Steward's reaction to his colleagues' preoccupation with differences in cultural content. Steward argues that this preoccupation has led to a general neglect of the important structural similarities which might accompany the overstressed differences. The preeminent task of multilinear evolution, he maintains, is to account for, to explain, these structural similarities. He believes that an analysis of historical sequences in different parts of the world will often demonstrate that similar mechanisms producing similarities in structure have been at work. For example, in a paper to which we referred in Chapter 1, "Cultural Causality and Law," published in 1949, Steward dealt with this issue on an empirical basis. He compared the high civilizations of the Old World with those of the New World and argued that the similarities in their social and political structures arose from essential similarities in their natural habitats and the techniques evolved for exploiting these habitats. In this case, as in others to be found in the body of Steward's work, it is apparent that the mechanisms of cultural development to which he attributes *primary* causal significance might easily be rephrased in terms of White's energy theory.

Although Steward has strong reservations about the fruitfulness of "grand" theories, he is forced in carrying out the strategy of multilinear research to employ propositions every bit as general as those used by White. For unless the investigator utilizes certain theoretical propositions to sort out the more crucial from the less crucial elements in any historical sequence, he is in danger of being swamped by the sheer variety and multiplicity of events involved. Often Steward writes as though his general theoretical propositions emerge by some process of induction from his multilinear investigations. Actually, however, they are logical constructions formulated prior to his researches. Indeed, without some such prefabricated theoretical stance his investigations would have become bogged down at their very outset by the infinite array of particularistic facts.

There are three related notions which together comprise the central element in Steward's approach to cultural evolution: (1) core institutions versus peripheral institutions, (2) the cultural type, and (3) levels of sociocultural integration.

Steward argues that in all cultural systems one can distinguish those institutions which are strategically crucial to the way the system is organized from those which are peripheral. The former, *core institutions*, are the ones most closely related to the way in which the culture adapts to and exploits its environment. Furthermore, while the core institutions of any culture may include ideological, sociopolitical, and technoeconomic elements, the technoeconomic factors figure most prominently in defining and forming the strategic features of any society.[17] Thus, once again the similarities between the theoretical positions of Steward and White are brought home to us.

Steward's conception of the relative causal weight of different cultural elements may be diagrammed in the following way:

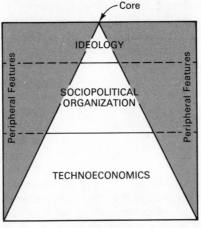

<hr />

[17] From the corpus of his empirical research it seems fairly clear that this is what Steward meant by the term *cultural core*. In at least one instance, however, he seems to entertain the possibility that such additional features as the esthetic, military, etc. might also be included in the cultural core. Harris has drawn attention to this seeming inconsistency in *The Rise of Anthropological Theory* (New York: Thomas Y. Crowell, 1968) pp. 660–61.

It follows, therefore, that while change may be initiated anywhere in the system—in the peripheral *as well* as in the core institutions—unless these changes react upon and transform the core institutions, the system as a whole will not undergo a change of cultural type. In one form, this process, defined by Steward as evolutionary, shows up time and again in the so-called underdeveloped areas of the world where many countries are caught up in ideological revolutions. These various ideological changes are now being employed as levers to bring about transformations in the core institutions. But in most cases the transformations are either partial or have hardly begun. They manifest—even to those of us who are self-consciously aware of the incongruities in our own culture—a curious juxtaposition of the old and the new, with the former predominating.

In Steward's view, cultures that have similar core features may be classified as belonging to the same general type. Since it is apparent that Steward is more concerned in his cultural typologies with structural features than with content, we equate his cultural type with what we have referred to earlier as a *structural* type.

If one groups Steward's cultural types and places them along a rough continuum of increasing sociocultural complexity, what emerges is a methodological framework for research and analysis. Steward calls this concept or methodological framework "levels of sociocultural integration." He distinguishes among three broad levels: family, tribe, and state, and defines each of these in terms of the largest autonomous sociopolitical unit engaging in collective action. Other evolutionists such as Elman Service in *Primitive Social Organization* (1962), Marshall Sahlins in *Tribesmen* (1968), and Morton Fried in *The Evolution of Political Society* (1967) have adapted and further refined Steward's concept. In place of family, tribe, and state levels, Service and Sahlins speak of bands, tribes, chiefdoms, and states; and Fried, who focuses on the evolution of inequality, discusses egalitarian, ranked, stratified, and state societies.

And finally, it is important to emphasize that Steward has always resisted the notion that his "levels" represent a precise empirical sequence. For him they are primarily a heuristic device for ordering data and dealing with problems of cultural transformations.

Some Recent Contributions

Recently Marshall Sahlins has suggested that the views of White and Steward on cultural evolution are complementary rather than conflicting.[18] He sees two ways of conceptualizing the evolutionary process. On the one hand, cultural evolution has yielded progressively higher levels of organization: systems exhibiting greater complexity and all-round adaptability. He calls this process or aspect *general evolution*. On the other hand, as new cultural types emerge, they undergo an inevitable process of radiation and adaptation to their specific total environments. Consequently, he refers to

---

[18] See Marshall D. Sahlins, "Evolution: Specific and General," in *Evolution and Culture*, eds., Marshall D. Sahlins and Elman R. Service (Ann Arbor: University of Michigan Press, 1960), pp. 12–44.

this process or aspect as *specific evolution*. Sahlins then goes on to say that White is interested essentially in general and Steward in specific evolution. We shall turn shortly to a more detailed look at Sahlins's views of evolution.

Earlier we remarked on the revival of interest in the concepts of evolution and development. It is also apparent from what we have said that there continues to be some dispute among anthropologists about the meaning of these concepts. But a careful reading of these controversies suggests that the disputes more often reflect different definitions and usages of the concepts than disagreements about substance.

But definitions, to paraphrase Lewis Carroll, are man-made. Therefore, it is less a matter of their being right or wrong than it is of their being more useful or less useful. Moreover, when anthropologists become embroiled in disputes about definitions, they move insensibly and inevitably from these quasi-objective considerations to reflections on the essential *nature* of evolution (Is it progressive? Is it reversible? Is it directional? Should it be equated with *any* kind of change?). In short, they become engaged in metaphysical discussions rather than scientific ones. And the quest to discover the *nature* of evolution, like the quest for a timeless and universally acceptable definition of evolution, is a hopeless one. What we consider the proper task of a scientifically conceived anthropology is to arrive at a conception of *evolution* or *development* (terms which we use interchangeably throughout) that will provide a useful framework for thinking about, researching, and explaining cultural change.

Despite the endless definitional disputes, all anthropologists would agree that minimally the concept of evolution implies directional change, rather than the kind of cyclical change that is described in Kroeber and Richardson's study of changing fashion in women's dress or any purely random change like, for example, a shift from punctate to incised pottery. As a matter of fact, Margaret Mead, in her *Continuities in Cultural Evolution* (1964), *defines* "*evolution*" as directional culture change—and leaves it at that.

But the notion of directional culture change is itself somewhat vague, and because of the vagueness it can easily be converted into a metaphysical principle. It is a notion that would appear, therefore, to be more appropriate to the speculations of the grand philosophers of history, like Hegel and Spengler, and Toynbee, than to a discipline with any scientific pretensions. Yet, even the more empirically minded social scientist investigating cultural change is constantly being confronted with situations where he is forced to make some judgment about the directionality of change. For example, in studying culture change we seem inevitably to be drawn into making a decision about when a society ceases to be one kind of system and becomes another kind of system. To be able to make such a judgment implies that we bring to our studies some conception of *kinds* of systems ranged in some sort of sequence of *probable* succession. The possibilities of change open to any society are never limitless: given a certain kind of structure and a specific set of historical circumstances, change in certain directions is more likely than in others. Thus, although the concept of directional change, like many of the concepts in anthropology, continues to have a certain porousness, its use need not necessarily lead us into a morass of metaphysical argumentation.

What we have been leading up to in the previous discussion is a distinction made a long time ago by Herbert Spencer: the distinction between cultural growth and cultural development. Growth, Spencer argued, is an additive process, whereas development implies the transformation of structures. More recently, Radcliffe-Brown, drawing upon Spencer's distinction, pointed out that change can take place within a structural type *or* it may involve a change from type to type.[19] Both kinds of change may be directional, but the second yields a transformation of society and the first does not.

The importance of this distinction may be illustrated with a recent study by Clifford Geertz of the history of changing agricultural patterns in Indonesia.[20] Geertz shows us that under the impact of the Dutch mercantile system, certain changes were set in motion in the traditional Javanese patterns of land use and community organization. Moreover, these changes seem to have been directional in nature. But the direction they took was toward a finer elaboration and complication of the pre-existing ecological patterns and community social structures. Geertz explains this process as a consequence of the Dutch rulers' interest in utilizing the traditional socioeconomic structures of the countryside for the production of certain cash crops. Since their purposes were better served by substantial preservation of pre-existing forms, the Dutch did not attempt to transform and integrate Indonesian structures into the commercial sector which they had organized on different principles from those applied in the rural hinterland. Borrowing a concept from Goldenweiser, Geertz characterizes the changes that took place in the Javanese ecological patterns as involutionary rather than evolutionary in nature. The implications of this trend of controlled adaptation for the future development of Indonesian society may be far-reaching; for, according to Geertz, the rural sector of Indonesian society seems to have dug itself (or been dug) so deeply into an ecological groove that it is hard to imagine the Indonesians making the transition to modernity (which they clearly are striving to do) without dismantling the entire traditional structure and building the system upon a different base.

All of which brings us back to Sahlins's distinction between general and specific evolution. The historical changes Geertz charts for Indonesian society would seem to fall under the rubric of specific evolution—that is, adaptational trends within a particular structural-ecological niche. If we are right in assuming that such changes can be characterized as specific evolution, then Geertz's study offers a case where accumulated specific evolutionary changes militate against the chances for a general evolutionary change.

On the other hand, specific evolution may be a creative process. For it is obvious that there can be no general evolutionary advance in the absence of cumulative specific evolutions. In other words, specific evolution *may* lead to involution or a tendency for the culture to dig itself in, as in Indonesia.

---

[19] See A. R. Radcliffe-Brown, *A Natural Science of Society* (Glencoe, Ill.: The Free Press, 1957), pp. 69–89.

[20] See Clifford Geertz, *Agricultural Involution: The Process of Ecological Change in Indonesia* (Berkeley: University of California Press, 1968).

And here the process is akin to what the biologists would call *specialization*—
e.g., the anteater is dug into a specific niche. *Or* specific evolution may lead
to more generalized and adaptive types—in short, to general evolution (stay-
ing with the biological analogy, we might refer to the appearance of mammals
as a new organic type emerging from particular reptilian lines).

Of course, anthropologists looking back on the history of culture (like
biologists looking back on the history of life) might, in post hoc fashion,
explain the decline of some cultures by reference to their overspecialization.
But what, in fact, does "overspecialization" mean? Can one look at a culture and decide whether it is so specialized that its potential for further advance is limited? And if one does make such a characterization, is it not clear
that what is involved is an implicit theory or perhaps a set of political or
moral judgments which should be made explicit before the characterization
can be evaluated?

The concept of specialization applied to human societies is not particularly
helpful or enlightening, for all societies are in some sense specialized. Their
institutions are geared, more or less successfully, to cope with—or, to put it
another way, to permit them to adapt to—a particular total environment.
To say that Bushman or Eskimo culture is any more or less specialized than
French or American culture really makes little sense. When Sahlins discusses
the relationship between specific evolution and the potential for general
evolutionary advance, he says:

> In fact a culture's downfall is the most probable outcome of its suc-
> cesses. The accomplished, well adapted culture is biased. Its design has
> been refined in a special direction, its environment narrowly specified,
> how it shall operate definitively stated. The more adapted a culture, the
> less therefore it is adaptable. Its specialization subtracts from its potential,
> from the capacity of alternate response, from tolerance of change in the
> world. It becomes vulnerable in proportion to its accomplishments. . . .
>
> In other words advanced and dominant cultures create the circumstances
> for their own eclipse. On the one hand, they themselves become
> specialized. Their development on a particular line commits them to it:
> they are mortgaged to structures accumulated along the way, burdened
> in Veblen's phrase, with the penalty of taking the lead. On the other
> hand, they restore adaptability to previously stable and backward people
> within their spheres of influence. These underdeveloped orders, rudely
> jolted from historyless equilibrium, may now seize "the privilege of
> historic backwardness" and overturn their submission by taking over the
> latest developments of advanced cultures and pushing on from there.[21]

There is a certain persuasiveness in Sahlins's argument. History is replete
with examples of societies whose institutions have become so frozen that
they inhibit or frustrate changes in a particular direction. But all societies,
advanced as well as simple, "are mortgaged to structures accumulated along
the way." And their burdens are not necessarily a consequence of their hav-

---

21 Marshall D. Sahlins, "Culture and Environment: The Study of Cultural Ecology," in
Horizons of Anthropology, ed. Sol Tax (Chicago: Aldine, 1964), pp. 138, 143–44.

ing taken "the lead." Today's underdeveloped world is full of peoples and cultures who are no less "mortgaged" to antique structures than peoples and cultures of the developed remainder.

If all-round adaptability—in the sense of controlling a wide range of environmental factors—is the measure of evolutionary potential, then the advanced societies seem to us to have a far greater potential than the less advanced.

Sahlins implies that his thesis is applicable to all cultures at all times and in all places. The thesis may have reasonable validity when applied to times past when cultures were simpler, more clearly dependent upon specific environments, and somewhat more isolated from one another. But when we look at the contemporary world with its high degree of global interdependence and interrelationships, it appears to us that it is more difficult to decide what constitutes specialization and what constitutes potential for evolutionary advance. Cultural systems can only be specialized with respect to something else—they are not in some absolute sense specialized. Certainly, advanced cultures cannot be said to be specialized with respect to their environments. For these cultures have developed such powerful and sophisticated devices for control of their habitat that they have become increasingly liberated from external environmental restraints. In this sense, therefore, it may be appropriate to describe these advanced populations as cultures that are in the process of *transcending* their environment.

While such current threats to the environment as air, water, and soil pollution appear to challenge this description, we must remember that these threats have been *created* by our culture and can only be corrected by the further application of cultural devices. Thus it is in reality the social, political, and economic organization (*cultural factors*) of industrial societies rather than the natural habitat or a lack of scientific and technical know-how that frustrates our attempts to solve these problems.

What Sahlins seems to mean by specialization, then, is that a culture's social, political, and economic arrangements have become ossified (that they lag) when they are not undergoing the kinds of changes that he would define as *adaptive*. But all of this implies some standard or criterion for judging the adaptability of the socio-politico-economic institutions. These standards remain implicit in Sahlins's schema.

It is true that advanced cultures may dilute their evolutionary potential by employing their social institutions in such a way as to frustrate structural changes. On the other hand, the relative economic poverty as well as the nature of the social institutions of many of the underdeveloped cultures may also function to delay or frustrate their evolutionary potential.

Structural Types. By now we trust it will be fairly evident that we are operating with the premise that an evolutionary approach involves the construction of structural types and the organization of these types into some logical sequence of increasing complexity—however one may define that complexity. In the preceding chapter we noted that typologies in general are not Platonically given but are constructs created to cope with particular issues and problems. Consequently, they may be as variable as are the issues and the problems themselves. A typology appropriate to the interests of one anthropologist or group of anthropologists may seem trivial or even useless to others. Thus, Ruth Benedict, who was primarily concerned with delineating the dominant theme around which a culture was organized, arrived at a typology based on what she termed "Appollonian" or "Dionysian" emphases (see *Patterns of Culture*). Although she may have used terms like "simpler" or "more complex" in dealing with her social types, these appear to have had no theoretical implications for her. In the absence of a more convenient nomenclature, she apparently used these nonrelativistic terms in a neutral sense. If we are correct in this assumption—and all the evidence points this way—Benedict's Appollonian-Dionysian typology has no evolutionary implications whatsoever. In point of fact, she seems at least uninterested in, if not positively antithetical to, the matter of cultural development or change. However, to anthropologists who *are* interested in such matters, a developmental typology has distinct heuristic value. Ordering the data in this way leads one to frame certain kinds of explanations which would never be suggested by a nondevelopmental scheme like Benedict's. A classical case familiar to all social scientists may be found in Max Weber's work on the origins of capitalism (*The Protestant Ethic and the Spirit of Capitalism*). Weber assumed that capitalism had developed out of precapitalist feudal society—an assumption which is both developmental and typological. In turn, this assumption enabled him to pose the question: Why should this have taken place in Western Europe rather than in highly sophisticated civilizations like those of India and China? Since Weber's type, capitalism, was defined in terms of economically rational behavior, he was led from this to seek an explanation of the early emergence of such behavior in the West rather than in China or India. As is well known, he attributed a major role in the development of capitalism to the psychological and ideological climate created by European or Western Protestantism. The nonappearance of capitalism in India and China was largely attributable in Weber's analysis to the absence of an encouraging ideological milieu—more specifically, to the lack of an ideology analogous to the "Protestant ethic." Had Weber not been thinking comparatively, developmentally and typologically, it is unlikely that he could have asked the questions he did, and even less likely that he could have come up with the explanations that emerged from his analysis.

Or to take an example from some recent evolutionary literature in anthropology, we might cite the band-tribe-chiefdom-state schema of Elman Service and Marshall Sahlins to which we referred earlier. When one thinks in terms of this broad framework offered by Service and Sahlins, one is led almost inevitably to raise questions about the basic organizational *structures* that may underlie a group of societies so ostensibly varied in terms of their culture *content*; one may then be led further to try to discover the conditions under which these types or organizational structures arise, are maintained, and become transformed.

In the preceding pages we have been talking about the heuristic advantages of a developmental taxonomy. Whether any such taxonomy reflects an *actual* temporal sequence or tells us anything about the continuity of change is, in the final analysis, a matter for empirical investigation. (It is worth reiterating here a point we made earlier: the empirical world need not be constrained by our logical constructions.)

Although the concept of stages (types) seems to be an inescapable one—as noted earlier even the non- and antievolutionists employ the language of developmental stages—we do not believe stage-thinking ought to be the central or sole issue in developmental analysis. To the nineteenth-century evolutionists, it *was* the primary issue, because in showing that cultural change (considered globally) had proceeded by a natural, stage-by-stage process, they hoped to remove miraculous intervention and causeless spontaneity from the study of cultural phenomena. But this battle has been won. It does not have to be fought over and over again. What we are saying here is that we ought neither to expect nor demand from an evolutionary orientation that its only purpose be to supply us with a "theory" of stages or a developmental taxonomy. If evolutionist formulations are to move beyond description, heuristics, and methodology toward acceptable scientific theory, then these formulations must specify the *variables or mechanisms* that may account for observed or postulated transformations of culture type. It is worth noting, at least parenthetically, that the natural-selection theory of biological evolution is a theory of mechanisms and not a theory of stages. However, it must not be forgotten that many contemporary evolutionists have not been indifferent to the search for "variables and mechanisms."

Evolutionist writings have focused our attention primarily on the broader aspects of culture change, features that have been either neglected or underplayed by other approaches. They have ordered data and speculation in such a way that certain important questions could be made more explicit. And it is in this respect that the contributions of the evolutionists have been most valuable to anthropology. Often evolutionism is treated or discussed as a theoretical "school" in anthropology as though it were somehow opposed to or at odds with other so-called schools or camps like functionalism, history, etc. But to the extent that anthropologists become concerned with producing scientific explanations for cultural phenomena, their efforts to understand such problems as cultural maintenance and cultural change will be accompanied by a convergence of method and technique. For, as we phrased it earlier, most anthropologists *have* been interested in the related questions, How do different cultural systems work? and How have they come to be as they are? It is true that, by and large, functionalists have tended to emphasize issues concerned with the former question; but any theory of maintenance must imply a theory of change. For to specify those critical and functionally related elements which maintain a system is to imply the elements which may be most crucially involved in its transformation. Recently, Pierre van den Berghe has pointed out how functionalism, the "dialectic," and evolutionism, despite their ostensible polemical and explanatory differences, seem to end up saying similar things about social change:

> Functionalism and the dialectic share an evolutionary notion of social change. For both Hegel and Marx, the dialectic process is an ascensional spiral towards progress. The functionalist concept of differentiation postulates an evolutionary growth in structural complexity and functional specificity analogous to biological evolution. . . . We are all aware of the pitfalls of organicism, the teleological implications of "progress," and the untenability of assuming that evolution is unilinear or has an

end-point (e.g. Marx's Communism or Comte's "positive stage"). Nevertheless, the convergence of the two theories on some form of evolutionism suggests that the concept of social evolution (in the minimal sense of change in discernible directions) may be inescapable, however ridden with problems existing brands thereof might be.[22]

One final and brief point about structural types. At one level these types may be viewed as simply classificatory devices constructed for the purpose of carrying out cross-cultural comparisons. But when used in the context of theory construction and testing, they come to be something more than a classificatory device; for they may implicitly contain theories or at least quasi theories. For example, if we wish to test the proposition that industrialism is functionally linked to the emergence of the conjugal or nuclear family as the basic kin unit in society, or if we would like to explore the possibility that a functional relationship exists between divorce rates, or pulmonary disorders, or suicide on the one hand and industrialism on the other, we must first isolate a range of societies that we consider to belong to the industrial type. But this entails isolating those critical elements of any system which lead us to define it as industrial. Once we have made a theoretical judgment concerning the core features of the industrial type, we have taken the first step toward formulating a broader theory concerning the probable conditions under which industrialism might arise. At the same time we may enlarge our understanding of those concomitant features which tend repetitively to be associated with the core elements that identify the phenomenon of industrialism itself. We presume it is for this reason that the philosopher of science Carl Hempel has argued that ideal types in the social sciences may be "theoretical systems embodying testable general hypotheses." [23]

Functionalism

For the past several decades functionalism, in one form or another, has been the dominant emphasis in anthropological studies, especially ethnographic research. (It is not, of course, coincidental that the rise to prominence of functionalism and of field work in anthropology should have gone hand in hand.) Certain of its tenets are basic to a theoretically oriented anthropology—specifically, the methodological dictum that one ought to explore the systemic features of cultures, i.e, look for the ways in which the institutions and structures of a society interconnect to form a system. The alternative, after all, is to conceive of culture as a congeries of discrete, disconnected traits which happen to appear here and there by historical accident.

It is this methodological phrasing of functionalism which Kingsley Davis seems to have had in mind when he argued that functionalism is *synonymous*

22 Pierre van den Berghe, "Dialectic and Functionalism: Toward a Theoretical Synthesis," *American Sociological Review* 28 (1963): 695–705.

23 Carl G. Hempel, "Problems of Concept and Theory Formation in the Social Sciences," in *Science, Language and Human Rights*, American Philosophical Association, Eastern Division (Philadelphia: University of Pennsylvania Press), 1: 77.

with sociological and anthropological analysis.[24] Yet, since all sciences are concerned with isolating systems conceptually and exploring the variables within such systems, this view of functionalism is not synonymous with social science alone but, in a broader sense, with all science. Thus, if this phrasing exhausted fully the analytic content of functionalism, it would be most reasonable to ask—with Davis—why it should be hailed as a distinctive method or special theoretical approach. It would be more appropriate to see it simply as a methodological maxim or precept orienting us to look for the interrelatedness of cultural phenomena and the unintended consequences of cultural acts.[25]

But there is usually much more to the functionalist's claim. In addition to his interpretation of functionalism as the methodology of exploring interdependence, there is a stronger phrasing of functionalism as a theory about cultural processes, about how societies work. Beyond their interest in tracing out the multifarious and often surprising ways in which the elements of a cultural system fit together, many functionalists believe they have created a body of theory which explains *why* these elements interrelate the way they do —and, even further, why certain cultural patterns exist or, at the very least, why they continue to persist. When Malinowski explained Trobriand magic in terms of it functioning to reduce anxiety in the face of the unknown, he purported to be telling us why magic existed in Trobriand culture as well as why it persisted. Similarly, Radcliffe-Brown seems to account for the very existence of Andaman religious ceremonies (as well as their persistence) in terms of their contribution to social cohesion. Melford Spiro, however, attempts to explain contemporary Ifaluk belief in malevolent spirits in terms of the way these beliefs function to displace aggression. Unlike Malinowski and Radcliffe-Brown, Spiro is careful to state that his explanation is not addressed to how the beliefs originated, but only to why they persisted in the face of what looks (to the outside observer) like their manifest dysfunctions.

Functionalism as a theoretical perspective in anthropology draws on the organic analogy—that is, it leads one to think of sociocultural systems as though they were a kind of "organism" whose parts are not only related to each other but, at the same time, contribute to the maintenance, stability, and the very survival of the "organism." Basic to all functional explanations, then, is the assumption, either open or implied, that all cultural systems have certain functional requisites, or necessary conditions of existence, or needs (whether these are phrased as social needs, à la Radcliffe-Brown or, ultimately, in individual biological terms, à la Malinowski)—all of which must somehow be met if the system is to continue as an ongoing concern. Presumably, if these functional systemic needs are not met, the system will disintegrate and "die"; or it will change into some other kind of system. In this sense, then, institutions, cultural activities, and other cultural complexes are understood or explained not merely by specifying their relationships to some larger system

---

[24] See Kingsley Davis, "The Myth of Functional Analysis as a Special Method in Sociology and Anthropology," *American Sociological Review* 24 (1959): 752–72.

[25] See I. C. Jarvie, "Limits to Functionalism and Alternatives to It in Anthropology," in *Functionalism in the Social Sciences*, ed. Don Martindale, American Academy of Political and Social Science Monographs (1965), no. 5.

in which they are implicated, but also by demonstrating that these relationships contribute to the maintenance of the larger system or some part of it.

As Eugene Meehan has pointed out, this mode of explanation gives rise to some sticky logical and empirical difficulties, the most prominent of which is trying to relate the concept of a *functional system* to any ongoing society:

> Functionalists are invariably faced with a difficult "boundary problem" when they seek to relate a system to empirical data. An unbounded system is not a system; systems exist only by virtue of being distinguished from the environment. Analytically, the boundary problem is readily solved. Empirically, it is very difficult. . . . Marion J. Levy, Jr., in his discussion of the point, rightly underlines the danger of adding the teleological fallacy to a functional explanation when seeking a solution to the boundary problem, i.e., equating functional necessity with the conditions of origin of the phenomenon to be explained.
>
> Finally, functionalists must deal with the hazardous problem of defining the properties of whole systems, or "states of the system," for a given point in time. Functional explanations *are* impossible if the state of the system cannot be stipulated clearly enough to provide a reference point for demonstrating the consequences of the particular event to be explained. To complicate matters further, functionalism has incorporated into its conceptual apparatus a number of concepts like "stability," "self-regulation," "homeostasis," and so on to such a degree that functional explanations often depend on the meaning attached to them. The difficulty again lies in the need to establish connections between the concept and the empirical data.[26]

Because anthropologists have traditionally dealt with small and relatively isolated societies, the boundary problem to which Meehan refers rarely presents itself to them as a matter for serious methological concern. They generally operate with certain implicit assumptions about the boundedness of the unit (village, hamlet, tribe, community) that they are examining. Robert Merton has referred to these implicit assumptions as (1) the postulate of the functional unity of society—everything is functionally related to everything else; (2) the postulate of universal functionalism—all cultural elements perform a function; and (3) the postulate of functional indispensability—every cultural element performs a function and no other element is capable of performing that same function. Merton says that all of these postulates must be rejected on empirical grounds: cultures are incompletely or only to varying degrees integrated; the same function can be performed by a variety of cultural items ("functional alternatives"); and many cultural elements may be functionally neutral or even dysfunctional—that is, they may produce stresses and strains which threaten the maintenance of the system.[27] In any case, all of these assumptions are matters for empirical investigation and cannot be decided on a priori grounds.

---

[26] Eugene J. Meehan, *Contemporary Political Thought: A Critical Survey* (Homewood, Ill.: Dorsey, 1967), pp. 164–65.

[27] See Robert K. Merton, "Manifest and Latent Functions," in *On Theoretical Sociology* (New York: Free Press Paperback, 1967), pp. 79–91.

In an attempt to clarify the concept of "function," Merton has also introduced a distinction between the manifest and latent functions of a cultural act or element. Manifest functions are "those objective consequences contributing to the adjustment or adaptation of the system which are intended and recognized by participants in the system"; latent functions, on the other hand, are those objective consequences of a cultural item which are neither "intended nor recognized" by the members of a society.[28]

When used in a descriptive context, Merton's distinction is helpful, since it enables us to separate conscious motivations from the objective and the unintended consequences of cultural acts. However, many functionalists have also wanted to employ Merton's distinction for explanatory purposes. Thus, they would say not only that a particular element has such-and-such latent functions ("unintended consequences"), but also that the cultural item persists (or perhaps exists) *because* of the latent functions it performs. Merton himself seems to believe that the concept of latent function will help us to explain at least the persistence, if not the origin, of a cultural arrangement. Discussing the Hopi rain dance, he writes:

> Hopi ceremonials designed to produce abundant rainfall may be labelled a superstitious practice of primitive folk and that is assumed to conclude the matter. It should be noted that this in no sense accounts for the group behavior. It is simply a case of name-calling; it substitutes the epithet "superstition" for the analysis of the actual role of this behavior in the life of the group. Given the concept of latent function, however, we are reminded that this behavior *may* perform a function for the group, although this function may be quite remote from the avowed purpose of the behavior.[29]

Merton then indicates how the concept of latent function will help us to account for the persistence of the Hopi rain dance despite the fact that rain does not always follow the ritual:

> Ceremonials may fulfill the latent function of reinforcing the group identity by providing a periodic occasion on which the scattered members of a group assemble to engage in a common activity. . . . Through the systematic application of the concept of latent function, therefore, *apparently* irrational behavior may *at times* be found to be positively functional for the group. Operating with the concept of latent function, we are not too quick to conclude that if an activity of a group does not achieve its nominal purpose, then its persistence can be described only as an instance of "inertia," "survival" or "manipulation by powerful subgroups in the society." [30]

In short, according to Merton, the Hopi continue to enact the rain dance not simply because they are mistaken in the belief that the ritual produces rain, but because it performs the latent function of promoting group solidarity. Merton's account leaves us uneasy. Somewhere, one feels, there is a gap in

[28] Ibid., pp. 105, 114–18.
[29] Ibid., p. 118.
[30] Ibid., p. 118–19.

the analysis, a hidden mechanism at work that we have not been told about. For how is it that the unintended consequences (latent function) of an activity can be the cause (or one of the causes) of the persistence of that activity? If we accept Merton's analysis, it turns out that the Hopi are not only "superstitious" but completely irrational as well. Not only does their rain dance ceremonial often fail to produce rain (it should be noted that some observers report that rain often *does* follow the ceremonials within a reasonable time), but they do not even know that it promotes group solidarity. Why, then do they continue to hold the ritual? At least two reasons occur to us: (1) It actually does, or they think it does or will, bring rain, and (2) They enjoy the ceremony, the getting-together, the ritual itself. Of course, there may be other explanations as well, such as fear of supernatural sanctions if the ritual is neglected, or custom, or a chance to pick up some tourist dollars, etc. In any case, the causes of the ritual and its persistence are products of conscious decisions and not necessarily the byproduct of hidden compulsions. The fact that the performance may indeed promote group solidarity may be defined as an *accidental* consequence and can in no sense, therefore, be said to account for the origin or the persistence of the ceremonial.

Oddly enough, however, and despite the apparent logical inconsistency of such a latent-function "explanation" of the event, many persons accept Merton's analysis of the rain dance as well as similar interpretations of other cultural phenomena. Clifford Geertz has detected a "mysterious" element in explanations of this kind as well as a kind of plausibility which may help to account for their acceptance:

> A pattern of behavior shaped by a certain set of forces turns out, by a plausible but nevertheless mysterious coincidence, to serve ends but tenuously related to these forces. A group of primitives sets out, in all honesty, to pray for rain and ends up by strengthening its social solidarity; a ward politician sets out to get or remain near the trough and ends by mediating between unassimilated immigrant groups and an impersonal government bureaucarcy. . . .[31]

The point can be made more generally. Whenever functional analysis attempts to move beyond the methodology of seeking structural relationships toward a *theory* about the origin or persistence of certain structures, it encounters the same kinds of logical limitations. Because the ascription of functions to particular institutions is always a post hoc affair, functional explanations have an air of reasonableness about them and seem to explain more than they really do. We are told, for example, that in society X the performance of certain rituals promotes social solidarity and therefore contributes toward maintaining the system of which they are a part. Let us ignore for the moment what is meant by "social solidarity" or "maintaining the system." We see the society in operation and we see the native performing rituals. To link the two in the above way seems perfectly plausible.

But in what sense have we explained rituals—either their origin or their persistence? Rituals may promote social solidarity, but so do a host of other

---

[31] Clifford, Geertz, "Ideology as a Cultural System," in *Ideology and Discontent*, ed. David E. Apter (New York: The Free Press, 1964), p. 56.

institutions, and functional explanations leave us in the dark about why society X may employ rituals for this purpose rather than one of its structural alternatives (it is true, of course, that the range of structural alternatives is never limitless). To argue, as has often been done in functional analysis, from some general systemic requirement or need to the presence of a specific institution which is supposed somehow to meet this requirement or need is logically inadmissable unless it can be demonstrated that the institution in question is the only one capable of performing the function attributed to it. But since, as we have already noted, the same social function may be performed by a variety of institutions, or since the same institution may perform a variety of functions, this would seem to be a very difficult undertaking at best. Even trying to account for the *persistence* of an institution in functional terms is an extremely chancy business, given the fact that other institutions may or can do the very same thing.

Culture Change

Another and common complaint about functional analysis is that since it is concerned with the self-maintenance of systems, it cannot account for structural change. To account for such change one has to weigh certain variables causally—that is, one has to make a judgment about which elements or institutions or structures are more basic, more "functional" than others. But this causal weighting, as we shall shortly try to show, can never come out of a strictly functional approach. In his classic essay, "Manifest and Latent Functions," to which we have already referred several times, Robert Merton attempted to remedy this situation by counterposing to the concept of *function* (positive function) the concept of *dysfunction* (negative function).[32] Thus, an institution or cultural activity is said to be *functional* when it contributes to the adaptation or adjustment of a given system and *dysfunctional* when it lessens such adaptation. What is more, the same institution can even have functional and dysfunctional consequences at the same time but, on balance, be more dysfunctional than functional or vice versa.

The major problem here is that one cannot tell when an institution is more functional than dysfunctional by simple empirical inspection. These are relative terms—relative to a set of theoretical judgments one holds about the nature of the society in question. Moreover, when Merton speaks of the overall adaptation of the system, one may legitimately ask: adaptation to what? For like function and dysfunction, adaptation is also a relative term and requires some theoretical standard against which it may be measured if the term is to be used in an empirically responsible fashion. In this vein, Raymond Firth tells us that one of the major problems in functional analysis is

> the difficulty from the observer's point of view of assessing functions in empirical situations. Much depends upon his view of the overall character of social relationships, and on the theory which he thinks applicable. For example, one can discuss the "protest functions" and "pressure

---

[32] Merton, "Manifest and Latent Functions," p. 107.

functions" of trade unions as introvert functions serving their own ends and maintaining their internal solidarity. One can see these as dysfunctional from the point of view of society as a whole, linked with various restrictive and disturbing practices. On the other hand, one can regard them as part of the general process whereby groups necessarily express themselves and work in society, giving confidence and energy to their members and gain to the society which relies on their efforts.[33]

Firth here raises one of the central problems in functional analysis—namely, how do we go about making functional statements scientifically acceptable? That is, how do we go about confirming or disconfirming them? As Meehan has reminded us, one of the major problems in attempting to substantiate functional claims is the failure or inability to specify just what it is that is being maintained or the mechanisms by which this maintenance is accomplished. Melford Spiro's discussion of the Ifaluk belief in malevolent spirits (*alus*) is an especially apt illustration of the more positive features of the functional methodology, as well as a testimonial to some of the difficulties posed when one attempts to derive theory or explanation from the methodology itself.[34]

Ifaluk is a small atoll in the Pacific (Central Carolines, Micronesia), with a population of some 250 persons. One of the most notable things about the culture, according to Spiro, is its ethic of nonaggression and its strong emphasis on mutual aid, sharing, and cooperation. An important aspect of Ifaluk religion is the belief in *alus*, who are believed to be the spirits or the souls of the malevolent dead. This belief, Spiro tells us, has a number of functions, positive as well as negative. On the manifest and positive level the belief provides the Ifaluk with a consistent and viable theory of disease as well as an explanation of other types of misfortune:

> The two areas of life over which the Ifaluk have no technological control are illness and typhoons, and the belief in *alus* serves to restrict the area of uncertainty. For it affords not only an explanation for illness, but also techniques for its control, minimizing the anxieties arising from intellectual bewilderment in the face of crucial life crises, and the feeling of impotence to deal with them.[35]

But these manifest and positive functions may be overbalanced, Spiro suggests, by the *dysfunctions* of the belief:

> The *alus* cause worry, fear and anxiety, as well as sickness and death, and by causing the death of individuals they can, potentially, destroy the entire society. *From the point of view of the people, it would be better if there were no* alus [emphasis added].[36]

Spiro then asks the question: "Why does such a manifestly dysfunctional belief continue to survive?" Note that the question he raises has to do with

---

[33] Raymond Firth, "Function," in *Yearbook of Anthropology*, ed. William L. Thomas, Jr. (New York: Wenner Gren Foundation for Anthropological Research, 1955), p. 245.

[34] See Melford E. Spiro, "Ghosts, Ifaluk, and Teleological Functionalism," *American Anthropologist* 54 (1952): 497–503.

[35] Ibid., p. 498.

[36] Ibid.

the *persistence* and not the *origin* of the beliefs. Spiro (as have many others, before and since) postulates that all human societies must find means for displacing and canalizing antisocial aggressive drives into more harmless "culturally sanctioned aggressive culture patterns." This, we are told, is an especially acute functional requirement for the Ifaluk because the society is small and confined and because the ethic of nonaggression plays such an important part in their world view and in the total organization of their society. If some cultural or institutional means for displacing aggression out-wardly did not exist, the aggression would probably be turned inward, leading to the disintegration of personality at the organismic level and to the whole-sale disruption of interpersonal relationships at the societal level. Thus, Spiro concludes that the belief in *alus* persists because it serves the very crucial *latent function* of displacing aggression into relatively harmless channels:

> The belief in *alus* has certain latent consequences of which the people are unaware, but which are vital to the functioning of this society and the preservation of its culture. The absence of this belief, *or of some other institution with the same functions* [emphasis added], would be dis-astrous for Ifaluk society, as we know it today.[37]

Finally, Spiro ends his essay with some observations concerning the *latent dysfunctions* of the belief in *alus*, observations which inevitably raise serious questions about his functional explanation of why belief in the spirits persists:

> The belief serves to drain energy from creative enterprise to that of de-fense against the *alus*; it serves to preclude investigations of alternative disease theories; it channels much economic activity into non-productive channels; finally, though it resolves many anxieties, it creates a very serious one in its own right—the anxiety created by the fear of the *alus* itself.[38]

In a friendly critique of Spiro's emphasis on the functional role of the belief in *alus*, William Lessa raises some interesting questions about alterna-tives which may serve the same purpose as the belief in malevolent spirits.[39] Since sorcery or black magic is encountered in other islands in the vicinity, and also, according to a trusted informant of Lessa, exists in Ifaluk itself, he asks, is it possible that Spiro may have overlooked or, perhaps, under-played the significance of sorcery as a functional alternative (as a means of displacing aggression) to the belief in *alus*? If this is so, Lessa concludes, Spiro's explanation for the persistence of a belief in *alus* is seriously impugned.

> If . . . black magic did exist on Ifaluk in 1947–1948 when Spiro did his research, it would undermine his argument that the people of the

---

[37] Ibid., p. 502. Note the similarity of Spiro's pattern of explanation to that of Murphy in his explanation of Mundurucú welfare to which we referred in chapter 1. Some of the same difficulties we pointed to in Murphy's theory—e.g., how does one tell that aggression or hostility is or is not being displaced?—also apply here.

[38] Ibid., p. 503.

[39] See William A. Lessa, "Sorcery on Ifaluk," *American Anthropologist* 63 (1961): 820.

atoll, who must avoid open social aggression because intimate cooperation is indispensable in a tiny society, have shunned sorcery and turned to the *alus*, or spirits, in giving release to their hostilities. While I am willing to agree that spirits may have psychological value as scapegoats, I feel that sorcery is fully as important. . . .[40]

In his rejoinder to Lessa, Spiro does assert that "numerous structural units, including sorcery, may serve this same function," adding that "in sum, although the article explicitly argues that the displacement of hostility from the in-group is a *functional* necessity for any society, it explicitly denies that the belief in evil spirits, as a means for serving this function, is a *structural* necessity, in Ifaluk or in any other society." [41] Spiro continues:

> Nowhere in the article is it either stated or implied that (a) the Ifaluk "turned to" spirits to satisfy certain functional requirements of their society, or that (b) by "turning" to spirits they would have to "shun" sorcery. Neither proposition is either part of the theory or deducible from it.
>
> First, since the displacement of hostility is interpreted as a *latent* function of the belief in evil spirits, I could not possibly argue that this belief either arose or persists "because intimate cooperation is indispensable. . . ." The argument asserts, instead, that however it arose and by whatever conditions it persists, this belief does in fact have this functional consequence. . . .[42]

Thus, Spiro ends up with the most modest of functional statements. To point up the unintended consequences of cultural acts certainly can be enlightening, and it is here that functional anthropology has probably had its greatest success. But to know something about the latent consequences of a cultural act hardly constitutes an *explanation* of that act, either of its origins or of its persistence.

In short, while Spiro may speculate fruitfully on the value or functions of an institution that seems to divert hostility away from the group and thereby apparently contributes to its survival as a social entity, he cannot argue from these postulated "consequences" to "causes." As Durkheim remarked long ago, only confusion can result from the failure to keep "function" distinct from "cause."

Functional Prerequisites

In 1950 a group of social scientists published, in a journal article, a generalized model of human society which included a list of the "functional prerequisites" of *all* human societies.[43] The authors justified "the inclusion

---

[40] Ibid.

[41] Melford E. Spiro, "Sorcery, Evil Spirits, and Functional Analysis: A Rejoinder," *American Anthropologist* 63 (1961): 822.

[42] Ibid., p. 823.

[43] See David F. Aberle et al., "The Functional Prerequisites of a Society," *Ethics* 60 (1950): 100–111.

of each prerequisite by the demonstration that in its hypothetical absence the society could not survive." The prerequisites they listed are (a) provision for adequate relationship to the environment and for sexual recruitment; (b) role differentiation and role assignment; (c) communication; (d) shared cognitive orientations; (e) a shared, articulated set of goals; (f) the normative regulation of means; (g) the regulation of affective expression; (h) socialization; (i) the effective control of disruptive forms of behavior.

Although Aberle and his colleagues attempt to draw a sharp distinction between culture and society, their effort does not help us to understand what it is of culture or society that survives or fails to survive. We know, for example, that Tasmanian society *and* culture were systematically and completely destroyed through the simple but bloody expedient of extermination of all Tasmanian aborigines. And we know, also, for example, that aspects of Roman culture persisted after the fall of Rome. But is it more accurate to say that Roman society ("a group of human beings sharing a self-sufficient system of action which is capable of existing longer than the life-span of an individual," in the words of Aberle et al.) failed to survive than to say that the "self-sufficient forms of action" were changed or transformed? Does such a change constitute nonsurvival? When American culture changed from an agrarian to an industrial type did American society fail to survive? These are some of the issues which are still unclear in the Aberle et al., discussion.

Of course there are plenty of historical examples of societies whose cultures have changed (indeed, it would be hard to find a negative case)—even examples of societies and cultures that have been transformed dramatically, and of others that have been completely absorbed. But, unlike organisms, societies rarely die. If, as Aberle et al. maintain, the "identity and continuity of a society inhere in the persistence of the system of action in which the actors participate rather than in the set of actors themselves," then virtually every structural change in the culture would mean the death of a society. The emergence of new cultural types would be synonymous with the death of societies.

Because it is difficult to find examples of societies that have died or cultures that have disappeared without a trace, it is, we believe, just as difficult to conceive of a society which disintegrated and terminated its existence because any one of the above list of "functional prerequisites" was not met. Thus, statements that appeal to such universal functional requirements, because they cannot be empirically verified, tend to be analytic (definitional) statements disguised as potentially synthetic (empirical) ones. They are, in other words, definitions of what is meant by the term *society*. It is for reasons such as these that Merton refers to "functional requisites" as "one of the cloudiest and empirically most debatable concepts in functional theory." [44] (Presumably for similar reasons, Merton tends to be suspicious of "organic functionalism," and tends also to avoid, wherever possible, the concept of "system." What Merton is concerned with may be referred to as "mechanical functionalism"—i.e., the way in which a group or an institution relates to another group or institution.)

Nor is it very enlightening to be told that the performance of certain

---

[44] Merton, "Manifest and Latent Functions," p. 106.

religious ceremonies promotes social solidarity or social cohesion when we are not told what these terms mean "operationally," or when it seems that part of what is meant by these terms is the coming together of people on certain occasions to perform religious ceremonies.

By now the point we have been emphasizing should be clear: trying to confirm statements of functional relationships and maintenance in anthropology raises logical and empirical difficulties not easily overcome. Since functional anthropology, as we indicated earlier, has utilized the organic analogy and has evidently drawn its inspiration from physiological analysis, it might be useful at this point to examine briefly the situation in the latter discipline. The notion that physiological analysis is synchronic and nontemporal is not strictly accurate. Physiologists are concerned with temporal processes, but over relatively short spans of time. They can assume that over longer periods such processes will be truly repetitive, the reason being that they take place within organic systems whose structures are relatively stable over enormous time spans (e.g., the process of respiration in the human species). This also enables physiologists to verify functional statements, either of the interdependence or self-maintenance kind, by showing that when the normal activity of some structure or process of the organism is interfered with, certain specific and observable effects follow: either certain compensatory mechanisms are called into play, restoring the organism to "homeostasis," or, if the interference is so great that the organism cannot compensate for it, the organism will behave abnormally and may even die. But it may be difficult if not impossible to find a special and distinctive body of functional theory in physiology. Rather, the existence of functional relationships are explained with reference to the theory of evolution. The biologist Ernest Caspari makes this quite clear:

> Function must be understood as a consequence of natural selection. The question of function turns out to be basically an historical one, the question of the origin of stabilizing mechanisms in the history of the species. The question of function becomes meaningful because natural selection has acted upon the organization of living organisms in such a way that greater stability of the system is produced.[45]

Like the physiologists, functional anthropologists are interested in temporal processes over short time spans, but unlike the physiologists they cannot assume that such processes will be recurrent whatever the time span may be. For cultural systems, unlike organisms, are subject to relatively rapid qualitative change. This raises the question: At what point does a culture cease to be one *kind* of system and become transformed into some other *kind?* That is, how are we to know whether or not a particular system or structure has indeed maintained itself and not changed into some other kind of system unless we have a clear conception in mind of *kinds* of systems, unless we are working with a *typology* of sociocultural structures? The idea

---

45 Ernest Caspari, "On the Conceptual Basis of the Biological Sciences," in *Frontiers of Science and Philosophy*, ed. Robert G. Colodny (Pittsburgh, Pa.: University of Pittsburgh Press, 1962), p. 144.

of structural types is important for functional analysis because it provides us with a methodological device for validating functional claims in the only way we can.

Minimally, the requirements for adequate functional analysis are (1) a conception of a system; (2) a list of the functional requirements of that system; (3) definitions of the various properties or "states" of the system being maintained; (4) a statement of those external conditions of the system which can conceivably affect these properties and which must, therefore, be controlled; and (5) some knowledge of the internal mechanisms by which such system-properties are maintained or kept within specific limits. These requirements are obviously and almost alarmingly stringent; and more often than not in dealing with cultural systems they cannot be met. For example, often it is not clear what property (social cohesion? group solidarity?) is being maintained "in a steady state," or even what "steady state" means. Moreover, since cultures are highly open systems, we are usually unable to specify with precision all the external conditions which might conceivably affect this or that property of the system. Nor can we usually identify and pinpoint those internal mechanisms by which the system functions, adjusts, and is kept in a steady state. In short, in our researches and explanations, we are not in a position to apply the kind of experimental methods utilized by the laboratory sciences.

But if we cannot duplicate precisely the substance of the experimental method of physiology, we can approach the *logic* of that method by employing *structural types* in the context of cross-cultural comparison. Thus, Merton, in speaking of the problems of validating functional relationships, remarks: "This requires, above all, a rigorous statement of the . . . procedure of analysis which most nearly approximates the *logic* of experimentation. It requires a systematic review of the possibilities and limitations of *comparative* (cross-cultural and cross-group) *analysis*." [46] And Leon Goldstein, who has also argued for the theoretical and methodological utility of structural types in functional analysis, points out that if functional statements are to be made "scientifically responsible," one must "show that their range of application is over a class of similar structures, rather than over haphazardly individual ones." As Goldstein states:

> To say of some activity that took place prior to or contemporaneously with some *unique event*, that it took place *in order* that the unique event could take place, is to say something that can never be subject to test. . . . If we take seriously and literally the view that the aim of each field expedition is to describe some sociocultural system which is unique and qualitatively distinct from any other such system, then we cannot responsibly make the kind of statement we find in the writings of the anthropological functionalists. Even though they often seem to be reasonable, if they are really made about unique systems there would seem to be no conditions under which we may expect to substantiate their claims.[47]

---

[46] Merton, "Manifest and Latent Functions," p. 108.
[47] Leon J. Goldstein, "Recurrent Structures and Teleology," *Inquiry* 5 (1962): 3–4, 5.

To think in terms of structural types demands a process of abstraction that will allow comparisons, one that shifts our attention away from the unique functional configuration and toward those functionally related institutions or cultural arrangements which somehow maintain a society within a given type. Our attention is also drawn away from the functional requirements of human society writ large toward the functional requirements of different structural types, i.e., toward those core institutions which make a society the *kind* of society it is. For as Ernest Gellner has commented: "The preoccupation with the truth that everything is, to some extent, functional, has obscured the even more important truth that some things are *far* more so than others." [48]

If we can discover that certain structures or functionally related elements are basic to the maintenance of particular structural types, then at the same time we have some idea about which structures are critical to the transformation of the type. It is here that functional and evolutionary concerns converge and tend to become merely a difference in emphasis or selective attention.

History

Just how history falls within the cluster of theoretical orientations included in this chapter may be a moot question. This, we believe, is due in part at least to the fact that the term *history* itself is used in a number of different ways. The common view is that historical events are events that occurred in the past and that historical knowledge is knowledge of these events. But this characterization of history as a "concern with the past" is not as straightforward or as clear as it might seem. For the past may refer to events that took place five minutes ago, or five years ago, or five hundred years ago, etc.

There are, however, some apparent differences in method between the way we try to recapture or reconstruct the past of five minutes ago versus the way we deal with the past of five years ago or of five hundred years ago. In dealing with the more recent past—say, within one's lifetime—there is the possibility that we may be able to draw on our own experience plus the reports and observations of informants and the evidence provided by documents. Thus, for example, when the historian Arthur Schlesinger, Jr., wrote his account of the Kennedy years, he drew on his own personal experience, on conversations with contemporaries, and on the available documentation. In dealing with the more remote past, however, direct personal experience is, of course, not available to us, and we must rely on the indirect evidence provided by artifacts, contemporary accounts, and other forms of documentation. But, as we all know, facts do not speak for themselves. Whether one draws on one's own personal experience, the accounts of living informants, the reports of dead informants (documents), or material evidence (artifacts), all these kinds of data require interpretation. In this sense, and despite the minor distinctions in technique just referred to, there are no significant differences between the methodologies

---

[48] Ernest Gellner, "Time and Theory in Social Anthropology," *Mind* 67 (1958): 184.

of recent and remote historiography. All history, according to some histor-
iographers, is ultimately contemporary history. That is, whether the events
dealt with fall within one's own experience or are derived from the experiences and accounts of others in the past, the interpretation is filtered through
the minds of the writers at the time of writing. But, as Goldstein has
observed, this view need not lead to a position of epistemological relativism,
for some reconstructions of the past *are* better than others:

> It sometimes happens that notwithstanding general agreement on what
> the evidence is, conceptions of what actually happened differ. The differ-
> ence is over what the past would have to be in order to best make sense
> of the evidence. The past that the historian evokes is not a real past
> as it was when it was present, but rather a construction of his own; not,
> to be sure, a free creation as in the writing of a novel . . . but a con-
> struction devised as the best explanation of the evidence he has. The
> historical event—the only historical event that figures in the work of
> historians—is an hypothetical construct. The historian does not look for
> evidence in order to explain the event, as if the event is clearly before
> him and he is required to make sense of it, but rather, he calls it forth
> for the purpose of explaining his evidence. And while one might want
> to say that the historical construction which most nearly describes the
> real past is the best or the truest account, how can we ever know? How
> can we ever test the event except in terms of our evidence? We can
> never compare conflicting accounts of what "really happened" then and
> there with anything but our evidence. I am not, to be sure, denying the
> metaphysical proposition that the past is or was real, but only observing
> that it is irrelevant to history.[49]

When one compares the work of historians with that of ethnographers,
one finds that both are engaged in a similar methodological enterprise. For if
we distinguish the ethnographer's raw observations in the field from the
report he later writes based on these observations, it is apparent that he is
engaged in a process very much like the one Goldstein ascribes to the
historian. An ethnographic report contains an analysis in terms of structures,
patterns, and institutions, all of which are a product of the ethnographer's
constructive synthesis and (hopefully) disciplined imagination. In short, the
field studies of the anthropologist are a kind of history and should be read
as such. Maitland was almost right when he said that "by and by anthropology
will have the choice between being history and being nothing," for

---

[49] Leon J. Goldstein, "Evidence and Events in History," *Philosophy of Science* 29
(1962): 177. Elsewhere in this same article (183) Goldstein says, "If one distinguishes
between the phenomenal panorama passing before the eye-witness and the report he makes
of what he observes, one could argue that the latter is rather like our historical event in
that it is possible to treat it as explaining the phenomenal panorama. Likewise, a sociological or ethnographic report may be treated as introduced for the purpose of making sense
of what the sociologist or ethnographer saw or experienced. In all of these cases there
seems to be a certain parallelism and one is at liberty to conclude that all events as
characterized in reports are hypothetical. The difference between historical events and
other kinds of events seems, then, to be even less than we commonly think. . . . When
we are concerned to explain an event as a state of affairs we are not required to make
distinctions of a logical character which depend upon the event's temporal location."

ethnography *is* history. It is what *was* when the ethnographer observed it or what *was* as described for the past by his informants.

The position we take with regard to historical and ethnographic analysis is that what makes history and ethnography distinctive is not so much their mutual interest in the past as their mutual concern with specific cultures considered as concrete systems located in time and space.

As we have indicated earlier, it is often difficult in dealing with concrete systems to find one's way through the welter of events that make up their concreteness. We cannot possibly describe everything, nor do we really want to. Always we are engaged in a process of isolating those elements of the system which are somehow more relevant to the problem at hand from those which are less relevant or altogether irrelevant.

Thus, if one is interested in more than the simple chronology or narrative of natural history, one must engage in a process of classifying, categorizing, and positing possible relationships among *types* of events. It is here that the functional and evolutionary perspectives must be wed to the historical. For it is only by bringing functionalism, evolutionism, and history together that we can take the first step toward the formulation of theories. Ordering the data in this way draws attention to those *types* of elements or events that contribute to our understanding of how concrete systems work, as well as why they work as they do. If we fail to place the historical events in a functional-evolutionary framework, our history will remain mere narrative or chronology. Thus, historical or ethnographic facts, like all facts, can only exist and have meaning as they relate to the theories or criteria of relevance that called them into being.

If the functional and evolutionary orientations are indispensable to the formulation of cultural theories, history plays an indispensable part in the verification of such theories. For history construed in its broadest sense as including both past and present varieties of culture is the only experimental situation anthropology can claim. And ultimately, if our theories are any good, they ought to be able to help us to explain the operation of concrete systems. There is one very important point, however, that anthropologists sometimes tend to forget—namely, that no theory, whether it be in the physical sciences or the social sciences, can possibly explain the operation of a concrete system unless the generality of the theory is restricted and supplemented by a statement of the relevant initial and boundary conditions of the system to which the theory is being applied. And it is history which provides us with the appropriate data for the formulation of such relevant restrictive conditions.

For example, Karl Wittfogel, in his well-known treatment of the rise of oriental despotism (see Chapter 1, footnote 18), has proposed, *inter alia*, a causal relationship in preindustrial societies between the construction, maintenance, and supervision of large-scale hydraulic works and the emergence of highly centralized political structures. Before we can begin to test or to apply this proposition to a concrete historical case, we must be able to specify certain relevant initial and boundary conditions. To begin with, we must of course be able to define the empirical features of the key terms: *large-scale hydraulic works* and *highly centralized, despotic political structures*. Moreover, we must be able to specify the unit to which the proposition applies—i.e., the area over which the despotic political structure exercises control. And, finally, we must be able to demonstrate that all *other* internal and external factors which might conceivably produce despotic political structures did not operate to produce these structures in the particular instance. Obviously, these logical requirements are stringent, and, as we have already pointed out, of a sort that anthropologists are rarely if ever in a position to meet; in most if not all cases, anthropologists have to be content with being able to state *some* of the relevant initial and boundary conditions of the systems they are attempting to understand and explain.

These limitations might be a source of despair for the anthropologist, especially when he compares his task with that of the physical scientist, who usually controls the initial and boundary conditions of the systems with which he deals. But it should be recalled that the physical scientist's greater theoretical precision stems from the fact that his propositions apply to idealized situations (e.g., bodies falling in vacuums, levers that do not wear or compress, etc.), or to artificially controlled situations such as those that prevail in the laboratory. It might comfort the anthropologist who is made uneasy by the theoretical uncertainties of his own discipline to realize that, when the propositions of the "exact" sciences are applied to systems which are neither ideal nor in the laboratory but exist *in nature*, the physical scientist is also confronted with serious difficulties in specifying all of the system's relevant initial and boundary conditions. Einstein once remarked that the theories of the physical sciences are more exact the more remote they are from the empirical world; and the closer they come to the empirical world the more approximate they become.

The anthropologist in his role as ethnographer is usually concerned with the current workings of a culture—with identifying a society's major structures and institutions, describing the way they work, and charting their interrelationships. But, unlike the physicist, he cannot assume that the phenomena, structures, and processes he studies will be stable and recurrent over time. If he seeks to explain why a society works as it does, he cannot disregard the past, whether that past be the past one year or one hundred years ago. However, it is only after one has examined the past that one is in a position to decide how and how much of that past is relevant to an understanding of the present. For while it is clear that all cultures show continuities as well as discontinuities with the past, less clear are the nature and identification of continuities and discontinuities and how much of the past one must reckon with in order to explain the present. Decisions of this sort always involve a process of selection and weighting of the alternatives and therefore imply theoretical judgments.

There was a time—from about 1915 to 1935—when the dominant methodological stance in American anthropology was "historical." Its leading figure, Franz Boas, was responsible for the training of such major anthropologists as Alfred Kroeber, Robert Lowie, Edward Sapir, Paul Radin, Ruth Benedict, Alexander Goldenweiser, and others. Boas and his students reacted strongly against the speculative formulations of the nineteenth-century evolutionists, and in so doing gave to American anthropology an anti-evolutionary bias that tended to dominate the discipline until the end of World War II. The evolutionists, as we have already indicated, had argued that cultural similarities were the outcome of the same basic and underlying causes, since the human mind reacted in similar fashion when confronted with similar environmental circumstances. It was this fundamental assumption that had provided the earlier evolutionists with the rationale for the use of the comparative method in charting the course of the evolution of culture. Boas rejected the rigidity of this assumption and was therefore highly critical of the evolutionists' methodology, pointing out that cultural similarities might be the product of dissimilar historical, environmental and psychological factors.[50]

In rejecting evolutionism, Boas came to advocate a special "historical" view of culture. In this view all cultures are made up of traits and trait complexes which are the product of *environmental conditions, psychological factors,* and *historical connections.* Drawing in particular on his studies of the spatial distribution of myths, folktales, and folklore, Boas noted that the elements of any culture were the product of complex historical processes involving, to a large extent, the diffusion and borrowing of traits and trait complexes from neighboring cultures.

Thus, the new historical method which Boas advocated was based upon

> "the careful and slow detailed study of local phenomena" within a "well-defined, small geographical area," with comparisons limited to "the cultural area that forms the basis of the study." Out of this study would emerge "histories of the cultures of diverse tribes." It was only by comparing these individual histories of growth that the "general laws" of human development could be discovered.[51]

It is not quite true, then, to say that Boas and his students thought it wholly impossible to discover broad regularities, laws, or recurrent processes in cultural phenomena. But they did not think it would be easy, and they were clearly skeptical of the attempt to frame such general statements until a great deal more of the ethnographic facts were in—facts which would provide them with a firmer inductive base for the formulation of such laws. Hence, the search for cultural laws or regularities was pushed off into the indefinite future. Furthermore, since the acceptance or rejection of any culture trait or complex was dependent ultimately, according to Boas, upon psychic factors, any regularities or uniformities of process—if they existed at all—reflected uniformities of mental processes; thus, cultural laws or regularities —should they ever be discovered—would in the final analysis turn out to be psychological in nature.[52]

---

[50] George W. Stocking Jr., "Franz Boas and the Culture Concept in Historical Perspective," in *Race, Culture, and Evolution: Essays in the History of Anthropology* (New York: Free Press, 1968), p. 210.

[51] Ibid., p. 210.

[52] See David F. Aberle, "The Influence of Linguistics on Early Culture and Personality Theory," in *Essays in the Science of Culture in Honor of Leslie A. White,* ed. Gertrude E. Dole and Robert L. Carneiro (New York: Thomas Y. Crowell, 1960), pp. 1–29.

In this respect, of course, the position of Boas and of those who followed him paralleled that of the evolutionists with their premise regarding the psychic unity of humankind. In point of fact, much of Boas's life work was devoted to documenting and propagandizing the validity of the evolutionist assumption about the psychic unity of man. Where he differed from his evolutionist predecessors, however, was in his skepticism about grand schemes of cultural development and in his concomitant concern for recording the details of particular cultures in time and place. It is for this reason that a number of anti-Boasian critics have charged him with giving a particularistic and relativistic emphasis to anthropology and, in this manner, discouraging efforts to arrive at a more generalizing, more "scientifically" oriented study of the history of man.

It should be remembered, however, that Boas' "historical" methodology and the school of thought he founded and led had an impact on the modern conception of culture in a number of important ways. In the first place, "Boasianism" shifted the anthropological perspective from the evolutionists' collective and global model or construct to a concern with the individuality or diversity of cultures. Furthermore, Boas's focus on cultural traits or elements led also to a kind of nonfunctional, fragmented view of culture, to what has sometimes been disparagingly referred to as the "shreds-and-patches" view of culture. In the final analysis, as Stocking reminds us, there is an essential duality in Boas's thinking about culture:

> The continuing duality in Boas' thinking on culture . . . is evident in remarks he made on tribal mythologies in 1898. "The mythologies of the various tribes as we find them now are not organic growths, but have gradually developed and obtained their present form by the accretion of foreign material." But although often adopted ready-made, this foreign material was "adapted and changed in form according to the genius of the people who borrowed it." On the one hand, culture was simply an accidental accretion of individual elements. On the other, culture—despite Boas' renunciation of organic growth—was at the same time an integrated spiritual totality which somehow conditioned the form of its elements. This latter interest in whole cultures and their psychological meaning in the "geniuses" of "peoples"—was also to have important implications for the development of the anthropological culture concept. When around 1930, American anthropology turned to problems of the patterning of cultural wholes and the interrelation of culture and personality, it may be argued that it was simply picking up the other thread of this duality.[53]

On the other hand, it is not difficult to see why the historical particularist emphasis of the Boas school and the fragmented view of culture (the "other thread" of the "duality" in Boas's conception of culture) led its stricter adherents into what might be referred to metaphorically as a theoretical dead end. For the Boasian view of history leads one to see each culture as the product of more-or-less unique historical circumstances and processes. And

---

[53] Stocking, "Franz Boas," p. 214.

it is impossible ever to generalize about the unique, the chance, the accidental.

We conclude this section with examples from the work of two contemporary anthropologists who, unlike the orthodox historical particularists, have used history in an evolutionary and functional framework to throw light on the present.

First, Elman Service, in an essay dealing with acculturative processes in the New World, identifies three distinct blocks of culture in contemporary Latin-America—what he calls *Euro-America, Mestizo-America,* and *Indo-America*.[54] In attempting to account for the differences among these major components of culture in Latin America, Service turns to the historical record. He shows that the policies and goals of the Spanish conquerors (the harnessing of Indian manpower for their own purposes) were uniform throughout Latin America, but that the impact and results of the conquest varied with the nature of the aboriginal organization. Utilizing Steward's concept of "levels of sociocultural integration," Service argues that in those areas where there were aboriginal states, we find today large Indian enclaves. This is his Indo-America. In those regions where there were tribal peoples organized in villages, a process of intermingling with the conquerors on a broad scale took place and yielded Mestizo-America. And those areas utilized by hunters and gatherers who were difficult to catch and subdue were ultimately depopulated and became what he calls Euro-America.

In Service's analysis the present is not seen as a by-product of whimsical or arbitrary choices in the past but as a consequence of historical processes involving conqueror and conquered under varying local and historical circumstances.

As a second example, Eric Wolf has identified a particular type of peasant community structure (the "closed corporate community") in both Mesoamerica and Java. He shows that a similar set of historical conditions—a society with an advanced commercial sector and a less advanced peasant sector—led to the emergence of this type of community structure in two widely separated parts of the world:

> It is my contention that the closed corporate peasant community in both areas represents a response to these several characteristics of the larger society. Relegation of the peasantry to the status of part-time laborers, providing for their own subsistence on scarce land, together with the imposition of charges levied and forced by semi-autonomous local authorities, tends to define the common life situation which confronts the peasantry of both societies. The closed corporate peasant community is an attempt to come to grips with this situation. Its internal function, as opposed to its external function in the social, economic, and political web of the dualized society, is to equalize the life chances and life risks of its members.[55]

---

[54] See Elman R. Service, "Indian-European Relations in Colonial Latin America," *American Anthropologist* 25 (1955): 411–23.

[55] Eric R. Wolf, "Closed Corporate Peasant Communities in Mesoamerica and Central Java," *Southwestern Journal of Anthropology* 13 (1957): 8–9.

Wolf shows convincingly that the conditions which gave rise to the closed corporate peasant community were the result of a series of parallel historic developments in Java and Mesoamerica:

> Both in Mesoamerica and Central Java, the conquerors occupied the land and proceeded to organize labor to produce crops and goods for sale in newly established markets. The native peasantry did not command the requisite culturally developed skills and resources to participate in the development of large-scale enterprises for profit. In both areas, therefore, the peasantry was forced to supply labor to the new enterprises, but barred from direct participation in the resultant return. In both areas, moreover, the conquerors also seized control of large-scale trade, and deprived the native population of direct access to sources of wealth acquired through trade, such as they had commanded in the pre-conquest past.

> Yet in both areas, the peasantry—forced to work on colonist enterprises— did not become converted into a permanent labor force. The part-time laborer continued to draw the larger share of his subsistence from his own efforts on the land. From the point of the entrepreneurial sector, the peasant sector remained primarily a labor reserve where labor could maintain itself at no cost to the enterprises.[56]

We could cite numerous additional examples of anthropological researches whose theoretical orientation could be labeled historical. For example, the pages of the periodical *Ethnohistory* include many cases where archival, elderly informant, and historical documentation are wedded to reconstruct past incidents and developments in the lives of a people or culture. An early piece by Clark Wissler, "The Influence of the Horse in the Development of Plains Culture," first published in *The American Anthropologist* in 1914, is also a case in point.[57] Often, too, as in the seminal series of Columbia University studies on a variety of Plains Indian cultures,[58] historical documentation

---

[56] Ibid., 12.

[57] Clark Wissler, *American Anthropologist* 16 (1914): 1–25. Obviously, other early investigators like Mooney, Cushing, Dorsey, Fletcher, and other Bureau of American Ethnology researchers were doing "history" even before Wissler. But, as Sturtevant notes in his excellent review-essay, "Anthropology, History, and Ethnohistory," "these were essentially natural-historical collectors of data, and what theorizing they attempted was largely insignificant for subsequent anthropology . . ." in *Introduction to Cultural Anthropology*, ed. James A. Clifton (Boston: Houghton Mifflin, 1968), p. 457.

[58] Cf. especially the following: Bernard Mishkin, *Rank and Warfare Among the Plains Indians*, American Ethnological Society Monograph no. 3 (1940); Oscar Lewis, *The Effects of White Contact Upon Blackfoot Culture with Special Reference to the Role of the Fur Trade*, American Ethnological Society Monograph no. 6 (1942); Esther Goldfrank, *Changing Configurations in the Social Organization of a Blackfoot Tribe During the Reserve Period*, American Ethnological Society Monograph no. 8 (1945); Joseph Jablow, *The Cheyenne in Plains Indian Trade Relations*, American Ethnological Society Monograph no. 19 (1951); Frank Secoy, *Changing Military Patterns on the Great Plains*, American Ethnological Society Monograph no. 21 (1953); Alexander Lesser, *The Pawnee Ghost Dance Hand Game*, Columbia University Contributions to Anthropology no. 16 (1933); and Margaret Mead, *The Changing Culture of An Indian Tribe*, Columbia University Contributions to Anthropology no. 15 (1932).

combined with an analysis of functional and ecological factors (see the section on cultural ecology, below) have employed history as a prime methodological or theoretical orientation with consummate skill to produce studies of individual tribes and the historical vicissitudes through which they passed on their way from a postulated precontact to a postcontact way of life or culture.

In these, and many other examples, the use of history as at least one among several orientations has provided a methodological focus for the investigator, a focus which enabled him to see, review, and analyze the data on change with insights that would clearly have been missing from any rigidly diachronic-functional approach.

In general, then, it may be said that those anthropologists like Service, Wolf, and others who are presently engaged in historical research or historical understanding (whether it be in their ethnographic endeavors or in a more directed and self-conscious effort to reconstruct the remote past in order to explain the present) are often concerned with the search for similarities, generalizations, and general processes which may pave the way to the formulation of broader theoretical statements.

Cultural Ecology

Cultural ecology is the last of those essentially methodological approaches (which we here call theoretical orientations) to be treated in this chapter. The cultural-ecological approach, methodology, or orientation has generally been a major concern of those anthropologists who are identified as cultural evolutionists. Although there are sound theoretical reasons why these two approaches have tended to go together, it is obvious that the association is not inevitable. One may think and write "ecologically" without the explicit use of an evolutionary framework or evolutionary tools of analysis. Or, contrariwise, one may be a "cultural evolutionist" without explicitly using ecology as an analytic tool. Thus, much of the work of anthropologists like Frederik Barth, Max Gluckman, Elizabeth Colson, and Clifford Geertz may be clearly labeled ecological and nonevolutionary—even if their ecological writings do have evolutionary implications. And, conversely, the writings of virtually all of the nineteenth-century anthropologists (as well as the sociologists) were strongly evolutionary in orientation and emphasis without being pointedly ecological—although again, one can discover certain ecological implications in their work.

Cultural ecology is characterized by a concern with adaptation on two levels: first with regard to the way cultural systems adapt to their total environment; and second—as a consequence of this systemic adaptation—with regard to the way the institutions of a given culture adapt or adjust to one another. (Note that the exploration of these issues is germane to all of the orientations dealt with in this chapter, since it leads one inevitably to raise questions of a functional-historical-evolutionary nature.) The cultural ecologist maintains that focusing on these adaptational processes allows one to see how different cultural configurations emerge, are maintained, and become transformed.

In general, cultural ecologists have tended to emphasize technology and economics in their analysis of cultural adaptation, because it is in these aspects of culture that the differences *among* cultures, as well as the differences over time *within* a culture are most apparent. Whether man's moral sense or the quality of his social life have changed or progressed over the past several thousand years is a moot question. But there is no disputing that man's control over his environment has increased enormously since the Paleolithic era. This increase may be largely attributed to improvements in the technological means available to man *and* to the growth of scientific knowledge. While modern cultures can afford to subscribe to certain moral philosophies that are 2,000 years old, for them to adopt a technology or to revert to a level of scientific knowledge that prevailed 2,000 years ago would (however desirable the prospect may appear to some) involve a total transformation of our way of life.

Although, as indicated, cultural ecologists have generally emphasized the dramatic role played by technological and economic factors in the adaptational process, it would be inaccurate to say that all of them believe these factors to be the *only* variables operative in cultural adaptation. Many ecologists have rightly drawn attention to the adaptive significance of nontechnological, noneconomic features of culture. Even Leslie White, who is a self-declared technological determinist in his ecological interpretation of cultural evolution, has pointed to the dialectic interplay of the various parts of culture, and to the often determinative role that may be played in given historical instances by ideological and sociopolitical factors. Or to cite another example, Eric Wolf has shown how certain ideological, psychological, and social features of the "closed corporate peasant community" ("the cult of poverty," "defensive ignorance," "institutional envy," and "leveling mechanisms" like the "political-religious system") serve to maintain the community's traditional adaptation in the face of what it perceives as outside threats to its corporate structure. And Charles O. Frake's view of cultural ecology places major emphasis on the native's conceptualizations and interpretations (i.e., ideological and psychological factors) of the environment. Vayda, Leeds, and Smith (and, more recently, Rappaport) have argued that religious and ceremonial activities may have important adaptive significance— e.g., the massive slaughter and consumption of pigs during certain ceremonials in the New Guinea highlands serves to maintain a long-run balance between the population and their food supply. And finally, Robert Edgerton has explored the relationships between personality and ecology.[59]

---

[59] See Leslie A. White, *The Evolution of Culture* (New York: McGraw-Hill, 1959), chapter 1; Eric R. Wolf, "Types of Latin American Peasantry: A Preliminary Discussion," *American Anthropologist* 57 (1955): 452–70; Charles O. Frake, "Cultural Ecology and Ethnography," *American Anthropologist* 64 (1962): 53–59; A. P. Vayda, A. Leeds, and D. B. Smith, "The Place of Pigs in Melanesian Subsistence," *Proceedings of the 1961 Annual Spring Meeting of the American Ethnological Society* (Seattle: University of Washington Press, 1961), pp. 69–77; Roy A. Rappaport, "Ritual Regulation of Environmental Relations Among A New Guinea People," *Ethnology* 6 (1967): 17–30; Robert B. Edgerton, "'Cultural' vs. 'Ecological' Factors in the Expression of Values, Attitudes, and Personality Characteristics" in *Man in Adaptation; The Cultural Present*, ed. Yehudi A. Cohen (Chicago: Aldine, 1968), pp. 309–14.

In general, it may be said that cultural ecology takes its inspiration from a long-range view of man, a view that sees man as a product of biological evolution, but a wholly unique product—unique because he comes to terms with his environment in ways that differ profoundly from those of all infrahuman species. At the infrahuman level, many species adapt in part to their total environment through a process of intraspecific and noncumulative learning. In the long run, however, their adaptation to the environment is dependent overwhelmingly upon a process of alterations in their genetic makeup and the mechanisms of natural selection. Hence, at the infrahuman level, adaptation may be said to be characterized by a more-or-less passive response of the given species to the ecosystem of which it is a part. Man, in adapting to his environment, does not undergo wholesale genetic alterations, but responds by playing an "active" role. In other words, while all infrahuman forms of life adapt to their environments substantially as given, man increasingly modifies and adapts his environment to himself. The enabling device is what we call *culture*—the primary mechanism through which man begins by adapting to and ends by controlling his environment. Increasingly, this environment in which he lives has become a cultural environment, so that whatever biological changes may occur in the species, the direction of causation seems to be much more from culture to biology, rather than the other way around.

Thus, *cultural* ecology, unlike *general* ecology, is not concerned simply with the interaction of life forms in a particular ecosystem, but with the way in which man, through the instrumentality of culture, manipulates and shapes the ecosystem itself. Cultural ecologists have stressed the point that different modes of manipulating the environment (nonpassive adaptation) have produced different kinds of cultural configurations and systems. Of course, most ecologists, general and cultural, would probably agree that man may very well wind up by manipulating himself off the face of the earth. But this too would be a consequence of cultural "adaptation" and not one of genetic change.

The Concept of Environment

It is apparent from the foregoing discussion that two of the central concepts of cultural ecology are *environment* and *adaptation*. Since there is considerable ambiguity in the use of these concepts, we should like here to examine them at least briefly. We do not believe that we can either completely dispel the ambiguities or resolve the difficulties of applying these terms operationally. Our more limited objective is simply to highlight some of the problems involved in using the terms in the context of explanation.

In popular usage, the word *environment* is generally equated with features of the natural habitat: climate, flora and fauna, soil, rainfall patterns, and even the presence or absence of subsoil minerals. There is a long tradition in Western intellectual thought, going back to Montesquieu and even beyond to the ancient Greeks, which attempts to account for cultural variation directly by reference to differences in the features of the natural habitat. But all contemporary cultural ecologists would reject any such mechanical use of environmental factors to account for variations in cultural arrangements. As they have often pointed out, a simple inventory of elements in the natural habitat will never permit one to predict the culture that may exist in a particular area at any given time.

Reacting against this simplistic environmental determinism, many cultural ecologists came to espouse a position which has been called environmental possibilism. In this view, the features of the natural habitat are seen as playing, not a determinative role, but a permissive or limiting role, offering opportunities in certain directions and inhibiting them in others. For example, the aboriginal Indian cultures of the Pacific Northwest, such as the Kwakiutl and Nootka, are usually referred to as hunting-and-gathering cultures. It has often been pointed out that, because they lived in an especially rich natural environment, they were able to achieve a level of sociocultural complexity nowhere matched by any hunters and gatherers in historic times. At the same time, it should be noted that these cultures had evolved a highly diverse and elaborate set of techniques for making use of the rich opportunities provided by their natural habitats. Indeed, some anthropologists have suggested that to refer to those Pacific Northwest Indians as hunters and gatherers is misleading, and that it is more accurate to call them "fish farmers."

We have used this rather simple example to illustrate the point that what constitutes an environmental opportunity or limitation can never be stated in absolute terms, but is always relative to the cultural means available for exploiting the possibilities of the environment. Thus, in a justifiable retreat from the simplistics of environmental determinism, cultural ecologists have turned toward a view which interprets environmental and cultural factors as part of a single interacting system, as in the following:

> A Javanese peasant's terrace . . . is both a product of an extended historical process of cultural development and perhaps the most immediately significant constituent of his "natural" environment. . . . Javanese rice terraces are closely integrated with modes of work organization, forms of village structures, and processes of social stratification. As one specifies more fully the precise nature of a people's adaptation from the geographical side, one inescapably specifies, at the same time and to the same degree, their adaptation from the cultural side, and vice versa. One delineates, in short, an ecosystem within which certain selected cultural, biological and physical variables are determinately interrelated. . . .

> This mode of analysis is of a sort which trains attention on the pervasive properties of systems *qua* systems (system structure, system equilibrium, system change) rather than on the point-to-point relationships between paired variables of the "culture" and "nature" variety.[60]

To return to the Pacific Northwest example, it is obvious that these tribes were "fish farmers" because fish were abundant in their environment. At the same time, the techniques and the practices that made fish available to them in such great quantities were culturally devised: they were the product of a

---

[60] Clifford Geertz, *Agricultural Involution* (Berkeley: University of California Press, 1968), pp. 9–10.

technology and sociopolitical organization that cannot be completely explained simply by the presence of fish.

It is apparent from the above examples that the environment that figures in the cultural ecologist's considerations is always a culturally modified environment. Such a formulation, we believe, implies an inescapable element of circularity: environment → culture, or culture → environment. For the interaction between the natural habitat and a cultural system inevitably involves a dialectic interplay of the elements or, in modern terminology, what is called *feedback* or *reciprocal causality*. But to accept the operation of reciprocal causality is not the same as saying that all elements in the system have equal causal impact. For when one looks at the interrelationship between cultural systems and their environments over time, it is clear that many features which constitute impediments or limitations for simpler technologies are often surmounted, or even turned into opportunities, by cultures with more advanced systems. Thus, the dense grass cover of the North American Plains was an impediment to hoe agriculture in aboriginal times. But with the use of the steel-tipped plow by Euro-Americans, this area became the breadbasket of a nation.

It is for these reasons that cultural ecology stresses the distinction between the habitat as given and the habitat as modified and utilized by man. And it is for these reasons also that, in assessing the interaction between the variables of the environment on the one hand and those of the culture on the other, most cultural ecologists would assign the greater causal weight by far to cultural factors. More and more of the natural habitat is being converted by man into a cultural environment. And even if the circularity of the cultural-ecological orientation can never be overcome, modern cultural systems have reached a point where they can (which is not to say that they will) either surmount or compensate for virtually any environmental deficiency or limitation.

One of the basic tenets of cultural ecology, then, is the distinction between the environment per se and the effective environment. By the *effective environment* we mean the environment as conceptualized, utilized, and modified by man. Some anthropologists see the way a culture utilizes its environment as a function of the way it perceives and conceptualizes this environment. They are led, therefore, to a phenomenalistic or cognitive view of cultural ecology. Thus, Edmund Leach writes:

> The environment is not a natural thing; it is a set of interrelated percepts, a product of culture. . . . What this environment is, is not discoverable objectively; it is a matter of perception. The relation between a society and its environment can be understood only when we see how the environment is organized in terms of the verbal categories of those who use it.[61]

---

[61] Edmund R. Leach, "Culture and Social Cohesion: An Anthropologist's View, in *Science and Culture*, ed. Gerald Holton (Boston: Houghton Mifflin, 1965), pp. 25, 37–38. See also Charles O. Frake, "Cultural Ecology and Ethnography," *American Anthropologist* 64 (1962): 53–59.

There is, of course, a strong measure of plausibility to Leach's statement. The apprehension of the environment, like the apprehension of all reality, is mediated through culturally provided conceptual categories. Thus, an examination of how a culture categorizes and conceptualizes its environment will tell us something about its taxonomic classification of nature. It may even tell us something about what its members attempt to accomplish with respect to their environment. But what they do indeed accomplish will depend not only upon the way the "environment is organized in terms of the verbal categories of those who use it," but also upon the objective properties of the environment and the knowledge and techniques a people have and use in coping with these objective properties. It is for this reason that most cultural ecologists, while acknowledging the kernel of truth in the position expressed by Leach, have been reluctant to espouse a completely cognitive, phenomenalistic approach to the environment.

The natural historian Marston Bates suggests a tripartite approach to the environment that includes Leach's environment as one aspect or view of the totality of the environment.[62] Bates speaks of the *operational* environment ("the sum of the phenomena that directly impinge on the organism"); the *potential* environment ("the sum of the phenomena that might conceivably impinge on the organism"); and the *perceptual* environment, which apparently corresponds to Leach's "perceptual" environment as applied to human societies.

The notion of the operational environment as utilized by cultural ecologists is largely a cultural environment in a double sense. It is a cultural environment first, because, as we have pointed out, it is increasingly the product of cultural interposition and tinkering, and second, because an important facet of the adaptation of *any* human society is its adaptation to other cultural systems that, in one form or another, impinge upon it. Every cultural system strikes a balance between the adaptation it makes to its "physical" environment on the one hand and to its "sociocultural" environment on the other. Often, for example, the key to understanding certain organizational principles of a culture, or the direction of change within it, is to be discovered by looking at its external relations, i.e., its interaction with other cultures. A quick look at changing culture patterns in many parts of the "developing world" should be enough to convince one of the accuracy of this proposition. However, we select our example from the more traditional anthropological literature. Both the tribal Tiv of West Africa and the tribal Nuer of East Africa are characterized by a social structure which anthropologists call "segmentary lineage organization." In both societies the basic living unit "on the ground" is a type of hamlet or "minimal lineage." But above the hamlet level, as one ascends the social structure, one finds lineages of larger and larger scope which progressively incorporate the kin units at the lower levels of the society. Except for the "minimal lineage," none of the higher or more inclusive lineages has a permanent organization. Each incorporative level comes into existence only when there is a dispute between lower-level structural units of like size and scope. In other words, the lineages of the Tiv and Nuer are

---

[62] See Marston Bates, "Ecology and Evolution," in *Evolution After Darwin*, Vol. 1, *The Evolution of Life*, ed. Sol Tax (Chicago: University of Chicago Press, 1960), 554.

lineages of "segmentary opposition." At the highest or most inclusive level, all members of the society may stand together in opposition to neighboring societies.

Marshall Sahlins has pointed out that both the Tiv and the Nuer have not only moved into areas *formerly* occupied by other peoples, but they have been consistently expanding at the expense of their neighbors.[63] He goes on to argue that a centralized political structure was most unlikely given the circumstances of Tiv and Nuer technology and the cultural patterns of adaptation. Consequently, the segmentary-lineage type of organization developed as an adaptive response on the part of these societies to their movement into a closed niche and their expansive thrust against the surrounding societies. The neighbors of the Nuer, the Dinka, are virtually indistinguishable from them with regard to many features of their culture. But because the Dinka, Sahlins tells us, were not faced with the same adaptive situation as the Nuer, they did not evolve lineages of segmentary opposition and have therefore steadily lost ground to the Nuer.

We are not so much concerned here with the empirical validity of Sahlins's argument as we are with the point of view expressed. The orientation is clearly cultural-ecological, but it is a form of cultural-ecological analysis which would have us look to what is happening at the borders of a society, that is, to how societies adapt to one another and compete with one another for the earth's resources. Indeed, one of the important lessons to be drawn from Sahlins's analysis is that it is often difficult to tell where one society leaves off and the other begins—a particularly critical methodological issue in the study of the contemporary world, where cultures have become so highly interrelated.

This brings us to our final point concerning the ambiguities built into the term *environment*. Repeatedly throughout this section we have used the words *system* and *environment* and have discussed the relationships between the empirical components to which these terms refer. We have talked as though we, along with other anthropologists, knew what the boundaries of these empirical components are, that is, as though we knew where *system* ends and *environment* begins. In point of fact, however, when anthropologists use terms like kinship *system*, political *system*, economic *system*, etc., they are usually invoking a methodological dictum: they are, in effect, saying that the phenomena they are dealing with have systemic attributes, that is, that they are ordered and interrelated. The question of the boundaries of these systems is generally only vaguely answered. But if one is concerned with the relationships between system and environment or the relationship among the institutions (economic, political, etc.) of a society, the question of defining boundaries becomes crucial. For example, if one is attempting to account for or to explain certain kinship arrangements by referring to features of the economic system, or to those of the political system, etc., it is important to be able to distinguish, at least minimally, one system from the others. Moreover, defining the boundaries of a system—any system—is not a simple matter. In an essay entitled "Definition of a System," Hall and Fagen point out that

---

63 See Marshall D. Sahlins, "The Segmentary Lineage: An Organization of Predatory Expansion," *American Anthropologist* 63 (1961): 322–45.

system and *environment* can be defined in much the same manner. Thus, they say:

> For a given system, the environment is the set of all objects a change in whose attributes affect the system and also those objects whose attributes are changed by the behavior of the system.[64]

They then go on:

> The statement above invites the natural question of when an object belongs to a system and when it belongs to the environment; for if an object reacts with a system in the way described above should it not be considered a part of the system? The answer is by no means definite. In a sense, a system together with its environment makes up the universe of all things of interest in a given context. Subdivision of this universe into two sets, system and environment, can be done in many ways which are in fact quite arbitrary. Ultimately it depends on the intentions of the one who is studying the particular universe as to which of the possible configurations of objects is to be taken as the system.[65]

It is relevant to note that the above quotations appeared originally as part of an introductory chapter in a book called *Systems Engineering*, published by the Bell Telephone Laboratories and presumably directed at an audience of physical scientists and engineers rather than social scientists. But despite the difficulties noted by Hall and Fagen in distinguishing *system* from *environment*, engineers seem to have had considerable success in defining the limits of the systems with which they are concerned. Defining the limits of the system in anthropology, however (or, indeed, in any of the social sciences), is a more complex matter. Engineers and physical scientists may generally bound their systems in the laboratory or other comparably controlled situations and, in this manner, they may delimit or control the variables relevant to the problem. While the anthropologist, like the engineer or physical scientist, may *seek* logical closure of the system with which he is concerned through the building of models, or the creation of structural types, or the comparison of systems within and among these types, the systems that he works with are *natural* rather than artificial systems. They are, therefore, highly open, and the number of variables that may be relevant to the operation of a particular institution or a "total" cultural system are beyond the anthropologist's control.

Nonetheless, despite the difficulties and ambiguities that we have noted with reference to the concepts of *system* and *environment*, these concepts are indispensable to the anthropologist in helping him to orient his thought and research. But in working with these concepts he must always keep in mind their lack of operational precision. Thus, the methodological advice offered by Ely Devons and Max Gluckman—while it does not provide a solution to this imprecision—seems to us to be the most feasible approach open

---

[64] A. D. Hall and R. E. Fagen, "Definition of System," in *Modern Systems Research for the Behavioral Scientist*, ed. Walter Buckley (Chicago: Aldine, 1968), p. 83.
[65] Ibid.

to anthropologists with regard to the problem of delimiting system and environment.[66] For Devons and Gluckman, like Hall and Fagen, suggest that the system and the environment must be conceptualized in an ad hoc manner—that is, that they must be bounded with reference to the demands of the particular problem with which the anthropologist is concerned. And, further, the anthropologist must always be prepared in the course of his work to redefine his system and redraw its boundaries.

The Concept of Adaptation

In the foregoing discussion we have dealt at some length with the environment as a key concept in the cultural-ecological orientation. In the course of this discussion we have referred many times to adaptation as a process relating cultural systems and their environments. It should be apparent by now that it is impossible to think of adaptation without reference to some environment or other.

We have already emphasized the notion of circularity (the reciprocity or feedback between culture and environment) that inheres in the cultural-ecological orientation. But to say that culture and environment interact within a single system is not to say that the causal influences are equal in both directions—we have also tried to emphasize that with technological advance the dynamic factor in the culture-environment equation has increasingly become culture and not the environment per se. Thus, as long as most cultural ecologists confine themselves to a description of the reciprocal interplay between culture and environment, no serious logical problems arise. However, when they move from description and from the use of the cultural-ecological approach as methodology toward its use for the purpose of specifying variables or framing theories and/or explanations, certain logical problems do arise.

Some of these problems stem not only from the fact that the environment may have a vastly different kind of impact at different levels of sociocultural and technoeconomic development, but from the additional fact that the very meaning of the term *environment* may differ over time. Cultural ecologists have not always been clear about this point. Julian Steward, however, has repeatedly emphasized—most notably in his article on "Cultural Ecology" for the latest edition of the *Encyclopedia of the Social Sciences* (1968)—the reciprocal decline in the "determinative" role of environmental factors as technology advances. In short, as environment itself becomes overwhelmingly a *product* of culture, attempts to explain culture *in terms of* environment become tautological. This is why we have referred to much of the work of contemporary cultural ecologists as circular. The same kind of circularity and the same logical problems appear when cultural ecologists use the concept of adaptation as an *explanatory* device.

Even in biological evolution, where adaptation plays such a central role in accounting for organic variation, this circularity is apparent and has been

---

[66] Ely Devons and Max Gluckman, "Conclusion: Modes and Consequences of Limiting a Field of Study," in *Closed Systems and Open Minds*, ed. Max Gluckman (Chicago: Aldine, 1964), pp. 158–261.

pointed out by philosophically minded biologists. Thus, the biologist finds it difficult to assign a precise meaning to the concept of adaptation without linking it to the fact that the species under discussion has survived and proliferated. For the biologist, survival as measured by reproductive success is evidence of adaptation, and extinction is after-the-fact proof of the failure to adapt. When the term *adaptation* is used as a descriptive label for a process (e.g., the appearance and radiation of a new species) that has taken place through time, it need not present problems. But when one tries to use the concept of adaptation as a device for explaining this process, the explanation becomes tautological. For the notion of survival is implied by the term *adaptation* in much the same way that being unmarried is implied by the term *spinster*.[67]

Anthropologists have not come off any better than the biologists in their use of the concept adaptation. The anthropologist sees a culture in operation and assumes that its carriers have made some sort of successful adaptation to their environment. Otherwise, of course, the culture would have disappeared, leaving, if anything, only an archeological memory of its existence and archeological evidence of its failure to adapt (i.e., to survive as a living culture).

Or maybe an anthropologist looks at two cultures in the same environment and finds that one is spreading at the expense of the other. Survival of the one is explained in terms of a "better adaptation" to that particular environment than that of the culture it is displacing; the evidence, or proof, is in the expansion. Or sometimes a culture (or a structural type) "proves" its "all-round adaptability" by expanding into a wide range of environmental zones or ecological niches. Needless to say, the principal evidence for this all-round adaptability is the fact of expansion.

What we would like to have, of course (as all of the above examples emphasize), is some effective measure of adaptation which is independent of the facts of survival and expansion. Leslie White has suggested that the adaptive effectiveness of a culture can be measured by its thermodynamic efficiency, that is, by the amount of energy it harnesses per capita per year and puts to work. Other anthropologists have tried to define adaptability in terms of greater complexity of structure—that is, the more adapted a culture,

---

[67] Biologists generally see adaptation as promoting "Darwinian fitness" which is equated with reproductive success, and this, in turn, means survival and proliferation. For example, the biologists Wallace and Srb tell us that when "animals and plants are *adapted* to their environments or to their modes of life [this means] that even casual observation reveals these organisms to possess particular characteristics that enable them to survive under the special environmental conditions in which they are found. . . . Imagine a species, a particular type of animal, that is not adapted to its environment. By definition it could not exist" (pp. 1–2). And: "I.I. Schmalhausen, an eminent Russian scientist, has pointed out, as evidence that individual adaptations are of evolutionary origin, that the physiological adjustments made by individuals in response to abnormal environmental conditions are often useless or even harmful. Adaptive responses as expressed by an individual's physiological changes are responses which through many generations have proven useful in allowing individuals to survive and reproduce; bizarre or unique environmental conditions, by definition, have never taken an important part in determining the nature of these reactions" (p. 9). Bruce Wallace and Adrian M. Srb, *Adaptation* (Englewood Cliffs, N.J.: Prentice-Hall, 1961).

the more structures it will include and the more differentiated, functionally specialized, and highly integrated these structures will be. But whether these measures of adaptation may be applied and made operational in the context of empirical research is still very much a moot point in anthropology.

Despite the logical difficulties associated with the use of the concept of *adaptation*, however, anthropologists cannot do without it. For, like the term *environment*, it is one of the most fruitful methodological concepts in all of anthropology. We should not be dismayed by the seeming paradox that some terms lack the definitional precision demanded of scientific concepts by the textbooks. For sometimes a hard-to-define or elusive concept can be very useful in orienting our thinking and our research in fruitful directions. Without the concepts of adaptation and environment, the conceptual tool kit of anthropology would be appreciably impoverished.

What Bates writes about the concept of environment might apply with equal force to the concept of adaptation:

> The idea of environment seems obvious and easy: it covers the surroundings, the setting of an organism; it is the sum of the forces acting on the organism from the outside, in contrast with the forces that arise from the inside, from the nature of the organism itself. But when we start to work with this contrast between inside and outside, we soon get into difficulties.
>
> The old "nature versus nurture" controversy is an example of one kind of difficulty. We now realize that the organism—the phenotype—is the end product of a particular genotype, a particular set of potentialities, developing in a particular context or environment. We cannot sort traits into two separate pigeon-holes, one labelled "hereditary" and the other "environmental." Everything about the organism is a consequence of the interaction of both. . . .
>
> Another kind of difficulty with the organism-environment contrast is illustrated in an extreme form by the human animal. When we investigate the environmental relations of the human species, what do we do about culture? Is culture an attribute of man or of the environment? . . . .
>
> The environment concept is thus a constant source of trouble, but I know of no way of getting along without it. One must go ahead and use it confidently—but also somewhat warily, keeping alert to the dangers. If we tried to avoid fuzzy and misleading words, I suspect that all verbal discourse would stop. This might make mathematicians and some kind of logicians happy, but it would be hard on the rest of us.[68]

Thus, as we have tried to show in this section, it is virtually impossible to be precise about any of the operating concepts (adaptation, environment, and system) involved in the cultural-ecological approach. Naturally, the imprecision leads to certain logical difficulties. And while we have emphasized some of these difficulties, we have done so not to denigrate the methodological utility of the approach, but to put the student on his guard, and also because,

---

[68] Bates, "Ecology and Evolution," pp. 552–53.

in the discussions of cultural ecology with which we are familiar, these logical and conceptual difficulties are often neglected.

Cultural ecology has been among the more suggestive and fruitful orientations in anthropology. Out of this approach has come a view of man as a species which, like other animal species, confronts the imperatives of adapting to and exploitation of the environment. The specific ways in which different peoples have at different times and in different places responded to this imperative, the cultural ecologists maintain, may provide us with at least a partial answer to the question of how these peoples organize their economic and social life, create religious rituals, and elaborate their artistic and philosophic beliefs as they do. The anthropological ecologist must always be a *cultural* ecologist, for he should never lose sight of the fact that man adapts primarily through the mechanism of his culture, and that, as a consequence, his mode of adaptation is unique.

Recently, however, some ecologically oriented anthropologists have expressed a somewhat different point of view. They assert that cultural-ecological studies have suffered by their failure to follow paths established by more general ecological studies. They advocate a unified ecological approach in which common principles and concepts would be applied to the study of both infrahuman species and man. Vayda and Rappaport, for example, write:

> An immediate methodological requirement for a more unified ecological approach is some measure of agreement about the kinds of units whose relations are to be studied. In addition to individual organisms, the units important to ecologists are populations (groups of organisms living within the given area and belonging to the same species or variety), communities (all of the populations within a given area), and ecosystems (either individual organisms, populations, or communities, together with their non-living environments). . . . Consistent with usage in ecology, the focus of anthropologists engaged in ecological studies can be upon human populations and upon ecosystems and biotic communities in which human populations are included. To have units fitting into the ecologists' frame of reference is a procedure with clear advantages. Human populations as units are commensurable with the other units with which they interact to form food webs, biotic communities, and ecosystems. Their capture of energy from and exchanges of material with these other units can be measured and then described in quantitative terms. No such advantage of commensurability obtains if cultures are made the units, for cultures, unlike human populations, are not fed upon by predators, limited by food supplies, or debilitated by disease.[69]

Judging from the above statement and other similar pronouncements—as well as from a number of empirical studies—what seems to have taken place in the movement from the "old" to the "new" ecology is a shift in emphasis away from *culture* as the object of study toward *populations of organisms* as the basic unit of analysis. With this shift, the importance of culture as a

---

[69] Andrew P. Vayda, and Roy A. Rappaport, "Ecology, Cultural and Noncultural," in *Introduction to Cultural Anthropology*, ed. James A. Clifton (Boston: Houghton Mifflin, 1968), p. 494.

mechanism of human adaptation has been downgraded somewhat, appearing now to be just "another feature" in man's behavioral repertoire.

We do not, of course, want to challenge in its entirety either the utility or the potential contributions of the new ecological perspective in illuminating certain adaptational features of human societies qua populations of organisms. If, for example, one is interested in demographic issues, the new ecological emphasis or perspective can certainly have both heuristic and analytic value for the researcher. However, what is not yet clear from the statements and the research of the new ecologists is how their unified or single ecological approach embracing man as virtually just another species of fauna in an ecosystem or biotic environment may help us to explain the emergence, maintenance, and transformation of *cultural* configurations. For one of the inevitable—and apparently intended—consequences of the "unified" approach would be to gloss over or diminish the basic distinction between *cultural ecology* and *general ecology*—a distinction whose importance we have emphasized repeatedly here because we believe it to be so fundamental to an understanding of cultural processes in general.

The significance of maintaining a clear conceptual distinction between cultural ecology on the one hand and general ecology on the other has been most cogently and crisply emphasized by the eminent biologist and Nobel laureate P. B. Medewar:

> There is one crucial distinction between endosomatic and exosomatic evolution. Ordinary evolution is mediated by the process of heredity. Exosomatic "evolution" (we can still call it "systematic secular change") is mediated not by heredity but by *tradition*, by which I mean the transfer of information through non-genetic channels from one generation to the next. So here is a fundamental distinction between the Springs of Action in mice and men. Mice have no traditions—or at most very few, and of a kind that would not interest you. Mice can be propagated from generation to generation, with no loss or alteration of their mouse-like ways, by individuals which have been isolated from their parental generation from the moment of their birth. But the entire structure of human society as we know it would be destroyed in a single generation if anything of the kind were to be done with man.[70]

Whatever the deficiencies of the old cultural ecology, it is and always was clearly concerned with issues having to do with the variation, maintenance, and change in these "exosomatic traditions"—in *culture*. In this concern it has raised a number of significant theoretical questions, drawn our attention to certain important types of variables, and warned the investigator that he "ignores this order of fact at his peril."

---

[70] B. P. Medewar, *The Uniqueness of the Individual* (London: Methuen, 1957), pp. 141–42.

Three Types
of Culture Theory

In the preceding chapter we discussed what we have called the four principal *theoretical orientations* in anthropology. We have tried to show that each of these approaches is usually identified with a particular "school" in anthropology. In point of fact, however, when an anthropologist of any persuasion moves from ethnographic description to explanation, he is inevitably forced to employ all four theoretical orientations, even though he may select one of these approaches for particular emphasis. In short, if the aim of the anthropologist is explanation and the formulation of theories, he will discover that each of these orientations logically implies the others and that, therefore, all tend to converge when applied to a similar set of problems.

But while these theoretical orientations may be indispensable in leading to the creation of theories, they do not by themselves constitute theories. A theory per se is addressed to the question of why (how) certain regularities of nature occur and must, therefore, contain a statement of the specific mechanisms and the relationship among the variables involved in the phenomena under investigation. In this chapter we shall look at the major types of theories that have emerged from the essentially methodological approaches of evolutionism, functionalism, history, and cultural ecology.

When an anthropologist gathers data in the field, he observes people doing such things as building canoes, tilling their fields, dancing in ceremonies, marrying, rearing children, divorcing, avoiding their mothers-in-law, and so on. But when he comes to writing up these observations, to describing the way the society functions, he employs a whole array of concepts and constructs not given by direct observation. These concepts and constructs have come down to him as a part of the accumulated intellectual armory of anthropology and its sister disciplines. Indeed, they play a major role in determining not only how he categorizes the materials of his observations, but how he chooses those particular aspects of culture on which he focuses his attention. One thinks, for example, of such basic constructs as status and role, of the organization of statuses into hierarchical or egalitarian patterns (i.e., ranking, stratification, class), and of the constellation of statuses and roles into institutional forms geared to performing specific functions. In attempting to explain both the form taken by institutions in different societal settings, and the way in which they relate to each other in the total structure of a given society, anthropologists have found it necessary to move beyond the concepts of status, role, and institution to an even higher level of abstraction—a level at which institutions are placed, for purposes of explanation, in certain analytic contexts called *subsystems*.[1] The major subsystems generally distinguished by anthropologists are *ideology, social structure, technoeconomics*, and *personality* (considered in both its social and psychobiological dimensions).

By a *subsystem*, therefore, we mean a set of variables or aspects of institutionalized behavior that can be analytically isolated for purposes of explaining, at least in part, how a society both maintains itself and undergoes change. The ideological subsystem of any society consists of all its beliefs, philosophies, values, and scientific knowledge. It should, therefore, be apparent that a society's subsystem of ideas, or its ideology, is not confined to any particular institution (school, family, business firm, factory, church, etc.) or major institutional order of that society. It should be equally clear, however, that certain societal institutions, such as universities, may be said to be more concerned with the ideological subsystem than with the technoeconomic, or the social structural, or the personality spheres. On the other hand, the university does perform functions that relate to all of the major subsystems.

But it is not only the university whose operations cross-cut all of a society's subsystems. For though each institution and institutional order in a society may be involved predominantly with one or another of the society's subsystems, its activities are likely to cross-cut all subsystems. Thus, one may encounter this kind of operational interweaving—institutional, institutional order, and subsystem—at every level of analysis.

---

[1] It might appear from these statements that we are describing the actual logical and psychological processes followed by each anthropologist as he confronts the empirical materials of his research. Of course, no anthropologist proceeds in such an "ideal" and orderly manner from the observation of raw, uninterpreted data through successively higher levels of abstraction. We write as if this were so only for purposes of exposition. Actually, every anthropologist begins his researches armed with the concepts and abstractions already provided by the discipline. He moves back and forth between the levels in accordance with the demands of his analysis.

While one of the achievements of anthropology has been to demonstrate certain significant relationships among institutions and institutional variables where none might have been suspected, anthropology as a theoretical science cannot be content to stop here. To say, for example, that phenomena A, B, and C mutually influence one another tells us nothing about the direction of causality nor about the relative weight that each of these elements contributes to the total interacting system. It is in the complementary process of identifying causality and assigning these relative weights that anthropology moves toward the creation of theory. When we look at how anthropologists (and, indeed, how all social scientists) have engaged in this joint process, what emerges is the four subsystems, each with its own assignment of relative weights and causality. Or, to return to the language of the preceding chapter: when confronted with the theoretical task of deciding which are the strategic or core features related to societal maintenance and change, anthropologists have responded by emphasizing variables selected from one or another of the subsystems. Thus, four major types of anthropological theory have emerged. If, as we pointed out at the beginning of this chapter, most anthropologists are eclectic in the use of the several *theoretical orientations*, this eclecticism extends also to their framing of specific *theories*. In practice, anthropological theorizing is a matter of emphasis. Even when a theory or an explanation stresses the causal significance of one of the subsystems it is likely to include some reference to the contributory impact of one or more of the remaining subsystems.

While some anthropologists have tended to assign greater causal weight to one or another of the subsystems, and others have been more eclectic in their causal analyses, there remains a third group. This latter group, seemingly overwhelmed by the complex interplay of all the factors in the total system, ends up by abandoning the attempt to assign causal weight to the variables of any one or any combination of the subsystems. In effect, what they seem to be saying is that the elements in *any* sociocultural situation are so multitudinous and so complex that cause-and-effect relationships can never be established. This view appears to us to be unsatisfactory on several grounds. In the first place, it is a methodological dead end. For if one starts out by assuming that the formulation or demonstration of cause-and-effect relationships is ultimately impossible, then one is never led to look for such relationships. Second, this position seems to assume that the only choice is between omniscience and complete ignorance—that if we cannot provide total explanations, we must abandon the attempt at *any* explanation. But there is a middle ground between omniscience on the one hand and complete ignorance on the other. To have some theoretical knowledge is better than to have none. A partial explanation is better than no explanation at all.

If we look at the work of some of the most creative social scientists of the past—such as Freud, Marx, Durkheim, Weber, Tylor, and Morgan—it is clear that one of the things that made their contributions both possible and valuable was their unwillingness to be intimidated by the complexities of causation in social phenomena. They concentrated on what they considered a few crucial variables, and they followed the causal significance of these wherever it led them in their search for explanations. Some of the explanations they came up with may have been partial, and some incorrect. But it is because they dared to advance causal explanations, even when these were derived from "incomplete" knowledge, that their work has had such a profound influence on all later generations of social scientists and represents collectively an enormous contribution to our understanding of man as a cultural animal.

Thus, while granting that "in reality" the variables of the four subsystems are interwoven, the formulation of theories requires that they be conceptually separated. Hence, for analytic purposes we shall treat each of the subsystems separately. We begin with technoeconomics.

Technoeconomics

In this section we have employed the term technoeconomic rather than the more familiar technology. Our rationale for so doing is that "technology" in popular usage generally refers only to the machines, tools, and weapons of a culture, whereas anthropologists, especially when they are engaged in formulating theories, almost invariably use the term *technology* to imply considerably more than these things themselves. As a matter of fact, in recent years the term *technoeconomics* has increasingly replaced *technology* precisely to emphasize the fact that tools alone do not make a technology. For when one "unpacks" (to use the philosopher's terminology) the ostensibly limited term *technology*, one finds that it includes *not only* the machines and tools employed by a given culture, but also the way these are organized for use, and even the scientific knowledge that makes them possible. Thus, while each of the above components of technology (*or technoeconomics*) is important, under differing cultural and historical circumstances one set of factors (e.g., the tools) may be more determinative than the others.

At simpler levels of sociocultural development, tools and the natural habitat (as Steward has shown so clearly in his discussion of patrilineal bands [2]) appear to play a very direct and important role in the shaping of a group's social and economic institutions (see p. 96, *infra*). At higher levels, economic factors and the sociopolitical arrangements associated with these factors tend to determine not only the rate and manner of growth of a given society's technical equipment (machines and tools), but also the ways in which that equipment may or may not be put to social use. Thus, Robert Heilbroner suggests that technological determinism may be "peculiarly a problem of a certain historic epoch—specifically that of high capitalism and low socialism in which the forces of technical change have been unleashed but when the agencies for the control or guidance of technology are still rudimentary." [3] He tells us, in short, that when technology (in this sense the machines and tools, and how they are used) is given more-or-less free rein to develop and to be used without much regard for the social implications of that development or use, we have a kind of technological determinism. When, however, social considerations intervene to determine how a particular complex of technical devices should be put to use, technology

---

[2] See Julian H. Steward, "The Economic and Social Basis of Primitive Bands," in *Essays on Anthropology in Honor of Alfred Louis Kroeber* (Berkeley: University of California Press, 1936), pp. 311–50.

[3] Robert Heilbroner, "Do Machines Make History?," *Technology and Culture* 8 (1967): 345.

ceases to be the determinant and becomes the servant of socioeconomic arrangements.

We would post a small addendum or extension to Heilbroner's analysis by way of clarification and emphasis. When he says that "the agencies for the control or guidance are still rudimentary," he is, we believe, referring not to "control or guidance" per se (for it is obvious that all technologies are controlled and guided), but to control and guidance in the interest of society at large rather than that of one or more favored groups within the society. In this sense, then, the decisions or lack of them, the social arrangements, or the very ideological position that supports or allows "free rein" to "rampant technological growth" are themselves the products of an existing socio-economic structure. And the determination to let the machines and the computers run rampant, as it were, is, in turn, therefore, an ideological and a power adjunct of the given socioeconomic structure.[4]

Hence, it would seem that whether a culture "decides" to let "technology" call the turn or whether it "decides" to control "technology" in the interest of "social betterment," the ultimate decision is a product of history and of socioeconomic arrangements with their accompanying ideologies. The effectiveness of these ideologies is, in either case, limited or determined by the various kinds of power they may or may not be able to exert.

Cultural Ecology and Technoeconomics: Orientation and Theory

Perhaps one of the most effective ways of illustrating what we have earlier referred to as the difference between a *theoretical orientation* and a *theory* is to examine the relationship between cultural ecology (a theoretical orientation) and specific technoeconomic theories. Many, if not most, anthropologists tend to see the cultural-ecological orientation and the theoretical concern with technoeconomic variables as virtually synonymous. There are several reasons why they equate the two: first, because they consider cultural ecology a theory rather than, in our terms, a theoretical or methodological orientation; and, second, because when they *have* moved from a programmatic or general methodological stance toward specific empirical hypotheses, the key variables they use for explanation are indeed overwhelmingly technoeconomic.

In the previous chapter we indicated why ecologically oriented anthropologists seem to be drawn inevitably to emphasizing a culture's material equipment as well as its environmental variables in their analyses of empirical materials. But despite the close relationship between cultural ecology and the material equipment available to a culture, the combination is neither

---

[4] Emmanuel G. Mesthene seems to be making substantially the same point when he says that "freedom of individual decision-making is a value that we have cherished and that is built into the institutional fabric of our society. The negative effects of technology that we deplore are a measure of what this traditional freedom is beginning to cost us. They are traceable less to some mystical autonomy presumed to lie in technology and much more to the autonomy that our economic and political institutions grant to individual decision-making" [*Technological Change* (Cambridge: Harvard University Press, 1970), p. 40].

necessary, exclusive, nor inevitable. Hypothetically, at least, there is no reason to suppose that other factors like the social and political organization, religious and philosophical beliefs, or personality traits may not have an adaptive impact equivalent to that of the material culture *cum* natural habitat.

It is considerations like these that have led us to make what we believe is a crucial and clarifying distinction between cultural ecology as a *theoretical orientation* and technoeconomic *theories*.

Technoeconomic theories, as we have pointed out, do not focus exclusively on the techniques and tools used by a society in meeting its economic needs. In short, the first part of the compound word (*techno*) refers to the technical or material equipment and knowledge available to a society, while the second part of the word (*economic*) stresses the arrangements employed by a given society in applying its technical equipment and knowledge to the production, distribution, and consumption of goods and services. Technology, in this arbitrarily limited sense, represents opportunity; economics the way in which that opportunity is applied socially. We believe this is the issue Marx was emphasizing when he distinguished between the "means of production" and the "mode of production."

Among the important implications of this distinction is that the impact of a society's technical equipment on the rest of the cultural system is always mediated through a set of socioeconomic arrangements. What is more, while a particular technology—in the narrower, colloquial sense—may set limits to the forms taken by these socioeconomic arrangements, it does not seem to determine them uniquely. For example, throughout much of aboriginal East Africa, the material culture was fairly uniform. Nevertheless, there existed sharp differences in socioeconomic structure between politically acephalous societies like the Masai and the Kipsigis, on the one hand, and the highly centralized kingdoms of Ankole and Shilluk on the other. Nor are such examples confined to the primitive world. Thus, operating from a similar material base, the socioeconomic structures of Japan, Sweden, the Soviet Union, and the United States are clearly dissimilar. Some social scientists have claimed that these dissimilarities are either superficial, transitory, or both. They would say that "in the long run" these superficial differences will vanish, and the socioeconomic structure of each of these countries will become indistinguishable from that of the others. This may indeed be so. Certainly, many of the recent developments that have taken place in the industrialized parts of the world seem to suggest that this is what is happening.[5]

"In the long run," we are told, convergence will win out. The same kinds

---

[5] George Lichtheim, however, believes that the apparent convergence of socioeconomic type between, for example, contemporary U.S. and the U.S.S.R., may be deceiving. Although their technological bases are very similar, the different uses to which this technology is put is in each case determined by widely differing types of social purpose and organization. This suggests to us that what are taken to be similarities or differences between two technoeconomic systems will depend on one's theoretical perspectives. As Lichtheim says: "To stay for a moment longer with the mixed economy and the welfare state: For all the latter's socializing tendencies, it differs radically from a genuinely socialist system, in that the public authorities do not themselves engage in production, but rather act to provide markets for commodities produced by privately owned industry and farming. To the extent that this distinction obtains, even Yugoslavia under a self-styled Communist

of tools and machines must yield the same kinds of social and economic institutions. Perhaps. In any case, "in the long run" and "transitory" are slippery terms. They can mean anything from years to centuries. And to people living under these transitory or converging circumstances, the differences may be anything but superficial. For example, the socioeconomic differences which distinguished Nazi Germany from England in 1940, each operating with the same kind of industrial equipment, may have been transitory, but the consequences of these differences were hardly superficial for the people of these countries and for the rest of the world.

To sum up: "in the long run," tools and machines may determine the form and functioning of all subsystems in a culture. But these material items never operate in isolation from the socioeconomic system—with all that that implies for utilizing, maximizing, encouraging, or suppressing the growth and expansion of the so-called technological realm.

Technoeconomic Determinants

The anthropological literature includes a great many studies demonstrating the impact of technoeconomic factors on the other subsystems of a society. Among the better-known cases of this type are those, for example, that deal with the transformation of North American Plains Indian culture following the introduction of the horse and, later, the gun. The horse made it possible for the Indian to exploit the rich animal resources (bison) of the American Plains in a way and to a degree that had not been possible before. Symmes C. Oliver, who has provided us with an excellent summary of much of the literature dealing with culture history and culture change among the Indians of the Great Plains, sums it up as follows: "It was a technological change, the introduction of the horse, that made the historic Plains culture possible. This basic technological change triggered a whole series of cultural modifications." [6] The tribes whose acquisition of the horse made it possible for them to move permanently out into the Plains came from varied cultural backgrounds. Some, like the Crow and the Cheyenne, had been primarily sedentary village horticulturalists. Others, like the Cree and the Comanche,

---

regime is not completely socialist. It is, however, unnecessary for a socialist system to dispense with pricing and the market. The fact that this has been done in the U.S.S.R. proves nothing except the mental rigidity of the planners. . . . A socialist system is compatible with a market economy, provided the basic decisions are made by the planners and provided the public sector is dominant, which in practice means that it must embrace large-scale industry and banking. Conversely, the mixed economy in western Europe is not socialist as long as governments merely act to ensure a high level of aggregate demand, thus providing the fuel for private investment." ["The Political Economy of Western Industrial Society," in *Readings in Introductory Sociology*, ed. Dennis H. Wrong and Harry L. Gracey (New York: Macmillan, 1967), p. 518]. See also: Peter Wiles, "Will Capitalism and Communism Converge," in *Scaling the Wall*, ed. George R. Urban (Detroit: Wayne State University Press, 1964), pp. 223–40.

[6] Symmes C. Oliver, *Ecology and Cultural Continuity as Contributing Factors in the Social Organization of the Plains Indians*, University of California Publications in American Archaeology and Ethnology, vol. 48, no. 1 (1962), pp. 67–68. This essay contains a good bibliography of the important works dealing with Plains Indian culture and history.

had been hunters and gatherers. Once arrived on the Plains, however, a cultural convergence took place. This is not to say that all differences in background were obliterated, for they were not. But there were clear convergences in social structure (toward a more fluid bilateral band organization, for example); in ideology (toward a growing emphasis on the warrior as an ideal type and toward a marked increase in the importance of the bison in religious ritual). And there are even instances of transformation in social personality. Thus, for example, a body of the formerly peaceful, "meek" hunters and gatherers of the Basin-Plateau area became the Comanche, fierce warriors of the Plains.

A well-known case study from another part of the world is Lauriston Sharp's account of the effects of the switch from stone to steel axes among the Yir-Yoront, a hunting and gathering tribe of Cape York, Australia. Sharp shows us how the introduction of the steel axe led to dramatic changes in "the realm of traditional ideas, sentiments and values"; how it proved to be "the root of psychological stress"; and how it "changed the character of relations between individual and individual" and between members of the group and those of adjacent peoples. According to Sharp, the steel axe was responsible for "a revolutionary confusion of sex, age, and kinship roles, with a major gain in independence and loss of subordination on the part of those able now to acquire steel axes when they had been unable to possess stone axes before." [7]

And, finally in this brief and limited sampling of "case studies," we turn to Ralph Linton's classic analysis of the Tanala of Madagascar. Linton asserts that a shift from dry rice cultivation to irrigated wet rice cultivation had a profound effect on all aspects of Tanala culture. From "self-contained . . . villages with their classless society and strong joint families," the Tanala were transformed into a "kingdom with . . . central authority, settled subjects, rudimentary social classes based on economic differences. . . . The transformation can be traced step by step and at every step we find irrigated rice at the bottom of the change." [8]

The Linton and Sharp researches referred to above deal with the impact of technoeconomic factors on other subsystems *within a single society*. The Plains Indian example is somewhat different: Oliver's synthesis of the empirical materials involves comparisons among a fairly large *number of societies within a region*, and he attempts to generalize on the basis of this intraregional comparison. He is clearly concerned with the factors which led to the emergence of a societal type in a specific historical setting. And among these factors technoeconomics looms large.

Other investigators using anthropological techniques and data have tried to frame technoeconomic generalizations and theories which go beyond a given case and even beyond a number of cases within a region. As a conse-

---

[7] Lauriston Sharp, "Steel Axes for Stone Age Australians," in *Human Problems in Technological Change*, ed. Edward H. Spicer (New York: Russell Sage Foundation, 1952), pp. 82–86.

[8] Ralph Linton, *The Study of Man* (New York: D. Appleton-Century, 1936), p. 353. See also Linton's chapter on the Tanala in *The Individual and His Society*, ed. Abram Kardiner (New York: Columbia University Press, 1939), pp. 251–90.

quence, their generalizations have wider comparative scope. Because of the broader scope, studies of this kind are most suggestive and, we believe, offer the greatest potential for the development of anthropological theory. This is not to say that single case or intraregional studies can not at times suggest broader generalizations or hypotheses. They can. But often they have been so tied to specific cultures and specific historical variables that it is difficult to generalize their findings, to convert these findings into more general theoretical propositions.

Thus, in a well-known paper to which we have referred earlier, Julian Steward argued that among hunters and gatherers one finds (despite many obvious differences in culture content) certain broad similarities in social structure.[9] In a sample of such groups from various parts of the world, Steward found that they were organized into small, politically autonomous bands. He maintains that the structural similarities are in each case generated by a direct response of the culture to its natural habitat and to the technical means available for the exploitation of this particular habitat. He distinguishes two subtypes within this major structural type. There are those groups whose subsistence depends largely on the hunting of small nonmigratory game. In turn, the success of this activity depends upon a small core of resident males who are familiar with the hunting territory. In combination, then, these factors "demand" patrilocality which, in its turn, produces what Steward calls "patrilineal band organization" (exogamous and virilocal). Those societies that depend upon herds of large migratory game like the bison, however, have evolved a somewhat different type of structure, which Steward calls the "composite band" (lacking exogamy and explicit postmarital residence regulations). In short, he uses his worldwide sample to formulate a general theory about the relationship between technoeconomics and social structure.[10]

Using a sample of 549 cultures, Meyer Nimkoff and Russell Middleton found that family types varied with certain technoeconomic arrangements.[11] They report that the characteristic type in hunting-and-gathering *and* in industrial societies is the conjugal, independent family. In horticultural or agricultural societies, however, they found that the basic unit is the joint or extended family. They believe that these correlations hinge upon certain specific technoeconomic variables such as the nature of the food supply, demand for family labor, physical mobility, and property. They write, for example:

> The association of the independent family with industrial society is usually accounted for mainly by characteristics of industry itself. One is the small demand for family labor. Unlike the situation in simpler economies, employment in industrial societies is provided by non-family agencies on the basis of individual competence, not family membership.

---

[9] See Steward, "Primitive Bands."

[10] For a critical view of Steward's thesis, see Elman Service, *Primitive Social Organization: An Evolutionary Perspective* (New York: Random House, 1962), pp. 66–76.

[11] See Meyer F. Nimkoff and Russell Middleton, "Types of Family and Types of Economy," in *Man in Adaptation: The Cultural Present*, ed. Yehudi A. Cohen (Chicago: Aldine, 1968), pp. 384–93.

Payment is in money, which is individualizing in its effects, whereas earlier labor was unpaid family labor, unifying in its influence. The modern industrial scene is also characterized by high rates of physical mobility, which separates the members of families and makes interaction more difficult.

The modern industrial society, with its small independent family, is then like the simpler hunting and gathering society and, in part, apparently for some of the same reasons, namely, limited need for family labor and physical mobility. The hunter is mobile because he pursues the game; the industrial worker, the job.

Property is more highly developed in modern industrial society than in the earlier agricultural society, but property is mainly in money, individually acquired, not in family-owned land.[12]

It is worth emphasizing here that the findings and the theoretical formulations of Nimkoff and Middleton complement and support Steward's thesis.

Drawing heavily on the theoretical formulations of Marx and Weber, and employing a wide range of empirical data gathered from all parts of the world, Karl Wittfogel has propounded a theory concerning the relationship between the construction, maintenance, and supervision of large-scale public works—particularly irrigation systems—on the one hand, and the emergence of strongly centralized, autocratic, and bureaucratic social structures—or what he calls oriental despotisms—on the other.[13] To attempt even a limited discussion of the controversy generated by this particular techno-economic thesis would require a book in itself.[14] For our purposes here, moreover, we are not concerned with the pros and cons of the controversy, with the apparent exceptions marshaled by Wittfogel's critics to assail his thesis, or with the durability of all or parts of his formulation. We are concerned, however, to point out that as a technoeconomic theory or generalization Wittfogel's thesis has stimulated an enormous amount of research. If this research leads to the formulation of better theories—i.e., theories that explain more of the facts—it has performed one of the very valuable functions of a theory and, in so doing, justified its existence.

In an attempt to operationalize White's energy theory of cultural differences and evolution—that cultures will vary, or advance, with the amounts of energy harnessed per capita per year and/or with the efficiency of the tools applied to the use of this energy (see p. 45, *supra*)—Marshall Sahlins has argued that Polynesian sociopolitical organization has varied with the natural habitat and the technoeconomic means of exploiting that habitat

---

12 Ibid., p. 393.

13 See Karl Wittfogel, *Oriental Despotism* (New Haven: Yale University Press, 1957).

14 A few examples from the rather large volume of published materials which have dealt with the Wittfogel thesis—either to support, modify, revise, or amend it—are as follows: Julian H. Steward et al., *Irrigation Civilizations: A Comparative Study* (Washington, D.C.: Pan American Union, 1955); Robert McC. Adams, *The Evolution of Urban Society* (Chicago: Aldine, 1966); Edmund R. Leach, "Hydraulic Society in Ceylon," *Past and Present* 15 (1959): 2–26; and Wolfram Eberhard, *Conquerors and Rulers: Social Forces in Medieval China* (Leiden: E. J. Brill, 1952).

(the strategy is that of Steward as well as White).[15] Sahlins attempts to demonstrate that higher levels of productivity will generate higher levels of sociopolitical complexity. That there is some correlation between level of productivity and the complexity of sociopolitical organization is a plausible notion for which there is abundant empirical evidence; and Sahlins's study clearly adds to the accumulated evidence in support of the thesis. But Sahlins wants to go beyond simple correlations; he proposes the following claim of causality: higher levels of productivity will yield surpluses which, in turn, generate higher levels of sociopolitical complexity. What he has done, therefore, has been to convert a functional relationship into a causal explanation. Yet despite the plausibility of his technoeconomic argument, certain problems remain. For one thing, Sahlins shows in a highly convincing manner that higher levels of sociopolitical organization are themselves responsible for calling forth higher levels of productivity. Thus, the argument seems to have an element of circularity in it. Moreover, it is at least conceivable that some other factors—like, for example, warfare, "great-man" leadership, special kinds of contact with outsiders or with "foreign" ideologies, etc.—may have been the catalysts for higher levels of productivity.

Many of the criticisms leveled against Wittfogel's hydraulic thesis suggest a relevant analog. Thus, some investigators have recorded extensive irrigation works (Hohokam in Arizona, China, Ceylon, Bali, etc.) without an accompanying despotism and highly centralized autocratic control. Moreover, despotisms and autocracies have developed in the absence of any apparent hydraulic influences. And, finally, do we have convincing evidence of technoeconomic *priority* over social-organizational, ideological, and/or personality subsystems in those cases where hydraulics and centralized despotic rules were found together?

Despite the wealth of comparative data contained in Sahlins's study, his account (probably because the data are not available) lacks the kind of historic depth that would confirm the case for the *priority* of technoeconomic factors as an explanation for the cultural divergence that follow initial settlement of the area.

If the above remarks carry any weight, then Sahlins' and Wittfogel's work would *seem* to leave the issue of causal priority somewhat up in the air. However, we think not, for in arguing for the causal importance of technoeconomic factors, one is not necessarily arguing against the thesis that other subsystems interact with it and may themselves play roles over time. Sahlins may be right when he says that technoeconomic factors yield more complex levels of social organization. He is not consequently *wrong* when he also shows that complex levels of sociopolitical organization may be used to alter the technoeconomic subsystems so as to achieve higher levels of productivity. John Harsanyi offers a lead to help us break out of the functionalist bind in which everything interacts with everything else by suggesting that we focus on degrees of institutional autonomy:

---

15 See Marshall D. Sahlins, *Social Stratification in Polynesia* (Seattle: University of Washington Press, 1958). See also Martin Orans, "Surplus," in Cohen (ed.), *Man in Adaptation*, pp. 204–14.

What does it mean to ascribe causal priority to one subsystem of the social system over another? It essentially means to assume that, while the main aspects of the first subsystem's development can be explained in terms of internal factors, i.e., in terms of interaction among its own variables, the second subsystem's development has to be explained in essential respects in terms of influences coming from the first subsystem. Obviously all parts of the social system and all parts of culture show some measure of relatively autonomous development, and on the other hand none of them can claim full autonomy. But the various subsystems seem to exhibit conspicuous differences as to the degree of autonomy they possess. Philosophy, art, religion, law, etc., may for a while apparently follow their own internal logic in their development, but soon this development takes an unexpected turn, old ideas are abandoned for no apparent good reason and new ideas emerge which in no way represent a further development of the old. If an attempt is made to explain these developments in terms of their internal logic alone they remain profound mysteries. But if we bring in external factors, such as social, political and economic changes, things become at once meaningful and understandable. The economic system (and even more so the larger system including, besides the economic variables, also technology, political organization and the size and composition of the population) shows a much higher degree of autonomy. If someone wants to explain capitalism as a product of Protestant ethics he has to find an explanation for the emergence of Protestant ethics itself—presumably in terms of the autonomous evolution of Christian theology. But Max Weber himself admits that Protestant ethics is by no means a logically necessary implication of Protestant theology; indeed he thinks that fatalistic ethics would have been logically more consistent with the doctrine of predestination. So the explanation of Protestant ethics in terms of autonomous theological developments fails at the very first step, and extra-theological social factors have to be invoked to explain why the early Puritans adopted the ethical attitudes so highly favorable to the development of capitalism. On the other hand, if we try to explain Protestantism as a result of the social conditions prevailing in late-medieval towns, we have no fundamental difficulty in explaining how these social conditions themselves emerged as a result of economic, technological and political developments.[16]

The phrases *technological determinism* and *economic determinism* are often used pejoratively to characterize and evaluate a particular work. The implication is that there is something simple-minded, mechanical, and not very imaginative about such works. Yet it is difficult to avoid some degree of technoeconomic determinism in any analysis of culture change. Of all the factors used by anthropologists to explain, technoeconomic factors are the most visible and easily apprehended. Thus, technoeconomic theories lend themselves more easily to substantiation or refutation than others. We believe this is why Marvin Harris can argue that the "cultural-materialist strategy" has been far more fecund than alternative strategies in anthropology: "The issue is what kinds of results have been achieved by following historical particularism, culture and personality, and the other emic and

---

[16] John C. Harsanyi, "Explanation and Comparative Dynamics in Social Science," in *Theory in Anthropology*, ed. R. A. Manners and D. Kaplan (Chicago: Aldine, 1968), p. 96.

idealist alternatives? Let those who know how to explain what the cultural-materialist strategy has thus far failed to explain step forward with their nomothetic alternatives." [17] Elsewhere Harris says:

> Cultural-materialist strategy requires that priority be given to research concerned with the material conditions of sociocultural conditions: cultural materialist hypotheses should be abandoned for cultural idealist hypotheses or for admissions of ultimate inscrutability only after the material circumstances have been given careful consideration.[18]

Virtually all anthropologists would agree that technoeconomic factors set limits to the variation in other structural arrangements of a culture. To the technoeconomic theorist these limits are thought to be somewhat narrow. To those theoreticians who favor causal explanations rooted in social structure, ideology, or personality, the limits are wide and these latter factors are believed to be of equal or greater causal significance.

It should be apparent from the foregoing discussion that our own position with regard to the causal weighting of technoeconomic factors might be termed "soft determinism." Thus, we find ourselves in substantial agreement with Robert Heilbroner, who says:

> Even when technology seems unquestionably to play the critical role, an independent "social" element unavoidably enters the scene in the *design* of technology, which must take into account such facts as the level of education of the work force or its relative price. In this way the machine will reflect, as much as mould, the social relationships of work.
>
> These caveats urge us to practice what William James called a "soft determinism" with regard to the influence of the machine on social relations. Nevertheless, I would say that our cautions qualify rather than invalidate the thesis that the prevailing level of technology imposes itself powerfully on the structural organization of the productive side of society. A foreknowledge of the shape of the technical core of society of fifty years hence may not allow us to describe the political attributes of that society, and may perhaps only hint at its sociological character, but assuredly it presents us with a profile of requirements, both in labor skills and in supervisory needs, that differ considerably from those of today. We cannot say whether the society of the computer will give us the latter-day capitalist or the commissar, but it seems beyond question that it will give us the technician and the bureaucrat.[19]

One final point should be stressed. To frame a technoeconomic theory which helps to explain certain features—say, of the social structure of hunters and gatherers—does not necessarily mean that the same kind of theory will have appropriate explanatory power when applied to other structural and

---

[17] Marvin Harris, *The Rise of Anthropological Theory* (New York: Thomas Y. Crowell, 1968), p. 662.

[18] Marvin Harris, Reply to review of *The Rise of Anthropological Theory*, *Current Anthropology* 9 (1968): 529.

[19] Robert L. Heilbroner, "Do Machines Make History?" 342.

societal types. In other words, it is not necessarily a single, all-encompassing theory of culture that we are after, but *theories* of culture. For example, in hunting-and-gathering societies the exigencies of making a living may give to technoeconomic factors an overwhelming causal importance relative to, say, ideological factors. But in a society like our own, where the manufacture and dissemination of ideologies and symbolic constructions through the mass media is an enormous enterprise, the impact of ideological factors may be much greater than in hunting-and-gathering societies.

At the risk of being repetitive, we feel we must stress once more the dialectic interplay of subsystems within the total cultural system. To those who are looking for certainty and neat, timeless theoretical formulations this will all be very unsatisfactory.

Social Structure

The structure of any entity—an atom, a molecule, a crystal, an organism, a society—refers to the more-or-less enduring relationships among its parts. Thus, the term *social structure* can be conceived of, in Radcliffe-Brown's words, as

> the continuing arrangement of persons in relationships defined or controlled by institutions, i.e., socially established norms or patterns of behaviors.[20]

Other theorists have conceptualized social structure somewhat differently. To Evans-Pritchard, for example, social structure is the configuration of stable groups; to Talcott Parsons it is a system of normative expectations; to Leach, a set of ideal norms or rules; and to Lévi-Strauss social structures are models. But, however social structure is viewed, a great deal of what is called social-structural theory is actually concerned with questions of how we can most usefully distinguish and conceptualize the various parts of a social system and the relationships among them. What are we to mean by *role*? What are the differences between an egalitarian lineage and a ranked lineage? What are the critical features of *caste*? The way we answer such questions may have important methodological and theoretical consequences. For example, if we think of *caste* in terms of its ritual and ideological attributes, then we will delineate it in one way and our search for explanations will take us in certain definite directions. On the other hand, if we think of *caste* in terms of its socioeconomic attributes, we will conceptualize it in a different way and seek our explanations in quite other directions. And whether we consider castes to be wholly unique to India or a phenomenon that may turn up in a non-Indian context will hinge upon what we take to be its defining characteristics.

Some social structuralists have attempted to illuminate societal structures

---

[20] A. R. Radcliffe-Brown, *Method in Anthropology: Selected Essays*, ed. M. N. Srinivas (Chicago: University of Chicago Press, 1958), p. 177.

by formulating certain underlying principles of organization. Thus, for example, a number of British anthropologists, in analyzing societies with segmentary lineages, have often spoken of the "segmentary principle" almost as if the people in question had a blueprint of their society in mind which they then proceeded to carry out. Radcliffe-Brown proposed several such structural principles to account for various features of kinship systems: the principle of the equivalence of siblings, the principle of lineage solidarity, and so on.

As short-hand descriptive devices intended to characterize certain attributes of a social structure, such principles can cause no mischief and may even be rather helpful. But if they are intended to serve as explanatory devices (and this is indeed the explicit or implicit assumption of some structuralists), their logical shortcomings are obvious. Since the principles are themselves derived from the very patterns of behavior they are intended to explain, to see them as having explanatory value is to engage in tautological thinking.

In their attempts to explain sociocultural phenomena, all social-structural theorists (who, by definition, operate with social structure as their master concept) tend to give precedence in one way or another to social variables over all others. They reject "culture" as a useful master concept, arguing that, unlike the concept of social structure, the concept of culture is much too broad and amorphous to serve as a useful analytic tool. "Look," they might say, "at all the difficulty cultural anthropologists have had simply trying to define *culture!* And who ever observed—much less recorded—the total life-ways of a people anyway?" As for structure, while it is true, they say, that one cannot observe it directly, one *can* observe social relations—that is, people interacting in social situations. As a matter of fact, when one engages in field research, one observes virtually *nothing but* people interacting in social situations. (Social situations are conceived broadly so as to embrace what we might normally think of as economic, religious, political relations, etc.) So the argument goes.

There is no logical reason why either the alleged fuzziness of culture as a tool of analysis, or the fact that social relations *are* largely what one observes in the field, should persuade social-structural theorists to view variables of the three other subsystems (technoeconomics, ideology, and personality) as aspects or epiphenomena of patterns of institutionalized social interaction. In any case, social structuralists have tried to interpret a society's ideologies, its technoeconomic arrangements, and even its range of personality types largely as aspects of role behavior and role relationships in all of that society's major social institutions: family, clan, church, school, factory, etc. In the final analysis, however, they are often led to explain role behavior and role relationships themselves with reference to factors from another of the subsystems—e.g., from ideology, personality, or technoeconomics.

Because most of these theorists have been concerned with delineating, through an examination of social interaction, a society's structures and the way these function vis-à-vis one another, they have had more success in dealing with problems of continuity and maintenance than with problems of change. Recognizing this essentially static nature of the concept of social structure, a number of these theorists have attempted to introduce into social-structural explanations a more dynamic element. Raymond Firth, for example, draws a distinction between *social structure* and *social organization*. *Social structure*, he notes, refers to the normative patterns of social behavior. But in the day-to-day acting out of these ideally assigned patterns, individuals rarely conform exactly to structurally defined expectations. In the performance of their social roles they may reinterpret, improvise, modify, or innovate. And these innovative social interactions may produce changes in the social structure. Firth puts it this way:

> The social anthropologist is faced by a constant problem, an apparent dilemma—to account for . . . continuity, and at the same time to account for social change. Continuity is expressed in the social structure, the sets of relations which make for firmness of expectation, for validation of past experience in terms of similar experience in the future. . . . At the same time there must be room for variance and for the explanation of variance.
>
> This is found in the social organization, the systematic ordering of social relations by acts of choice and decision. . . . Structural forms set a precedent and provide a limitation to the range of alternatives possible— the arc within which seemingly free choice is exercisable is often very small. But it is the possibility of alternatives that makes for variability. A person chooses, consciously or unconsciously which course he will follow. And his decision will affect the future structural alignment. In the aspect of social structure is to be found the continuity principle of society; in the aspect of organization is to be found the variation or change principle—by allowing evaluation of situations and entry of individual choice.[21]

Firth looks for the sources of structural change largely within the social system itself. More specifically, he is led to locate the sources of such change in role behavior and the patterns of role relationships. But when Firth says that structural changes are produced by reinterpretations and modifications in role behavior, is he uttering anything more than a simple redundancy? For, after all, are not roles an inextricable aspect of any social structure? And, therefore does not structural change, by definition, mean a shift in role behavior? It seems to us that Firth would probably not dispute this formulation. Yet he certainly intends to advance more than this tautological statement. Nevertheless, it is difficult to put one's finger on just what more he is claiming. Given the fact that the possibility of variations in role behavior is a constant feature of all human societies, and given, further, the fact that structural change is continuous neither in time nor space, there must be some additional factor which will account for this discontinuous pattern of change. The logic of Firth's argument leads, we believe, to the conclusion that unusual, innovative, or deviant personalities are the ultimate source of modifications in role behavior and, therefore, in social structure. What is more, to account for the discontinuous pattern of change, Firth must countenance the likelihood that such creative personalities have tended to

---

21 Raymond Firth, *Elements of Social Organization* (London: Watts, 1951), pp. 39–40.

cluster fortuitously at different times and places.[22] All of which, of course, may be true, but it is difficult to see how one would go about proving the case, for or against. Thus, the most basic explanatory factors in the whole theoretical schema—patterns of individual choices and decisions—appear to be beyond our empirical grasp, a most unsatisfactory state of affairs.

One can have no quarrel with Firth's formulation as *description*. For it is clear, as he indicates, that structural change comes about as a result of individuals exercising choices and making decisions. Nor can one question his assertion that the choices open to an individual are neither limitless nor whimsically given. The range of choices open to an individual in a given society are always contained within a matrix provided by the structure itself, whether that structure be relatively stable or not. But to say all of this is to pose the problem and not to provide an explanation of it. The choices and decisions that interest anthropologists are those that have *social* meaning or content—they are not the random choices and decisions of individuals but the ones that seem to fall into patterns. Since this is so, we would want to know what it is that determines that choices will be patterned in one way rather than another.

Firth tells us that variation and "free play" are properties of social structures in all cultures. Moreover, people in every society are making choices all the time. Most often, their choices result in little or no structural change. Sometimes, however, their cumulative choices lead to dramatic structural changes. A satisfactory explanation, then, should be able to tell us why certain choices *do* and others *do not* yield structural change. And in order to explain "patterns of choice" one must refer either to the institutional structure of the society or to creative or deviant personalities—or to some combination of the two. Firth seems to opt for the combination when he says, for example:

> The structure provides a framework for action. But circumstances provide always new combinations of factors. Fresh choices open, fresh decisions have to be made, and the results affect the social action of other people in a ripple movement which may go far before it is spent. Usually this takes place within the structural framework, but it may carry action right outside it.[23]

A little later, however, Firth tells us:

> Organization is concerned with roles, but not with these alone; it also involves that more spontaneous, decisive activity which does not follow

---

[22] We are not claiming that Firth advances the proposition in this form. Indeed, he seems explicitly to reject it: "From the great range of theoretical treatment in the field of social development, an anthropologist should perhaps select Kroeber's monumental *Configurations of Culture Growth*. But as Kluckhohn and others have pointed out, this work, with its stress on the roles of clusters of exceptional individuals, falls far short of a sociological theory" ["Comment on 'Dynamic Theory' in Social Anthropology," in *Essays on Social Organization and Values* (London: Athlone Press, 1964), p. 27]. This leaves the major explanatory factor in Firth's schema unclear. Below, we spell out why we think this is so.

[23] Raymond Firth, "Social Organization and Social Change," in *Essays on Social Organization and Values* (London: Athlone Press, 1964), p. 35.

simply from role playing. . . . Ultimately, the social structure may have to give way through a concatenation of organizational acts.[24]

It is apparent that Firth's schema *must* include an element of "spontaneous, decisive activity." If this were not so, then all choices would be structurally given, and the entire distinction between social structure and social organization would be pointless. But it is difficult to see how a "spontaneous, decisive activity" can be tested empirically. It is one thing to end up with explanations that are beyond empirical demonstration, quite another to start out by conceding unprovability—i.e., by anchoring our explanation in nonverifiable assumptions.

The key question, then, is: Which is the more promising strategy of explanation: (1) that individual decisions, conscious or unconscious, lead to modifications in role behavior which in turn produce structural change? or (2) that when new cultural devices, traits, or elements emerge within or impinge upon a social structure from "outside," certain structural alternatives which were not previously available may open up? We become aware of these changes at the level of social relations when we observe individuals opting for the emerging structural alternatives and, in so doing, modifying their role behavior. We are persuaded by the evidence that this latter interpretation makes the most sense.

In any concrete, empirical situation the two processes (structural changes and choice-making) are interrelated and go on simultaneously. But there is more than nit-picking or logic-chopping involved in the distinction we have made. We believe there is an important difference in emphasis (and in the consequences for explanation) between the two strategies, since the kinds of factors we choose for purposes of explanation will, in turn, depend upon which of the two strategies we have chosen. One must, we believe, decide whether choices are to be treated, for explanatory purposes, as dependent or independent variables. Firth appears to hedge in this matter by saying that sometimes they are one and sometimes the other, or maybe they are a little bit of both. We consider this formulation unproductive, in that it is ultimately more descriptive in character than explanatory, and prefer what seems to us the more clearcut second alternative or strategy of explanation.

An example of the kind of evidence that persuades us to favor this interpretation comes from the Kipsigis of East Africa, a herding-*cum*-horticultural people, who moved in a relatively short time from a condition of communal land ownership to one in which virtually all land became privately owned.[25] The change clearly implies concomitant changes in role behavior and relationships and in the social structure of the tribe. Moreover, it can be demonstrated that a series of individual decisions and choices were involved in bringing about the shift. And, finally, while we know that the transformation in patterns of land holding and land use were completed in less than a generation, we know also that the traditional patterns of com-

---

24 Ibid., p. 45.
25 See R. A. Manners, "The Kipsigis of Kenya: Culture Change in a 'Model' East African Tribe," in *Contemporary Change in Traditional Societies*, ed. Julian Steward (Urbana: University of Illinois Press, 1967), 1: 205–360.

munality in land use, with minimal private ownership, had prevailed for at least a few hundred years before the changeover. It is conceivable that the change may be explained by a "fortuitous clustering," around the 1930s, of innovative deviants who looked at the land and decided—individually, and for unknowable personal reasons—to lay claim to various pieces of it. If so, their actions involved the creation of new social roles and new patterns of social interaction—a new social structure. Or it is possible that the "new way" of *looking* at the land was triggered by something else, even if the earliest responding personalities were deviant.

It is possible, for example, that the introduction of the plow, maize, markets, missionaries, manufactured goods, the hut and poll tax, money, and the establishment of tea, flax, and coffee estates owned by white settlers were some of the factors responsible for altering the perceptions of the innovators, and thereby their social roles and relationships and, ultimately, the structure of Kipsigis society itself. The settlers required labor to work their cash crops; this labor force could not feed itself but had to be fed with maize produced by tribespeople not working on the estates. The plow facilitated the cultivation of maize in relatively large acreages; new shops and markets displaying such delectable items as manufactured cloth, steel knives, sugar, glass beads, steel needles, etc. were opened; and private missionaries from the United States preached the virtues of hard work, private initiative, and private ownership of land. Moreover, the hut and poll taxes eventually had to be paid in cash, so that the Kipsigis either had to go to work for the whites or to produce maize to obtain the necessary cash. The overwhelming majority chose the latter alternative, and manipulated traditional land-use patterns—with fences to keep out livestock—into annually expanding areas of cultivation followed by assertions of private and permanent ownership.

The social structure of the Kipsigis tribe underwent a profound transformation. The change was a product of cumulative individual choices, but the same choices had not been made before the imposition of British rule and the structural, technoeconomic, and ideological changes that accompanied that rule. Surely, the alterations in patterns of social interaction that followed are more likely to have been the result of that complex of introduced changes (however we cut up the "pie" of causation) than of the fortuitous clustering of deviant, mysteriously motivated innovators.

Several observations of a more general nature are suggested by the preceding discussion. Much structural "theory," as we have pointed out, is concerned with the task of identifying the major structural features of a society and determining how they fit together to form an overall pattern. Yet, while this task of mapping the structures of different societies has informed us on the range of structural possibilities, and has even contributed in important ways to our understanding of how these structures work, such models do not by themselves constitute theories or provide explanations. If these models are to serve as theories, they must tell us something about the factors and conditions that produce, maintain, and change this or that structure.

When structuralists, as we have tried to indicate, attempt to move beyond description to the framing of theories, they commonly look to social relations and social interactions or, following the influential work of sociologists like Max Weber and, more recently, Talcott Parsons, to what is called social action. It is precisely here, however, that certain difficulties arise. For in order to give these concepts explanatory value, what invariably seems to occur is that the investigator "smuggles" into them elements of the very phenomenon he is trying to explain. In effect, circular reasoning provides the *illusion* of explanation. It is probably for this reason that Percy Cohen, himself a social-action theorist, prefers to conceive of social-action theory as a mode of inquiry and an *aid* to explanation rather than as a distinctive device for explanation. Cohen writes:

> In all sociological [anthropological] inquiry it is assumed that some features of social structure and culture are strategically important and enduring and that they provide limits within which particular social situations can occur. On this assumption, the action approach can help to explain the nature of these situations and how they affect conduct. It does not explain the social structure and culture as such, except by lending itself to a developmental inquiry which must start from some previous point at which structural and cultural elements are taken as given.

> The criticism that action theory, in itself, explains very little, is valid. Action theory, as such, is a method. It is a set of near-tautological assumptions which structure the mode of cognition of social inquiry which is, on the whole, concerned with the conditions and the products of social interaction.[26]

And again:

> Theories or models of interaction do not permit one to derive from them very much about the nature of social systems. The obvious reason for this is that the content of interaction is governed by the social structure or system in which it occurs.[27]

Thus, Cohen points up the methodological difficulties of trying to explain social structures by remaining conceptually within the analytic confines of social structure. Robert Nisbet has made the same point very forcefully but in a slightly different way:

> Any effort to reduce structural changes to microscopic variations of role or behavior within a structure is doomed to futility. . . .

> Here I take the liberty of quoting from an article I wrote thirteen years ago on the subject of social structure and change: "The chief danger of contemporary functionalist approaches seems to me to be in search for causes *within the social system*, as though the social system were, like a biological entity, governed by autonomous, inner drives toward cumulative change. There is the added fact that these alleged causes take on increasingly, a psychological character. Both tendencies—the search for inner autonomous causes of change, and the concentration upon psychological processes as causative forces—seem to me unfortunate. . . .

---

[26] Percy Cohen, *Modern Social Theory* (New York: Basic Books, 1968), pp. 93–94.
[27] Ibid., p. 125.

"Instead of dealing with the problem of structural change in historical and institutional terms, which is to say in terms of the total of the structure to its environment (temporal and spatial), we find sociologists and ethnologists, first, seeking the causes of change in alleged autonomous mechanisms within the structure, and second, throwing the weight of causal analysis upon such actually *derivative* phenomena as psychological stresses and strains within the social structure." [28]

Many structuralists are fully aware of the logical difficulties and theoretical shortcomings of social action-interaction theory. As a consequence, they have been driven, explicitly or implicitly, to go *outside* social structure in the search for variables that might explain social structures and sociocultural arrangements. As we indicated in our earlier discussion of Firth's formulation, his argument must lead him ultimately to ideological and psychological factors, and, more specifically, to innovative personalities in order to explain how role behavior is restructured. Similarly, other structural theorists have been led to frame their explanations in terms of values, themes, religious philosophies, technoeconomic arrangements, and relationships to the natural habitat. If the structural theorist responds that these variables, as he conceives of them, are aspects of social structure, then we need not engage him in controversy over what impresses us as a minor methodological preference. We would only point out that in making this claim he will have moved very close to our conception of culture with its internal analytic distinction among the various subsystems. For whether one views these variables as comprising subsystems of culture or as aspects of social structure capable of interacting with one another and exerting an independent causal influence on social structure, the end result, as far as theoretical explanation of sociocultural phenomena is concerned, is much the same.

The Determinative Role of Social Structure

In the foregoing pages we have been discussing social structure primarily from a particular point of view—i.e., social structure conceptualized in terms of *social action, social interaction,* and *role behavior.* This way of thinking about social structure naturally focuses attention on individuals or social actors who "act out" the structure, and has in general led to the kind of "microscopic" analysis to which Nisbet refers. On the descriptive level, this approach makes eminently good sense because it is, after all, the acting and interacting of individuals that we observe in our researches in the field.

But even description must contain some degree of analysis, and once one moves beyond simple, raw observation of the social scene, one must move to a somewhat higher level of abstraction and deal with groups and institutions. The key question, then, is: Do groups and institutions have a "reality" of their own—i.e., one not reducible to the individuals who make them up? It must be stressed that this is a methodological rather than an ontological question. That is, the question properly phrased might read as follows: Can statements about the properties of institutions be derived from statements

---

[28] Robert A. Nisbet, "The Irreducibility of Social Change: A Commentary on Professor Stebbins' Paper," *The Pacific Sociological Review*, 8 (1965), 15.

about the properties and behavior of the individuals who make up the institutions? But starting with individual social actors and trying to construct the institutions of any society has generally proved to be nothing more than a tautological procedure. The main reason for this, as Percy Cohen indicates, is that the very content and pattern of social action and interaction is a reflection of the properties of the aggregate phenomena of social structure. Thus, trying to deduce or understand the nature of the macrostructure from the nature and behavior of the social particles (individuals) is like "looking through the wrong end of the telescope." When used for purposes of "explanation"—either of how the structure operates or of what is its impact on other subsystems within the society—the telescope entry has led to the kind of questionable formulations proposed by Firth. Consequently, we find these kinds of formulations lacking in explanatory power.

Probably this is why S. F. Nadel, who views structure in terms of roles and role analysis, asserts that his theory is not a theory in the explanatory sense of a set of connected generalizations from which "observable consequences logically follow." Rather, he tells us, it is theory in the more restricted sense of "a body of propositions (still interconnected) which serve to *map out* the problem area and thus prepare the ground for its empirical investigation by appropriate methods." [29]

But theorists who have conceptualized social structure macroscopically—that is, in terms of the functioning groups and institutions rather than in terms of their individual actors—have tried to formulate theories in which the structural features and variables are used for explanatory or causal analysis.

For example, during the late nineteenth century the agrarian economies of China and Japan both came under the impact of Western industrial societies. Within half a century or so Japan had industrialized to a rather remarkable degree while China had not. Marion Levy has made a good case for the differences between traditional Chinese and Japanese family structure as a pivotal factor in explaining the different rates of modernization in the two countries.[30] In China, he reminds us, an individual's primary allegiance was to his family. Allegiance or obligation to the state was secondary. Nepotism was an obligation; it was built into the system. Thus, a man who was upwardly mobile was expected (and himself expected) to carry with him as large a portion of his family as possible. What is more, the laws and traditions governing inheritance demanded that all sons share equally. Under these conditions, capital that might have been accumulated for systematic large-scale investment was constantly being dispersed. Thus, while other factors and variables may also have played their part in defeating or discouraging any efforts of the Chinese state to reorganize its social economy, it is fairly clear that family obligations of a particular kind, including the patterns of inheritance, were a significant deterrent to that reorganization.

Japan's success in accomplishing a rapid reorganization of its social economy, on the other hand, Levy also attributes in large part to the nature of the family structure. In Japan the family fitted into a hierarchical, feudal

---

29 S. F. Nadel, *The Theory of Social Structure* (London: Cohen and West, 1957), p. 1.

30 See Marion J. Levy, "Contrasting Factors in the Modernization of China and Japan," in *Economic Growth: Brazil, India, Japan,* ed. Simon S. Kuznets, Wilbert E. Moore, and Joseph J. Spengler (Durham, N.C.: Duke University Press, 1955).

framework. Thus, a man owed loyalty not only to the head of his family, but also to the lord who was superior to his family head and then, through a series of higher lords and princes, ultimately to the emperor himself. Primogeniture was the characteristic pattern of inheritance, thus allowing for the accumulation and concentration of wealth. Finally, in Japan the practice of adoption was fairly common, making it possible for talented young men to rise in the social hierarchy without at the same time incurring the obligation of carrying other members of their family with them. These traditional patterns facilitated the state's ability to demand—and receive—from the populace the kind of response and the sacrifices that early industrialization seems to require, whereas in China efforts to reorganize the economy conflicted with the more parochial interests of the family.

Or, to take another example closer in space and time. In his well-known and highly controversial study of black ghetto life,[31] Daniel Moynihan sees the structure of the black family and its attendant life style as major impediments to the ability of blacks to improve their lot in American society. On the face of it, the causal role assigned by Moynihan to the family would seem to contradict the "theory of family structure" outlined by Nimkoff and Middleton and discussed in the previous section. But the formulations are not wholly incompatible. For as Lee Rainwater has convincingly demonstrated, the black ghetto family structure—its matrifocality, its psychological and ideological concomitants—is an adaptive response to the socioeconomic conditions in which Blacks find themselves.[32] But having made this adaptation to a set of penalizing social and economic circumstances, the pattern does indeed set certain (if transitory) limits on the "possibilities for subsequent adaptations." As Rainwater notes, "it is the individuals who succumb to the distinctive family lifestyle who experience the greatest weight of deprivation and who have the greatest difficulty responding to the few self-improvement resources that make their way into the ghetto." [33] Rainwater then goes on, however, to point out that the ghetto family structure is only semiautonomous and its causal impact only partial: "It is tempting," he says, "to see the family as the main villain of the piece, and to seek to develop programs which attack directly this family pathology," [34] yet "if we are right that present Negro family patterns have been created as adaptations to a particular socioeconomic situation, it would make more sense to change the socioeconomic situation and then depend upon the people involved to make new adaptations as time goes on." [35]

---

[31] See Daniel Patrick Moynihan, *The Negro Family: The Case for National Action* (Washington, D.C.: Office of Policy Planning and Research, U.S. Dept. of Labor, 1965).

[32] See Lee Rainwater, "Crucible of Identity: The Negro Lower-Class Family," *Daedalus* [vol. 95, no. 1 of *The Proceedings of the American Academy of Arts and Sciences*] (Winter 1966), 172–216.

[33] Ibid., 173.

[34] Ibid., 207.

[35] Ibid., 208. We are not, of course, arguing here for the "pathological" nature of the black ghetto family. Nor are we predicting whether or what kind of "new" family structure might ultimately emerge under a set of changed socioeconomic circumstances that would truly lift the black population out of its disprivileged and second-class status. All that we are saying here is that, with regard to the present structure and circumstances of the

The Political Dimension

Depending on the way they are conceptualized and emphasized, political institutions may also be seen as a structural variable having determinative or *causal* impact. In a comparative analysis of the relation between political power and the economy in stateless societies (particularly chiefdoms) Marshall Sahlins has shown that once *positions* or *offices* in which power inheres emerge (rather than power being merely an attribute of personal characteristics), then such political positions (or those who occupy these positions) react upon the structure of the economy, reorganizing it into larger networks of production and distribution having characteristics which differ significantly from those of the earlier economy.[36]

Sahlins, as we indicated above, is talking here primarily about chiefdoms, societies where political institutions are not yet fully crystallized and distinguished from the kinship system. When, at a higher level, a set of political offices becomes *fully* separated from the kinship system, and the society is organized largely on territorial rather than on kinship principles, we have what is called a *state*. Under such a state or nation-state type of organization, political factors come to have even greater causal importance than they manifested at the level of the chiefdom.

Yehudi Cohen has given us a series of general propositions which emphasize the change in causal priorities at different levels of cultural development —in particular, the growing importance of the political factor:

> Technological change underlies institutional change in stateless societies; conversely, changes in non-technological (especially political) institutions underlie technological change in nation-states. In the latter case, institutional changes stimulate technological developments, and the latter in turn lead to accommodations in family and kinship systems, in many aspects of law and social control, in religion and values and ideologies. Thus the direction and sequence of events in evolutionary adaptation undergoes a reversal in societies that are integrated into nation-states from the sequence that is observable in stateless societies.[37]

Statelessness constitutes a set of limiting conditions for technological

---

"black family in the ghetto," we agree with Rainwater when he reminds us that that structure (whatever its present impact) got the way it did because of historical and contemporary factors in the institutional world in which the ghetto is embedded. Whether, in the long run, there will be "new" patterns, and whether these will approximate or differ from existing middle-class white "ideal" models is not for us to say. Adaptation in ghetto "family structure," under conditions of true socioeconomic equality, may yield entirely new family, household, or other constellations. But these, too, will not be immune to the effects either of their past or to the impact of the "world outside." Nor, we must add, will the structure of the "white family" be immune from these same influences.

36 See Marshall D. Sahlins, "Political Power and the Economy in Primitive Society," in *Essays in the Science of Culture in Honor of Leslie A. White*, ed. Gertrude E. Dole and Robert L. Carneiro (New York: Thomas Y. Crowell, 1960), pp. 390–415.

37 Yehudi A. Cohen, "Adaptation and Evolution: An Introduction," in *Man in Adaptation: The Institutional Framework*, ed. Yehudi A. Cohen (Chicago: Aldine Atherton Press, 1971), pp. 17–18.

advance because there is no stimulus for the production of gross de-
ployable surpluses in such societies. States on the other hand, encourage
the harnessing of more efficient extrapersonal sources of energy in the
interest of the production of surpluses, largely for the benefit of the ruling
classes. The political institutions of a state embody only the potentials
for technological advance and do not guarantee that it will occur, but
technological advance is always severely limited in the absence of a
unifying state.[38]

Finally, Cohen notes that even values and ideologies may come to play a
role in nation-states that they do not exert with the same force in stateless
societies:

> Distinctive national strategies develop in a nation principally in re-
> sponse to politically stimulated factors in the habitat rather than to
> natural elements as in stateless societies. . . . Values and ideologies are
> among the most important tools in the different substrategies in a
> national society, and this is an important aspect of its complexity.[39]

The above generalizations about the increasing importance of political
factors as societies become more complex might seem to controvert our
position with regard to the determinative weight we assigned (with certain
qualifications) to technoeconomic variables in the preceding section of this
chapter. But the two subsystems actually work in conjunction. For if politics
in the contemporary world is about anything at all, it is certainly "about"
the control of the technoeconomic sphere and how the economic pie is to
be cut up and distributed.

One of the major points we have tried to emphasize in this section on
social structure may be applied as well to the other subsystems treated in
this chapter. To use Marxist terminology: certain aspects or subsystems of
culture which may be considered parts of the "superstructure" (i.e., epiphenomenal with regard to their origin) tend, once they have come into
existence, to take on a life of their own and may even exert a powerful causal
or determinative impact on the infrastructure itself. Or to make the same
point in a more modern terminology: what is a dependent variable in one
context may become an independent variable in a different context.

Ideology

In this particular section we use the term *ideology* to refer to the
ideational realm of a culture. Thus, under this rubric we include values,
norms, knowledge, themes, philosophies and religious beliefs, sentiments,
ethical principles, world-views, ethos, and the like. We are using the term in
the neutral and general sense intended by its originator, de Tracy, who, in
the late eighteenth century, coined "ideology" to embrace what he called

---

[38] Ibid., p. 17.
[39] Ibid., p. 19.

"the science of ideas." Since that time, owing particularly to the influence of such thinkers as Marx, Freud, and, more recently, Mannheim, the term has come to mean something quite different. When used in the modern and more restricted sense, *ideology* usually refers to a system of ideas that may serve to rationalize, exhort, excuse, assail, or account for certain beliefs, actions, or cultural arrangements. Thus, today when one characterizes a system of ideas as "ideological," what is usually implied is that the ideas are partisan—that is, rather than being objective they are framed to support (or attack) some cause. In this sense, the special pleading of ideology is contrasted with the neutrality of genuine knowledge. And the ideologue is said to use and even to tailor the facts to bolster his ideological position rather than modifying his system of ideas when the facts demand it. Most modern investigators, therefore, take great pains to distinguish ideas-as-knowledge from *ideology*. Arthur Schlesinger, Jr., for example, writes that it is

> useful [to distinguish] between *ideas* and *ideologies*. Ideas are particular insights; ideologies are ideas crystallized into universal systems. Ideas are relative, ideologies absolute. . . . Where some men accept the confusions of experience, others require the notion of ultimate rationality in the universe; these yearn for a single, fundamental, all-encompassing, all-explanatory pattern which man can apprehend and which equips him with a body of principles adequate to all the contingencies of politics and life.[40]

Because the term *ideology* now has these particular connotations, we would have preferred a more neutral term for the ideational sphere of a culture. But to the best of our knowledge there is no single term less awkward than, say, *ideational sphere* or *ideational realm*, which expresses what we mean by *ideology*. Thus, in this section we have tried to restrict the use of the term to its older, neutral, and nonjudgmental sense.

Man is preeminently a conceptualizing and symbolizing animal. Indeed, as Leslie White has remarked, he is the only creature capable of being killed by a symbol. It seems reasonable to assume, therefore, that the symbolic systems or ideologies by which man explains and orders his social and natural universe would play some role in the way his societal structures are maintained as well as in the way they are changed. But the question, *How much of a determinative role do ideological factors play in cultural maintenance and change?* has been, and continues to be, among the most controversial issues in anthropology—indeed, in all of social science. This issue has been highly controversial, in part because extrascientific considerations of a moralistic nature have been injected into the discussion. Since ideas are creations of the human mind, to assert the importance of ideology many writers believe, is to strike a blow for free will and the essential autonomy of

---

[40] Arthur Schlesinger, Jr., *The Crisis of Confidence* (New York: Bantam Books, 1969), p. 47.

man. On the other hand, views that play down the role of ideology or that treat ideas as largely epiphenomenal are often assailed as "deterministic" and, therefore, as diminishing the intrinsic worth of man. Thus, discussions of the role of ideologies in culture have often moved beyond the purely scientific question of assessing the causal weight of ideological factors in cultural systems into more emotion-laden areas.

In part this issue has continued to generate debate because the elements of the ideological subsystem are particularly subjective in nature, and therefore allow the widest latitude for personal interpretation. As an illustration, consider those instances in the anthropological literature where different investigators have presented widely divergent interpretations of the same society. Among the better-known cases of this sort—indeed they have become *causes célèbres* in anthropology—are the differing accounts of the village of Tepoztlan by Lewis and Redfield (pp. 24–25, *supra*), and the varying interpretations of the Pueblo Indians, particularly the Zuni. One of the principal sources of the contradictions in these cases was the differing interpretations of the ideological subsystem of these societies, especially as that ideology is reflected in the quality of interpersonal relations and the social personality of the people in question.

Anthropologists have attempted to mediate these conflicting interpretations of ideology in much the same way that they have gone about reconciling the occasionally discrepant accounts of a society's technoeconomic arrangements or its social structure—that is, by restudies and by comparison with other societies of the same structural type. In the case of Tepoztlan, the Redfield and Lewis accounts, as we remarked earlier, have been compared with accounts of other Mexican peasant communities as well as with accounts of peasant communities in different parts of the world. And in the Pueblo case, investigators have pointed out certain crucial empirical materials which seem to have been overlooked or ignored by some of the interpreters of the Zuni ethos.[41] Out of all this has emerged a partial resolution of the contradictory interpretations and a broader consensus among anthropologists about what the ideological structure of these societies is *really* like.

What we have been saying is that, to a large extent, the determinative role of ideological factors has been a highly debatable issue because anthropologists have had more difficulty in conceptualizing the ideological subsystem of societies than they have had in coping with the technoeconomic, social structural, or even personality subsystems.

Of course, not all areas of ideology confront anthropologists with the same degree of difficulty. When they deal with naturalistic, matter-of-fact knowledge, they are on much firmer ground. For one thing, such knowledge is frequently tied to specific tasks, so that the investigator does not have to engage in a long chain of inference to get at the knowledge. What is more, people are generally able to verbalize this kind of knowledge quite clearly. It is when anthropologists attempt to deal with the more elusive and highly inferred ideological entities and structures—like values, themes, world-view, and ethos—that they encounter the greatest methodological difficulties. To conceptualize such ideological elements involves a high degree of inference;

---

[41] See John W. Bennett, "The Interpretation of Pueblo Culture: A Question of Values," *Southwestern Journal of Anthropology* 2 (1946): 361–74.

and as the chain of inference lengthens, the room for personal interpretation increases, and the possibility of applying empirical controls diminishes.

**Methodological Problems
in Delimiting the Ideological Subsystem**

Since ideologies are subjective, we can have no access to them through direct observation. They must be inferred from some form of behavior or other: from what people say or from observations of people interacting in different social situations. And although simpler societies generally lack a body of written literature that might help one to get at their ideological structures, here one does have the advantage of dealing with a relatively homogeneous subsystem, one shared by most members of the society.

In literate and modern societies, on the other hand, one's observations of various forms ·of overt behavior and the verbal statements one gathers can be supplemented by a kind of content analysis of written and visual sources: newspapers, magazines, novels, memoirs, television, radio, and the like. But the very richness of these sources and the circumstances that give rise to these riches often constitute a mixed blessing. For such societies may be highly differentiated in terms of region, class, race, religion, ethnicity, and the like. And in dealing with the variety of written and visual materials one may be led to wonder which group's values, norms, themes, sentiments, and philosophies are being expressed. Indeed, whether we can even speak of *the* ideological structure of a modern society or must speak instead of a variety of ideological structures becomes an important conceptual issue.

In trying to get at the subjective, ideological phenomena which lie behind overt behavior, the investigator is forced to make several critical methodological decisions. First, how much weight should he give to the verbal statements of his informants? When people tell us why they act as they do in this or that situation, are they telling us the "real" reasons? Or are they ignorant, consciously deceptive, rationalizing, presenting the official version, or merely telling us what they think we want to hear?

To take a different sort of problem, do we admit as ideological phenomena only those elements and propositions consciously held and verbalized by a people? Or do we allow the possibility that a society's structure and behavior may, in certain respects, be determined by unconscious values, covert themes, and implicit principles; and that these are so pervasive and basic to the society and, at the same time, so deeply internalized that the people themselves cannot verbalize them? [42] Some anthropologists would deny uncon-

---

[42] Albert K. Cohen warns against the incautious and sometimes overzealous use of the unconscious as an explanatory catchall: "There is nothing remarkable about having, let us say, a tendency, and not being conscious of it. It may be quite another thing, however, to say that there is a tendency 'in the unconscious.' This expression may be defended as a figure of speech, not to be taken seriously, but it is a dangerous one. It suggests a place, a region of the mind—sort of a cave, perhaps—where sinister forces contend in darkness. Such metaphors have a way of beguiling the imagination, so that presently one finds himself constructing a geography of this mysterious place: its boundaries, its topography, its laws, its population, its principal products. This wealth of implication simply does not follow from the idea that there are things about ourselves that we take note of and indicate to ourselves, and others that we do not." [*Deviance and Control* (Englewood Cliffs, N.J.: Prentice-Hall, 1966), p. 72].

scious principles, etc., a place in the anthropologist's analytic and explanatory framework. S. F. Nadel, for example, cautions us that "uncomprehended symbols have no part in social inquiry; their social effectiveness lies in their capacity to indicate, and if they indicate nothing to the actors, they are, from our point of view, irrelevant, and indeed no longer symbols (whatever their significance for the psychologist or psycho-analyst)." [43] And Monica Wilson, in much the same vein, emphasizes that in her work on Nyakyusa ritual she employed only "Nyakyusa interpretations of their own rituals, for anthropological literature is bespattered with symbolic guessing, the ethnographer's interpretations of the rituals of other people." [44]

V. W. Turner, however, argues for the opposite approach. He writes:

> How, then, can a social anthropologist justify his claim to be able to interpret a society's ritual symbols more deeply and comprehensively than the actors themselves? . . . The participant is likely to be governed in his actions by a number of interests, purposes, and sentiments, dependent upon his specific position, which impair his understanding of the total situation. An even more serious obstacle against his achieving objectivity is the fact that he tends to regard as axiomatic and primary the ideals, values and norms which are overtly expressed or symbolized in the ritual. . . . The anthropologist who has previously made a structural analysis of Ndembu society, isolating its organizational principles, and distinguishing its groups and relationships, has no particular bias and can observe the real interconnections and conflicts between groups and persons, in so far as these receive ritual representation. What is meaningless for an actor playing a specific role, may well be highly significant for an observer and analyst of the total system. . . . I con-

---

[43] Quoted in V. W. Turner, "Symbols in Ndembu Ritual," in *Closed Systems and Open Minds*, ed. Max Gluckman (Chicago: Aldine 1964), p. 27.

[44] Quoted in ibid., p. 27–28

In a review of Mary Douglas's *Purity and Danger: An Analysis of Pollution and Taboo* (1966), Melford Spiro says: "Symbolism, in the language of Madison Avenue, is 'very big' in contemporary anthropology. Still, I must confess that I am becoming weary of symbolic analysis when, as is so often the case, it proceeds neither from a general theory of symbolism, from which the meaning attributed to a symbol can be logically deduced, nor from a set of psychological data on social actors, from which the putative meaning of the symbol is empirically induced. In the absence of both bases for the derivation of meaning, symbolic analyses become arbitrary, and conviction of their validity must stem from the persuasiveness of the argument. . . .

"Douglas is relentless in her insistence that the social system is the universal symbolic referent not only for rituals of pollution but for all ritual. Thus, in rituals designed to produce genital bleeding in males, 'what is being carved in human flesh is an image of society.' And when these rituals are performed publicly in moiety- and section-divided societies, they 'are concerned to create a symbol of the symmetry of the halves of society.' These notions, I readily admit, would never have occurred to me. How in the world *does* an incision in the penis symbolize an image of society? Why should society be symbolized in, of all places, the penis? Still, as a student *manqué* of the human mind, I am quite prepared to believe that anything can symbolize anything; and if either a set of data or a strong argument were to be produced in support of the symbolic equation, penis equals society, I would be quite prepared to believe it" [*American Anthropologist* 70 (1968): 391–92].

And further on the subject of the inescapable phallic symbol, Victor E. Frankel reminds us that "Freud himself had been wise and cautious enough to remark once that sometimes a cigar may be a cigar, and nothing but a cigar. However, his epigones are less cautious and feel less inhibited" [" 'Nothing But—,' " *Encounter* (November 1969), p. 51].

sider it legitimate to include within the total meaning of a dominant
ritual symbol, aspects of behavior associated with it which the actors
themselves are unable to interpret, and indeed of which they may be unaware, if they are asked to interpret the symbol outside its activity-
context.[45]

As we indicated in Chapter 1, we would in general subscribe to Turner's
methodological position. It seems to us that Turner correctly emphasizes that
an anthropologist who relies wholly on the native viewpoint for his interpretation of a society's structure and behavior may come out with a distorted or even an erroneous view of that society. The argument that a native
really knows his culture better than anyone not a member of the culture is
of course true. It is true in the same sense that a person who has never had
measles cannot *really know* what it is like to have measles. But there may
be a profound difference between experiencing a phenomenon and having
knowledge of that phenomenon. Thus, to have had measles does not necessarily mean that one knows anything about the pathology of the disease or
how to treat it.

At the same time, however, it seems to us that in dealing with ideological
structures and their subjective meanings, the anthropologist is confronted
with special problems in interpretation and empirical validation. To conceptualize such structures in terms of their unconscious values, covert themes,
and the like is to compound these difficulties. What does it mean, for example, to say that a pattern of social behavior is "governed" or "determined"
by values, themes, or principles of which the persons involved are totally unaware? To be sure, there is ample evidence to show that people are usually
not aware of the factors that have produced the institutional arrangements
of their society; nor will they be aware of many of the (unintended) consequences of their social actions, nor of the "psychodynamic origins" of their
individual behavior. But the steps, logical or empirical, by which the investigator moves from an unperceived value or principle to the concrete patterns of
behavior said to be ruled by such unperceived values are generally unanalyzed,
and may even be unanalyzable. Because the postulated "values," "principles,"
etc., do not yield easily to empirical verification, it is often difficult to determine what the empirical referents of such conceptions as unconscious
values and covert themes are. Are they intended as intervening variables, or
as hypothetical constructs? If the former, then they are concepts which con-
veniently summarize observed behaviors; if the latter, they posit some un-
observable process or entity which is intended to explain behavior. Thus,
"intervening variables" have no "factual-content surplus" beyond the empirical data they serve to summarize; whereas "hypothetical constructs" add
something to the empirical data which constitute their support and, therefore, "their actual existence should be compatible with general knowledge and
particularly with whatever relevant knowledge exists at the next lower level
in the explanatory hierarchy." [46]

---

[45] Turner, "Symbols in Ndembu Ritual," pp. 28–29.
[46] Kenneth MacCorquodale and Paul E. Meehl, "Hypothetical Constructs and Intervening Variables," in *Readings in the Philosophy of Science*, ed. Herbert Feigl and May
Brodbeck (New York: Appleton-Century-Crofts, 1953), p. 610.

The influence of ideological factors on other cultural components operates through a process of psychological conditioning, that is, through the impact of ideas on human behavior. Yet, as Melford Spiro observes: "The theoretical grounds for investigating any ideological system (including religion) with causal efficacy are shaky indeed, and one is usually left unconvinced by these interpretations." [47] He goes on to remark that this is so because we often do not know at what "level" the social actors have learned or internalized the ideology of their culture.

Spiro distinguishes five "levels" of ideological learning which may help one to account for the differential impact of ideology on other cultural variables or subsystems: (1) either through formal instruction or informally an actor has *learned about* some aspect of his culture's ideology; (2) actors have not only learned about certain ideological constructs but they also *understand* and can use them correctly in the appropriate social context; (3) understanding certain constructs, the actors also *believe* them to be true and valid; (4) the constructs have a certain *cognitive salience* in that they are used by actors as a guide in the structuring of their social and natural worlds; (5) in addition to their cognitive salience, the constructs have been *internalized* by the actors so that not only do they serve as guides but they serve also to initiate behavior.

The inference one may draw from all of this seems quite clear: even when we "observe" an ideological concept or set of concepts in action, we cannot know anything about the cognitive salience or degree of internalization of the concept or concepts. Hence, to assign causal efficacy to ideological factors often proves a most elusive and controversial matter.

Consider norms and values, for example—certainly among the most widely used explanatory concepts in all of social science. An investigator observes a certain regularity of behavior in a society—men do the hunting and women tend to the children and the household—and from this he infers the existence of a norm. Then, of course, he notes other regularities of behavior from which he infers still other norms.

In referring to these regularities of behavior as norms one may intend only to draw attention to the fact that all or most people in the society behave in this way. But more commonly the term *norm* refers to how people believe one *ought* to behave in this or that situation—e.g., men ought to be the hunters and women ought to tend to the children and the household. More than likely, then, when our hypothetical investigator infers the existence of a series of norms, he is using the term in this latter sense. And sometimes, when he checks his list of norms, he may see (or construe) a similar theme running throughout the norms. This in turn suggests that the norms reflect a common value, e.g., male dominance. So far, all our investigator has done is to describe and classify his observations and the inferences he has drawn from these observations; in other words, he has summarized a range of diverse

---

[47] Melford E. Spiro, "Buddhism and Economic Action in Burma," *American Anthropologist* 68 (1966): 1163.

observational data under the rubrics *norms* and *values*. If we were to ask him what this society is like, and if he were to respond that the people have such-and-such values and that their normative structure was of this or that particular nature, we would get an idea, in fairly compact form, of what the society is like.

But anthropologists with a strong interest in the value-norm aspect of the ideological subsystem want, like all anthropologists, to do more than simply classify and describe their data. They want to explain.

Thus, having inferred certain norms from behavior and certain values from norms, they may then explain the process by reversing the order of derivation: norms come from values and behavior is determined by norms. Thus, the circle is complete. It should be obvious, however, that if one is going to use values to explain a particular behavior pattern, the evidence for the values must be independent of the norms which suggested the values to the investigator in the first place, and independent also of the behavior the values were formulated to explain. For example, if in culture X one observes that in a streetcar males always get up and give ladies their seats, always tip their hats to ladies on the street, and always hold doors open for ladies to pass through, one may conclude that this behavior is "normative-ought" as well as "normative-do." Such norms may also suggest that this culture *values* male chivalry. But the norms cannot then be said to derive from the value, male chivalry. Nor can the existence of the value be demonstrated by pointing to the fact that men give ladies their seats in streetcars, etc. The confirming evidence for the value must be sought in other behavioral data. The same logic would apply in the case of the validation of norms and their use as explanatory factors. Judith Blake and Kingsley Davis have made this point most tellingly:

> In practice, we tend to find the best evidence of values in the norms themselves. If people manifest a dislike of cheating in examinations, of dishonest advertising in business, and of unnecessary roughness in sports, we infer something like a value of "fair competition." Such a process of reasoning may help us to insert the motivational linkages and thus integrate a body of diverse information. At bottom, however, it is a classification. Its usefulness does not extend to causal explanation, because the inferred value comes only from the specific norms themselves and hence cannot be used as an explanation of these norms. In other words, unless we have evidence independent of norms themselves, we cannot logically derive norms from values. Independent evidence, if obtainable, may show that so-called values are non-existent, that they are consequences of the norms or that they derive from a third factor which is also responsible for the norms.
>
> Presumably if one's interpretation is in terms of norms rather than values, one is on firmer ground. Yet the difficulty of proving the existence of the norm is great. As a consequence, there is a tendency to take regularities in behavior as the evidence of the norm. When this is done, to explain the behavior in terms of the norm is a redundancy.[48]

---

[48] Judith Blake and Kingsley Davis, "Norms, Values, and Sanctions," in *Handbook of Modern Sociology*, ed. Robert E. L. Faris (Chicago: Rand McNally, 1964), pp. 460–61.

For these reasons Blake and Davis suggest that we abandon the use of "values" as causal agents in sociological and anthropological analysis and treat them instead as "sheer constructs by which we attempt to fill in the subjective linkages in the analysis of social causation." [49]

Among the consequences of a too-heavy reliance on "normative sovereignty" is that it may lead one to espouse a blueprint theory of society—the notion that a people start out with a system of ideas, themes, norms, values, etc., and then proceed to create institutions based upon them. While all views or conceptions of how a society functions may have their shortcomings, it seems to us that the "blueprint" view of society suffers from some especially heavy logical liabilities. For, as Blake and Davis have noted, it may lead us into a theoretical cul-de-sac:

> The emphasis on values and norms leads, as critics have been quick to point out, to deficiencies in the scientific understanding of real societies. The gravest deficiency arises, ironically, in the failure to deal adequately with norms themselves. As long as cultural configurations, basic value-attitudes, prevailing norms, or what not are taken as the starting point and principal determinant, they have the status of un-analyzed assumptions. The very questions that would enable us to understand the norms tend not to be asked, and certain facts about society become difficult, if not impossible, to comprehend. . . . The origin and appearance of new norms and their constant change—again facts of social existence—become incomprehensible under an assumption of normative sovereignty.
>
> . . . The deceptive ease of explanation in terms of norms or value-attitudes encourages an inattentiveness to methodological problems. By virtue of their subjective, emotional, and ethical character, norms, and especially values, are among the world's most difficult objects to identify The assumption that for each society there is one norm or one value regarding a given aspect of behavior is in most instances untrue. Insofar as an investigator uses norms or values as explanatory principles for concrete behavior, he therefore tends to be explaining the known by the unknown, the specific by the unspecific. His identification of the normative principles may be so vague as to be universally useful, i.e., anything and everything becomes explicable.[50]

At the beginning of this section we indicated that we were using the term *ideology* in a more inclusive sense than is usual. The preceding discussion, however, has concentrated upon certain aspects of the ideological subsystem. We have not, for example, treated the whole area of naturalistic and scientific knowledge. The importance of this knowledge is clearly beyond dispute. What is more, it does not confront the investigator with the same kinds of serious methodological problems that one encounters in dealing

---

In preparing this section, we have leaned heavily on this essay. We recommend it highly to any reader interested in the way ideological concepts such as *norms* and *values* have been used in anthropological and sociological analysis and theorizing.

[49] Ibid., p. 461.

[50] Ibid., p. 463.

with the more abstract and elusive features of the ideological subsystem. For this reason we have focused on those aspects of ideology which have been both widely used by anthropologists as explanatory factors and have also been controversial—i.e., values, norms, themes, ethos, and the like.

Our treatment of this more controversial side of ideological subsystem has been largely critical. Once again, our purpose has been to alert the student to some of the difficulties that occur in a crucial area of social-science inquiry, not to diminish the potential explanatory importance of ideology. To say that the issues present difficulties in their handling is not to recommend their dismissal. For clearly, idea-systems may have adaptive significance comparable with those of technoeconomics, social structure, and personality. And whether idea-systems can be said to exercise a determinative role vis-à-vis the other subsystems is a matter that cannot be decided by fiat, but must be empirically determined.

In a fairly recent study, Alvin Gouldner and Richard Peterson attempted to do precisely this.[51] More specifically, working with a large sample of world cultures and using sophisticated quantitative techniques and devices, they attempted to assess the relative causal weight that could be assigned to the variables of the subsystems technology, social structure, and ideology (or what they call the "moral order"). They wanted to know which variables account for the greatest "variance" in the total system. They found that social-structural variables had the least causal and predictive value. Technology had the greatest causal and predictive value, with ideology not far behind. But the combination of technology and ideology seemed to account for the greatest variance in the total system. Now, as Gouldner and Peterson point out, their study was intended as a methodological experiment and does not *prove* anything. One could quarrel, for example, with the way they coded the various items of culture in order that they might be quantified. But the study does suggest that ideology—even in the more restricted sense in which Gouldner and Peterson use it as referring principally to the normative structure or moral order—has a causal impact that should not be downgraded in framing explanations of cultural maintenance and change.

"The Logic of the Irrational"

A great deal of explanation in anthropology has been concerned with demonstrating what Ely Devons and Max Gluckman call the "logic of the irrational." [52] In other words, whereas many of the institutions of primitive societies may strike the casual observer as bizarre and irrational, the job of the anthropologist is to show that behind this irrationality these institutions are actually rational, even though the participants themselves may not be aware of that rationality. Explaining the rationality of the irrational frequently leads the anthropologist to the ideological subsystem. Sometimes, as in Evans-

---

[51] See Alvin W. Gouldner and Richard A. Peterson, *Notes on Technology and the Moral Order* (New York: Bobbs-Merrill, 1962).

[52] See Ely Devons and Max Gluckman, "Conclusion: Modes and Consequences of Limiting a Field Study," in *Closed Systems and Open Minds,* ed. Max Gluckman (Chicago: Aldine, 1964), pp. 254–59.

Pritchard's account of Azande witchcraft,[53] the native interpretation of the phenomenon is taken as the anthropologist's interpretation. Thus, in Evans-Pritchard's view, Azande witchcraft represents a native theory or explanation of why misfortune strikes a particular person at a particular time and place. If, for example, a man is killed by a falling tree, the Azande know very well that it was the tree and not a witch that crushed the man's skull. But the question the Azande wants answered is why *that* man should have been under *that* tree at the precise moment that it fell. The theory of witchcraft "explains" the coincidence and provides the answer.

But other investigators have tried to account for the logic of the irrational by probing beneath these surface explanations and speculating about deeper "hidden" or "unperceived" ideological factors. Their ideological explanations spill over into the area of psychology and become, in effect, psycho-ideological in nature. In these types of explanations one often encounters, explicitly or implicitly, such conceptions as latent, covert, or unconscious values, norms, themes, etc.—conceptions which actually straddle what we have here called the ideological and personality subsystems.

Melford Spiro's functional analysis of the persistence of Ifaluk belief in ghosts, it will be recalled (see pp. 61–63, *supra*), illustrates a type of explanation which combines variables from each of the above subsystems, since it emphasizes the Ifaluk need to displace aggression as well as the need to maintain and strengthen the social ethic of nonhostility. Spiro's account also includes another and somewhat different ideological-psychological explanation—namely, that the belief in malevolent spirits provides a consistent theory of disease and natural misfortune. This disease-and-natural-misfortune interpretation derives from a different generalization than the aggression-displacement hypothesis favored by Spiro in his analysis—from the general proposition that all people have a need to *know*, to *explain* the world and to make it intelligible in order to cope with it as effectively as their cultural equipment allows. The Ifaluk belief in malevolent spirits, whatever else it may do, apparently serves that function. Thus, one may assume that these beliefs persist because they have never been effectively challenged by an alternative belief or set of beliefs that can help the Ifaluk to cope more efficiently.

It is interesting to note that in a more recent paper by Spiro, in which he discusses religious ideology, he argues most lucidly for precisely this latter point of view—namely, that the ideology-*cum*-explanation theory of religious beliefs persists because it "works." As a matter of fact, Spiro expresses the same kind of concern about Merton's latent functional explanation of the Hopi rain ceremonies, for example, that we remarked upon in an earlier section. (Note that in the following quotation Spiro explicitly rejects the kind of latent-function explanation upon which his earlier analysis of Ifaluk beliefs rests.)

---

[53] See E. E. Evans-Pritchard, *Witchcraft, Oracles and Magic Among the Azande* (Oxford: Clarendon Press, 1937). See also Max Gluckman, "The Logic of African Science and Witchcraft: An Appreciation of Evans-Pritchard's *Witchcraft* . . . ," *Rhodes-Livingston Institute Journal* (June 1944): 61–71.

Thus, despite Merton's incisive analysis of functional theory, it is highly questionable if the persistence of Hopi rain ceremonies is to be explained by the social integration to which *he* (Merton) thinks their performance is conducive (their real, but latent, functions), rather than by the meteorological events to which *Hopi* think they are conducive (their manifest, but apparent, functions).

The Hopi belief in the efficacy of their rain-making ritual is not irrational —although it is certainly false—because the conclusion, rain ceremonies cause the rains to fall, follows validly from a world-view whose major premise states that gods exist, and whose minor premise states that the behavior of the gods can be influenced by rituals. That the premises are false does not render them irrational—until or unless they are disconfirmed by evidence. But all available "evidence" confirms their validity: whenever the ceremonies are performed it does, indeed, rain. Hence, given their "behavioral environment" . . . Hopi beliefs are not irrational; and given their ecological environment, the apparent function of these ceremonies is surely sufficient explanation for their persistence. . . .

If it is not sufficient, however, no appeal to unintended sociological functions will provide us with a better explanation—indeed, as we have already seen, it can provide us with no explanation at all. For how can the function of social solidarity explain the practice of these—or of any other—rituals? Notice that the objection to such an explanation is not that social solidarity may not be an object of desire—there is no reason why it cannot; and it is not that social solidarity is not achieved by the practice of these rituals—it often is. The objection, rather, is that the achievement of this end is *not* the desire which the practice of *these* rituals is intended to satisfy. Surely, not even the proponents of this type of explanation would suggest that Hopi rain ceremonies, sacrifices to Kali, exorcism of demons, celebration of the Mass, and the like are practiced with the conscious intention of achieving social solidarity. Is it suggested, then, that this is their unconscious intention? I would doubt that anyone would make this suggestion, for this suggests that if the efficacy of these rituals for the attainment of their designated ends were to be disbelieved, they would nevertheless be performed so that their solidarious functions might be served. This argument surely cannot be sustained. I can only conclude, then, that the persistence of these rituals is explicable by reference to what, for anthropologists, are their apparent, rather than their real, functions.[54]

Now all of this sounds like a harkening back to the nineteenth century, to the intellectualist views of, for example, Tylor and Frazer in their treatment of ideas about the supernatural. And indeed it is. But the current fashion in anthropology tends to depreciate these ancient Tylorean assumptions and to interpret primitive ideologies in largely symbolic and expressive terms (à la Victor Turner and Mary Douglas) rather than in cognitive or intellectualist

---

[54] Melford E. Spiro, "Religion: Problems of Definition and Explanation," in *Anthropological Approaches to the Study of Religion*, ed. Michael Banton, Monograph no. 3 (London: Travistock, 1966), pp. 113–14.

terms. Spiro, Robin Horton, and a few other "neo-Tyloreans" object to this presently dominant mode of interpretation because it encourages its anthropological adherents to play the game (well-known in literary criticism) of thinking up ingenious symbolism to explain this or that aspect of the ideological system. But the link between the symbol and that part of the culture it is alleged to symbolize is often tenuous to say the least. Evidence and empirical verification are often entirely lacking, and it is only the ethnographer's imagination that fills in the spaces between the act, the actor, and the consequences. In the absence of a more general sociological or psychological theory of symbolism, it is difficult to see why people in any society do not express certain features of their culture more directly but seem to prefer always to take the roundabout symbolic route.

As Robin Horton writes:

> An extreme illustration . . . is provided by Edmund Leach's *Political Systems of Highland Burma.* . . . Leach maintains that Kachin ideas about *nats* (spirits) are nothing but counters in the language of political argument; and it is precisely this contention which convinces one that his analysis is unreal. One cannot help protesting that if the *nats* are nothing more than counters in the power game, why do Kachins waste so much time talking about them? Why do they not couch their political arguments more directly? [55]

Horton then goes on to comment in a similar vein about John Middleton's analysis of *Lugbara Religion*:

> Reading this book . . . one gets the same feeling of unreality as one had from Leach. Why do these people not get on with [their] politics? Rereading [*Lugbara Religion*] with the intellectualist analysis put in before the political, one immediately regains a sense of reality. Now it becomes obvious why the old men spend such a lot of time talking about ancestral power and witchcraft when they are struggling for political position. It is because these ideas mean so much to Lugbara as intellectual tools for making sense of the world, that they are such powerful instruments in the hands of the politicians. If they meant nothing in intellectual terms, they would be nothing in the hands of the politicians. . . . [56]

Horton sums up this general argument as follows:

> It is clear that social anthropologists have been seriously misled by the glib phrase "manipulation of ideas." What politicians manipulate is not ideas, but people's dependence on ideas as means of ordering, explaining, predicting and controlling their world. Only a prior analysis of the nature

---

[55] Robin Horton, "Neo-Tyloreanism: Sound Sense or Sinister Prejudice?," *Man* 3 (1968): 626. For further discussion of these issues see R. Horton, "African Traditional Thought and Western Science," *Africa* 37 (1967): 50–71, 155–87; Edmund R. Leach, "Virgin Birth," *Proceedings of the Royal Anthropological Institute* (1966–67): 39–49; and Melford E. Spiro, "Virgin Birth, Parthenogenesis and Physiological Paternity: An Essay in Cultural Interpretation," *Man* 3 (1968): 242–61.

[56] Ibid., 626.

of this dependence can pave the way for an adequate grasp of the scope and limitations of manipulation.[57]

Finally, Horton goes on to point out that intellectualist or cognitive emphases in the interpretation of ideologies and belief systems complement rather than preclude other types of interpretation such as those which stress social or psychological functions. But if one treats belief systems as really *meaning* what they say ("We dance because that is the way to bring the rain"), one is offering a wholesome corrective to explanations based on hypotheses regarding the role of such elusive concepts as unconscious symbolism or latent functions.

In this section we discussed some of the methodological and theoretical issues involved in constructing ideological explanations of sociocultural phenomena. Our treatment was not intended to be exhaustive, both for reasons of space and because of the breadth and complexity of the subject. We have not, for example, even touched upon such matters of interest to anthropologists as Whorf's hypotheses concerning the relationships between the grammatical structure of a language and the way a people view their world; nor have we said anything about Durkheim's conception of "collective representations." [58] But many of the same kinds of logical problems that we have discussed would apply with equal force to these formulations.

In dealing with ideology, the anthropologist must, to some extent, rely on the information and insights provided by his informants. And all anthropologists have found that there are often inconsistencies between the expressed norms, values, and ideals of a culture and the actual behavior of the people. This sort of thing occurs so commonly that it has become almost a custom in the literature to refer to it as the "conflict between the real culture and the ideal culture." Since it is difficult, if not impossible, to predict the "real" from a knowledge of the "ideal" in any culture, anthropologists have looked for the intervening factors which would bridge the gap between the two. When they have not been able to find these explanatory factors in the more empirically grounded subsystems of technoeconomics and social structure, they have often filled the hiatus by positing certain ideological processes taking place in the mind of the native. In this respect, then, ideological becomes psycho-ideological or psychological. And as we indicated earlier, the anthropologist may end up with much the same sort of explanation when he attempts to bridge the gap between the ostensible irrationality of an institution and its underlying rationality. While we certainly do not wish to condemn these efforts at explanation, we must once again emphasize our belief that they involve difficulties which must be recognized.

Despite all the cautions and reservations we have expressed regarding ideological—and especially psycho-ideological—*explanations*, we do not for a moment question the *impact* of ideologies on cultural systems—as crucial factors in either promoting *or* inhibiting change. However an idea or ideas

---

57 Ibid., 627.

58 See Benjamin Lee Whorf, *Language, Thought and Reality: Selected Writings of Benjamin Lee Whorf,* ed. J.B. Carroll (Cambridge, Mass., and New York: The Technology Press of M.I.T. and John Wiley, 1956); and Emile Durkheim, *The Elementary Forms of the Religious Life,* trans. J.W. Swain (London: Allen and Unwin, 1915).

may have originated, once the ideological structure (or superstructure) has come into existence it may take on "a life of its own." Thus, we believe that there is indisputable evidence that this structure may come to exert autonomous causal influence on the rest of the cultural system.

In other words, it is reasonable to suppose that under certain circumstances ideologies may play an important and even critical determinative role, whereas in other situations they may be of lesser importance. Then, as Gouldner and Peterson point out, the question becomes: What is the *relative* causal weight that may be assigned to ideological factors in explaining a *particular* sociocultural system or range of sociocultural systems? To pour a great deal of time and effort into trying to find out whether "ideas" are really *the* "prime movers" in cultural development strikes us as a fruitless endeavor.[59] Nor, it seems to us, should we become involved in endless metaphysical debates about "idealistic" versus "materialistic" views of the universe. These labels may have a place in polemical philosophical jousting, but they may also be misleading. Marx, for example—who has been called many things but never, to the best of our knowledge, an "idealist"—was fully aware of the causal role of ideas, as Robert Merton's interpretation of Marxist doctrine makes clear:

> In the making of history, ideas and ideologies play a definite role: consider only the view of religion as the "opiate of the masses;" consider further the importance attached by Marx and Engels to making those in the proletariat "aware" of their "own interests." Since there is no fatality in the development of the total social structure, but only a development of economic conditions which make certain lines of change *possible* and probable, idea-systems may play a decisive role in the selection of one alternative which "corresponds" to the real balance of power rather than another alternative which runs counter to the existing power-situation and is therefore destined to be unstable, precarious and temporary.[60]

And by way of looking at the other side of the materialist-idealist issue, the conceptual framework of the contemporary sociologist Talcott Parsons usually impresses students as "normative-idealistic" in its explanatory import, since it emphasizes norms and values as causal factors. Yet when Parsons confronts the problem of explaining culture change, he can, as Gouldner notes, be quite "materialistic":

> Parsons' stress here on the economic-occupational structure is surprisingly reminiscent of a Marxian analysis. If such a convergence between Parsons and Marx exists, it is certainly not because Parsons is a Marxist. Parsons converges with Marx because he confronts himself with a problem essentially similar to that which Marx had persistently committed himself, namely, the introduction of planned change in a society.[61]

---

[59] See Elman R. Service, "The Prime-Mover of Cultural Evolution," *Southwestern Journal of Anthropology* 24 (1968): 396–409, and Marvin Harris "Monistic Determinism: Anti-Service," *Southwestern Journal of Anthropology* 25 (1968): 198–206.

[60] Robert K. Merton, "*The Sociology of Knowledge,*" in *Social Theory and Social Structure*, rev. and enlarged ed. (New York: Free Press, 1957), 478–479.

[61] Alvin W. Gouldner, "Theoretical Requirements of the Applied Social Sciences," in

And, finally, Robert Heilbroner, in discussing social change, points out that there are "limits" to the kinds of changes a society's "core structures" can tolerate. If these limits are exceeded, a new type of society, or what Heilbroner refers to as a new "social order," emerges. And it is at these limits that ideology plays its crucial role:

> One meaning we can give to the idea of "limits" is very simple: It is those boundaries of change that would so alter the functional base of a society, or the structure of privilege built on that base, as to displace a given social order by a new one. To be sure, the exact line as to what constitutes a vital infringement on the body of a society is by no means easy to draw, and it is precisely here, at the margin of change, that ideology plays its decisive role in admitting or excluding particular alterations in a social structure.[62]

Personality:
Social and Psychobiological Dimensions

So far in this chapter we have dealt with three subsystems of culture, each of which has been utilized by one group of anthropologists or another to "explain" cultural variation. We have, in effect, implied that anthropologists may be divided into theoretical camps, with members of each camp assigning greater causal weight to one or another of these subsystems—techno-economics, social structure, ideology. We turn now to a fourth camp, to those anthropologists who consider personality variables as significant in accounting for cultural stability and change.

But because the subsystem of personality (or, as it is variously labeled, culture and personality, personality in culture, psychological anthropology, etc.) is, like the other subsystems already discussed, a vast and complex field, we propose to focus our discussion on two major theoretical and methodological issues which are inevitably involved in any attempt to utilize personality variables for purposes of explaining cultural phenomena. The first of these issues is whether personality variables should be considered an integral part of the cultural system on a par with variables of the other three subsystems, or considered as analytically external to the cultural system and, therefore, causally nonsignificant. In other words, while man and culture are obviously inseparable, can we take the position that it is personality that *causes* culture? Or may we assume, for explanatory purposes, that the human psyche and personality are either constants or dependent variables and, therefore, irrelevant in accounting for cultural stability and variation? We shall return to this matter below.

The second issue is related to the first: If personality variables are considered an integral part of the cultural system, to what extent do they exert a causal influence on the rest of the system? If one sees personality in this

---

The Planning of Change: Readings in the Applied Behavioral Sciences (New York: Holt, Rinehart and Winston, 1961), p. 91.

62 Robert L. Heilbroner, *The Limits of American Capitalism* (New York: Harper Torch, 1967), pp. 66–67.

way, then the same kind of theoretical questions raised in our discussion of the other subsystems should apply to that of personality.

It should be clear that these two issues are closely related because the second issue—the more theoretical one of assigning specific causal weight to personality variables—will depend upon the view that one takes of the first— the more methodological one of whether personality variables lie within the cultural system and must therefore be considered an integral part of any explanation of that system. Thus, before we turn to the details of those explanations which have emphasized personality variables, we should take a look at what we have referred to as the more methodological issue. For it is obvious that if one employs personality causally—i.e., to explain culture— one must first examine the relationship of psychological—and even psychobiological—variables to sociocultural phenomena. These are questions that did not arise in our discussion of the other subsystems. In short, the more general issue to which we must first address ourselves relates to the autonomy both of psychology and of cultural anthropology.

A Methodological Note

It is commonly asserted that the boundaries between the academic disciplines are highly artificial and permeable; that they have resulted in part from historical accident and are perpetuated by universities largely as a matter of administrative convenience. Within recent years this view has been emphasized particularly with respect to the social sciences. One frequently hears the assertion that since all the social sciences are concerned with explaining the same phenomena—social institutions and human behavior— they ought to be more formally integrated. Hence the popularity of such phrases as "the behavioral sciences" and even the establishment in some universities of supradepartments like "human relations" and "social relations."

It is true, of course, that the emergence and development of the social sciences (and indeed, of all the academic disciplines) have been affected by factors from the wider cultural environment—factors like changes in the economic structure, or the growth of the modern university with its increasing administrative complexity. But it does not follow from this that the boundaries between the social science disciplines are either *wholly* arbitrary or mere matters of convenience. There is a rationale behind the division of labor that now characterizes the social sciences. And this rationale reflects the internal development of each of the disciplines over time.

All of the social sciences are broadly concerned with human behavior. But to say this is not particularly illuminating; for many of the nonsocial sciences like human physiology, biochemistry, and psychophysics may also be said to be "concerned with human behavior," or at least with certain aspects of human behavior. What distinguishes each of these disciplines is not that each deals with different events, for, indeed, many of the events or things with which the various disciplines do deal are identical. Rather, each is distinguished by the fact that it conceptualizes these events or things in different ways. Or to put it another way: because each discipline asks different questions, each will focus on different aspects of those events or things it is looking at. Thus, a biologist, a psychologist, and an anthropologist observing the same event may conceptualize and explain it in quite different ways. Each of the investigators will literally derive different phenomena from the very same event.

The general point we wish to make is that an event or a thing is what it is. Strictly speaking, there are no physical, biological, psychological, or cultural things or events in the world. It is we who conceptualize them in different ways in order to answer certain specific kinds of questions. Suppose that, for example, although it is her customary pattern to do so, a woman leaves her home one morning having forgotten or neglected to "make up her face." Unexpectedly, she finds herself in a social situation that "demands" makeup. She suddenly realizes her error, becomes embarrassed, and blushes. How should we characterize this relatively simple sequence of events: as physiological, psychological, or cultural? It is, of course, all of these at once and, depending upon our interests and purposes, we will conceptualize it in different ways.

Thus, the autonomy of a discipline does not depend upon its dealing with a particular chunk of reality as its own special and private concern. No discipline, whether it belongs to the physical, the biological, or the social sciences may claim this kind of proprietorship over an event or a thing. Rather, the autonomy of a discipline stems from the fact that it has a set of problems and questions which are its special concern. The kind of questions a discipline puts to reality determines the way it conceptualizes this "reality." Thus, the concepts and terms of a discipline define its "phenomena," and the generalizations and theories generated by that discipline explain those phenomena.

As we noted in our introductory chapter, the problems with which anthropologists are generally concerned fall under two broad rubrics: How do different cultural systems work? and How have they come to be as they are? The subject matter of anthropology, as defined by its basic concepts, includes such things as lineages, rituals, segmentary states, supernatural beliefs, redistributive networks, irrigation states, postmarital residence patterns, magical practices, closed corporate peasant communities, periodic markets, and so on. These are the kinds of phenomena anthropologists have tried to describe and explain. Moreover, because they have been concerned with the maintenance and change of *total* systems, they have dealt with *all* of a culture's subsystems and the way these interrelate. In this respect their work has differed in important ways from the work of the political scientist or the economist who (at least until quite recently) concentrated upon one or another subsystem in industrialized societies. Thus, anthropologists have often dealt with questions that did not concern other social scientists. And because they have generally carried on their inquiries among non-Western or nonliterate cultures which were of no apparent interest to the economist, political scientist, etc., they have had to develop skills that would enable them to cope with *all* of a society's institutional orders.

As long as anthropologists confined their efforts to small-scale societies, this "holistic" approach seems to have worked pretty well. But whether this same approach can or should be applied to the study of more complex situations is another matter (and a question to which we shall return in Chapter 5).

In taking the "holistic" approach to "simpler" societies, the anthropologist has often raised institutional questions similar to those asked by the sociologist, the political scientist, and the economist in their studies of "more complex" societies. Consequently, the anthropologist has often borrowed concepts and propositions that were developed by these other disciplines. Sometimes this borrowing has proved fruitful, but at other times the process of lifting concepts out of the theoretical context of another discipline and applying them to phenomena for which they were not formulated has created confusion. The upshot of this borrowing and of its obverse—the use of anthropological concepts by other disciplines concerned with aspects of human behavior and culture—is that each of the so-called cultural sciences now enjoys only a relative degree of autonomy. And even this restricted autonomy seems to be declining somewhat as the disciplines converge on current studies and problems of development and underdevelopment. Nevertheless—as even a brief look at some of the products of recent interdisciplinary research will show—there are still some significant differences among anthropologists, political scientists, and economists—for instance, in the way they conceptualize and attempt to explain a particular problem.

If the autonomy of cultural anthropology is increasingly limited in its relationship to the other *cultural* sciences, the logical distinctions that separate cultural anthropology from psychology (a "noncultural" social science) seem to be even greater. When, for example, an anthropologist writes about a hydraulic state or a redistributive economy, a political scientist or economist will have no difficulty in translating the analysis into the terms of his own discipline. The anthropologist is referring to certain institutional arrangements, and whether it is the ruler or the welfare state that functions as the major redistributive agent, the arrangements themselves can be viewed as a similar order of phenomena. The psychologist, on the other hand, is concerned primarily with identifying and explaining *intraorganismic* psychic mechanisms and processes. These "psychic phenomena" may be panhuman in scope and operation (e.g., basic needs or the relationship between frustration and aggression) or they may characterize only a certain type of personality configuration (e.g., the authoritarian personality). And while the psychologist *is* concerned with the extraorganic sociocultural environment as it may produce, affect, or modify psychic processes, he is generally *not* concerned with explaining the origins or functioning of the cultural environment as such.[63] Thus, "psychological reality" is reality as it is conceptualized by the discipline of psychology. The phenomena of the discipline are defined by its basic concepts and terms such as *drives, repression, conditioned reflexes, basic needs, ego strength, habit strengths, cognitive maps,* and the like. In other words, the "phenomena" that concern the psychologist are of a different order from those that concern the cultural anthropologist.

---

[63] We are dealing with logical distinctions between modes of questioning different ways of conceptualizing "reality" and the explanatory systems that these produce. We are not concerned with those particular psychologists whose special interests seem to take them "outside" their field. Thus, while it is true that some psychologists have attempted to explain the rise and fall of sociocultural institutions in psychological terms (e.g., Freud, Roheim, etc.), it seems to us that their formulations have rarely been convincing.

What, then, does it mean to say that sociocultural phenomena should be explained in psychological terms? Those who adhere most strenuously to this view assert that "collective concepts" like lineage, church, school, state, caste, class, etc., are nothing more than convenient fictions. Such sociocultural institutions, it is argued, have no "reality" independent of the individuals who make them up. Or, as Robert Lynd pointed out, it is people and not institutions who vote, enamel their fingernails, and believe in capitalism. Thus, if "individuals" are the only reality, then it follows that statements about sociocultural institutions ought to be "reduced to" or "explained by" statements about the psychological functioning of individuals. But to effect such a "reduction" we need some logical way of making the transition from statements about drives, basic needs, cognitive maps, and the like to statements about lineages, ritual organization, political structure, etc. Or, to phrase it another way, we must be able to demonstrate empirically that, given such-and-such *psychological* conditions, one may expect certain institutional arrangements to arise.

Clearly, any attempt to explain sociocultural phenomena in *wholly* psychological terms does not, at least for the present, seem to be feasible. Institutions are *organized,* they have a *structure,* and it is the purpose of anthropological explanation to account for the particular patterns of organization of, as well as the maintenance and changes that may take place in, such structures. When investigators try to explain these structures in terms of the psychological attributes of individuals, they have invariably found it necessary to conceptualize the individuals in terms of their social personality. And a critical aspect of this social personality is the variables of the very institutional structures they are trying to explain. For example, our hypothetical investigator may try to account for the organization of a lineage in terms of the psychological behavior of its individual members. But at some point he will have to include a review or summary of the statuses occupied by the lineage members and the roles they perform. Status and role, however, are features of the lineage organization one is trying to explain and *not* of the psychological organization of the individuals per se.

Because attempts to reduce statements about sociocultural phenomena to statements about the psychological behavior of individuals have invariably foundered on such logical difficulties, many psychologically oriented investigators favor a less extreme variety of personality or psychological explanation. Thus, they may temper their explanatory claims with the qualification that this kind of reduction ought, "in principle," to work out. The "in principle" seems to involve two related aims or assumptions. One of these is that we ought to work toward a greater rapprochment between anthropology and psychology; the second appears to hold out the hope that a greater degree of reduction will be possible as the disciplines mature in the future.

Now, while social scientists often speak of "reductionism" in disparaging terms, as though the reductionist were trying to "explain away" the variety and complexity of sociocultural phenomena, reductionism is actually a sound methodological procedure—provided always that the logical and empirical steps for getting from psychological phenomena to sociocultural phenomena can be filled in. For if one of the "ideal" goals of science is to subsume a wider and wider range of phenomena under a contracting corpus of explanatory principles and theoretical generalizations, then clearly reductionism is one of the goals of science. Secondly, to say that the reduction of sociocultural phenomena to psychological explanation is not now feasible says nothing about whether a greater degree of reduction may not be feasible in the future. The reduction of one discipline, wholly or in part, to another discipline does not hinge on the metaphysical constitution of the world. Rather, as we have tried to indicate, it depends upon the logical relationships between disciplines, and these may change through time. Thus, it is conceivable that in the future sociocultural phenomena may be *more* explainable in psychological terms than they are at present. This will depend upon the future development of the two disciplines and is, therefore, an empirical matter. But looking at the present stage of development of these disciplines and the directions in which they seem to be moving, any such reduction appears to be a long way off.

Considerations like those just discussed have led many social scientists to reject reductionism and to espouse the position that sociocultural phenomena constitute an automonous level of analysis in which psychological variables are irrelevant. The classic statement of this position is contained in Emile Durkheim's *Rules of the Sociological Method*. In anthropology Alfred Kroeber and Leslie White, among others, have reiterated Durkheim's thesis and argued for the independence of cultural analysis from psychology—what Kroeber, borrowing a term from Spencer, called the "superorganic" view of culture. White, probably the most articulate and consistent modern spokesman for this view, puts the case for the autonomy of culture this way:

> Some anthropologists would readily grant the irrelevance of *anatomical* traits to an interpretation of cultural differences, but would insist upon not only the relevance but the importance of psychological factors. The personalities, character structures, minds, egos, or ids of peoples or individuals will, they argue, shape their cultures. But if *personality, mind,* etc., be defined as biological phenomena, as functions of the neuro-sensory-muscular-glandular-etcetera system, then their argument is wholly lacking in scientific support. If, however, they define personality and mind as products of human social experience, i.e., as culturally determined, then they are saying that culture causes or determines culture, but through the medium of human biological organisms, which is precisely what we are maintaining here.

> Secondly, let us consider a large population, a tribe or nation, for example, over a considerable period of time, such as the people of England between A.D. 1066 and 1866, or the people of Honshu between A.D. 1850 and 1940. We observe in each case that the culture has changed greatly. The populations, as biological organisms, have, however, undergone no appreciable change, either anatomically or psychologically. We cannot, therefore, explain the cultural changes by invoking the biological factor; we cannot explain a cultural variable in terms of a constant, biological or otherwise. Nor would we be aided in the slightest degree by taking the human organism into consideration. Here as before the biological factor is irrelevant, and consequently it should be disregarded. In both of these examples, therefore, the independence of culture from its biological

carriers, or substratum, from the standpoint of logical analysis and for purposes of scientific interpretation, is again demonstrated.[64]

When White denies the relevance of psychological factors in explanations of cultural phenomena, he has in mind, as these examples indicate, questions involving relatively broad cultural differences and historical changes. But many anthropologists insist that there are certain other questions with which we must deal where psychological variables *are* relevant. These investigators would not deny the autonomy of sociocultural phenomena as a level of analysis; nor would they explain such phenomena in wholly psychological terms. What they do maintain is that there are "anthropological" issues and problems where psychological variables, especially personality factors, must be explicitly included as integral parts of our explanations. For example, in his classic study, *Suicide*, Durkheim demonstrated that varying rates of suicide (especially what he called "egoistic suicide") in different societies were determined by the degree of integration of certain critical social institutions, such as the family, the church, and secondary associations like political parties. Now, despite his disavowal of the relevance of psychological factors, Durkheim, as Alex Inkeles points out, had to "posit a general theory of personality—namely that man's 'psychic constitution' needs an object transcending itself" [65] in order to get *from* the degree of integration of particular social institutions to varying rates of suicide. Unless this psychological step is explicitly included in the explanation, we will have difficulty in understanding how a low degree of integration of certain key institutions can be the *cause* of higher rates of suicide.

This more modest and restricted phrasing of the relationship between psychological variables and sociocultural phenomena is quite different from the stronger "reductionist" claims, and cannot be dismissed as either irrelevant or premature. For it is perfectly reasonable to suppose that personality factors *may* play a role in the maintenance and/or change of cultural systems. How *much* of a role they do in fact play, and what causal significance can be assigned to this role is a matter for empirical investigation.

The Old Culture-Personality School

Although it may sometimes appear that an interest in psychological phenomena is relatively recent in anthropology, it should be noted that from its very beginning as a systematic field of inquiry anthropology has been concerned with mental processes. For example, the "psychic unity of mankind," among the earliest and most fundamental axioms of the discipline, is, of course, an assumption about panhuman mental processes. Thus, in adhering to this assumption anthropology was led away from racial, biological, and genetic explanations of cultural differences to explanations of these differences in sociocultural terms. Once they had accepted the premise that

---

[64] Leslie A. White, *The Evolution of Culture* (New York: McGraw-Hill, 1959), pp. 13–14.

[65] Alex Inkeles, "Personality and Social Structure," in *Sociology Today: Problems and Prospects*, ed. Robert K. Merton, Leonard Broom, and Leonard S. Cottrell, Jr. (New York: Basic Books, 1959), p. 252.

mental processes were essentially identical for all humankind, many of the early anthropologists went on to speculate about the *nature* of these mental processes. Tylor, for example, in his classic two-volume work, *Primitive Culture*, sought the origins of animism, and ultimately of all religion, in the mental processes of *Homo sapiens*. Nevertheless, and despite the underlying assumptions about panhuman mental processes, Tylor and those anthropologists who followed him (down through the first two decades of the twentieth century) had available to them only the psychological constructs and formulations of that period. And these did not seem to lend themselves to an analysis of social life. It was not until the appearance of the Freudian synthesis that anthropology was supplied with a dynamic and all-embracing theory of human personality which seemed capable of providing the link between psychic processes and sociocultural systems. The growing popularity of Freudian psychology during the 1920s and '30s gave an enormous impetus to personality and culture theorizing in anthropology. Many observers have suggested that the time was ripe for a new theoretical emphasis. Nineteenth-century evolutionism had been battered into temporary insensibility by Boas and his followers. And, ironically, the historical particularism and extreme relativism fostered by them as a counter to evolutionism seems to have exhausted its theoretical possibilities. The functionalism of Radcliffe-Brown and Malinowski had not yet crossed the Atlantic in any force. Then along came Freud.

Under the impact of the highly systematized Freudian psychology many American anthropologists began to focus on child-rearing practices in different cultures, to explore the effect of these practices on the emergence of different personality configurations, and, ultimately, to explore the relationship between group personality and sociocultural institutions.

Two theoretical constructs emerged from this early work in what some writers have called the "old school" of culture-personality: "basic personality structure" and "modal personality." The notion of a "basic personality structure" was developed by the psychoanalyst Abram Kardiner in collaboration with the anthropologists Ralph Linton, Cora DuBois, and others in a series of seminars at Columbia University during the late 1930s.[66] In their view, all of society's institutions are either primary or secondary. Among the primary institutions, the most important is the family with its associated patterns and techniques of child rearing. These child-rearing practices give rise to a constellation of personality traits which are shared by all members of a society— i.e., the *basic personality structure*. The personality structure, in turn, determines the form and content of the society's secondary institutions or "projective systems." Kardiner's secondary institutions included art, religion, mythology, folklore, patterns of thought, etc. Thus, the Kardiner schema posited and emphasized *early* socialization practices as independent variables and saw the direction of causation as going from these practices to basic personality structure and from there to magical-religious structures and ideological systems. It should be pointed out that while Kardiner apparently included subsistence patterns among the so-called primary institutions, in his theoret-

[66] See Abram Kardiner, *The Individual and His Society* (New York: Columbia University Press, 1939), and Abram Kardiner, R. Linton, J. West, et al., *The Psychological Frontiers of Society* (New York: Columbia University Press, 1945).

ical discussions he tended to concentrate on family structures and patterns of child rearing, and concerned himself only in passing with economic arrangements. As a matter of fact, Kardiner was never very clear about any of the primary institutions other than the family and its principles and practices of early socialization.

Shortly after the publication of the first Kardiner volume (*The Individual and His Society,* 1939), some investigators pointed out that even in small-scale societies there are differences in personality type for which the Kardiner formulation fails to account. These investigators, most notably Cora DuBois of the original seminar, were thus led to reformulate the basic personality concept by adding a statistical dimension to it. This revised concept was labeled *modal personality,* and referred to the statistically *most common* personality type found in a society. However, the direction of causality in this revised schema was much the same as it had been in the earlier Kardiner formulation: from early socialization patterns to modal personality and thence to the rest of culture, which was seen either as projections of or accommodations to the modal personality type.

Although applied initially only to small-scale societies, the concepts of basic and modal personality were later applied to societies of much greater complexity, like nation-states. Of course, an interest in "national character" goes back at least as far as Thucydides and Herodotus. But the concepts of modal and basic personality appeared to offer a more precise scientific tool for dealing with the mystique of national character than the impressionism of earlier comments and observations. Consequently, when the conduct of World War II seemed to require more exact knowledge of the character of the populations engaged in the struggle, various agencies of the U.S. federal government turned to anthropologists of the culture-and-personality persuasion for assistance. More specifically, these agencies supported anthropological investigations into the national character of a wide range of nation-states and ethnic communities. This interest and support survived the war years. The product of all this government research as well as the corollary research it apparently stimulated is a large corpus of literature dealing with the basic and/or modal personality of the Japanese, Russians, Germans, British, Poles, Bulgarians, Roumanians, Chinese, East European Jews, and Americans.

A review of these researches into the basic and modal personality of primitive and national cultures prompts four general observations: First, most of the anthropologists involved in these investigations tended to view culture and personality as so intimately related and interdependent as to constitute merely different labels or, at most, different ways of looking at the *same* phenomena. But, as David Aberle notes, the failure to treat culture and personality as analytically separate and autonomous systems (or subsystems) "destroys the field of culture and personality by providing it with nothing to relate to anything else. To the degree that culture and personality are identical, there is no interaction between them." [67]

Second, unlike the psychologists who seem to be concerned primarily with

---

[67] David F. Aberle, "The Influence of Linguistics on Early Culture and Personality Theory," in *Essays in the Science of Culture,* ed. Gertrude E. Dole and Robert L. Carneiro (New York: Thomas Y. Crowell, 1960), p. 26.

individual (private) personality, these anthropological investigators were for the most part interested in group (public) personality and the relationship between group personality and culture. In general, they did not even question the *existence* of a group personality, assuming instead that each culture exhibits a dominant personality type. Thus, rather than asking *whether* a society could be characterized in terms of a basic or modal personality type, they were led to ask *what* is the nature of its basic or modal personality.

Third, although some of the earlier investigators used Rorschach and other projective tests or devices for delineating the basic or modal personality structure, for the most part these theoretical constructs were derived or inferred from various cultural materials (myths, folktales, literary works, movies, popular songs, etc.) and institutional arrangements (especially family organization and child-rearing patterns). Since these investigators then tried to use the modal personality characteristics to explain the cultural arrangements, behavior, and institutions from which they had been inferred, their analyses proved tautological and their attempts at explanation circular. Alex Inkeles and Daniel Levinson in their excellent discussion of the methodology of modal personality studies point out that the delineation of the modal personality of a society, if it is to move beyond impressionism, requires certain rigorous techniques: the drawing up of a population sample of individuals, the use of psychological testing devices, and the working out of a psychological population profile for certain personality characteristics.[68] These are stringent requirements—especially as applied to large social units. It seems to us that their very stringency may explain why, as Inkeles has noted, "no one has ever tested a national population or even a major sub-population using either an adequate sample or adequate psychological instruments. All assertions or denials of national, subnational, regional or class differences of major magnitudes, therefore, remain mere statements of faith." [69]

Finally, many of the early culture-personality writers were interested not only in working out the effects of culture upon personality but also in demonstrating the impact of personality upon culture. And when they moved, in this latter endeavor, from statements about correlation to statements about causation, these tended—as we noted in the case of Kardiner—to go from socialization patterns to basic or modal personality, and then to the institutional arrangements and ideological structure of a society.[70] Because of the

---

68 See Alex Inkeles and Daniel Levinson, "National Character: The Study of Modal Personality and Socio-Cultural Systems," in *Handbook of Social Psychology*, vol. 2, ed. G. Lindzey (Cambridge, Mass.: Addison-Wesley, 1954).

69 Inkeles, "Personality and Social Structure," pp. 267–68.

70 Some personality and culture investigators have actively denied the imputation of any such causal chain to their work. For example, in the debate about the early swaddling of Russian children or the rigid toilet training of the Japanese, Geoffry Gorer and Margaret Mead have denied that they were arguing in causal fashion from the swaddling or toilet training of Russian and Japanese children to adult Russian and Japanese personality, and then to the wider institutional framework of contemporary Russian and Japanese society. All they were attempting to do, they argue, was to show the processes by which an infant born into Russian or Japanese culture becomes a Russian or a Japanese and that swaddling and toilet training seemed to be among the more important determinants of adult character in each case. But numerous critics maintain that they did, in fact, attempt to do more than this. These critics have cited specific passages from Gorer's work in which he

Freudian emphasis in virtually all of this work, the possibility that critical influences on adult personality might postdate early childhood was rarely entertained or seriously explored. Thus, socialization usually meant *early* socialization.

If one accepts the linkage between child-rearing practices and patterns of adult personality; and, further, if one believes that a society's institutions must accommodate themselves to the adult personality structure, then theories employing socialization as an independent variable seem entirely possible. For, in this view, when socialization patterns are relatively stable, the dominant values, beliefs, and attitudes of a society will be internalized by its members and they will generally be motivated to maintain and perpetuate the system. Or, again from this point of view, when socialization patterns become differentiated or undergo change, deviants or even a new personality type will emerge which will, in turn, exert pressures for institutional change in the society.

Despite a surface plausibility, there are certain objections that might be be raised to this schema. First of all, if we treat socialization as an independent variable, we have no way of explaining why different cultures should exhibit different patterns of child-rearing. What is more, it seems impossible to find an unequivocal empirical example of a society in which a major institutional change followed a change in socialization patterns. As a matter of fact, the weight of the empirical evidence suggests the opposite—that changes in socialization, where they have occurred, generally *follow* major changes in a society's institutional structure.

If, as we are suggesting, the causal impact of socialization on institutional change is in doubt, then the role of socialization in the *maintenance* of cultural systems may also be problematic. As Bert Kaplan has pointed out, there is empirical evidence to suggest that a cultural system can maintain itself despite a high degree of noncongruence between its institutions and the personality characteristics of its members (and, presumably, its socialization patterns). He writes:

> One interesting conclusion which can be drawn from observations of noncongruence such as that existing in the Soviet Union is that the social system as a whole nevertheless persists. Even drastic noncongruence does not seem to disrupt the society's functioning. This should warn us against being too certain of the dependence of societal functioning upon the support of particular personality characteristics. Noncongruence undoubtedly results in strain among individuals, and in inefficiency in the social system, but so long as the necessary tasks get done it is not fatal or perhaps even serious.[71]

appears clearly to be offering causal explanations of various sociocultural institutions by using adult Russian and Japanese personality and, ultimately, early child-rearing practices as major explanatory devices.

See Victor Barnouw, *Culture and Personality* (Homewood, Ill.: Dorsey Press, 1963), chap. 8; also Margaret Mead, "National Character," in *Anthropology Today*, ed. A. L. Kroeber (Chicago: University of Chicago Press, 1953) for a good bibliography.

[71] Bert Kaplan, "Personality and Social Structure," in *Theory in Anthropology*, ed. R. A. Manners and D. Kaplan (Chicago: Aldine, 1968), p. 321.

What Kaplan is saying here is that noncongruence-without-disruption can and does occur because an individual may *learn about* the prevailing values, beliefs, and attitudes of his society without ever internalizing them, i.e., without making them a part of his personality.[72] Thus, a person may function with a high degree of efficiency in the army while holding beliefs, sentiments, and attitudes diametrically opposed to the aims and the purposes of the military. There is no reason to suppose that the same sort of phenomenon may not obtain in the wider society.

Cultural persistence or maintenance cannot, then, be seen simply as a function of socialization patterns. To an overwhelming extent, the maintenance of a culture depends upon its relationship to its enviroment-writ-large as well as upon the way its various institutional orders interconnect to form a system. It seems to be something like this that David Aberle had in mind when he commented: "Socialization itself explains the how, not the why of stability and never explains major features of change." [73]

Although we have referred in the preceding paragraphs to just a few specific studies, our remarks are intended to apply to a broad spectrum of work produced by the "older school" of personality and culture writers. On the other hand, the reservations and criticisms expressed do not apply to all of the work done by the pioneers in this field. For a number of these investigators into the relationship between cultural and psychological phenomena were clearly aware of the methodological and conceptual weaknesses we have noted, and in their explorations into modal personality they attempted to compensate for these apparent deficiencies.

Thus, Anthony Wallace's rigorous approach to modal personality, among the Tuscarora and Ojibwa Indians represents such an effort.[74] Having defined modal personality in statistical terms, Wallace administered Rorschach tests to his subjects and found that 37% of the Tuscarora sample fell within his definition of the modal range. Five percent of the Ojibwa fell within the modal range prescribed for the Tuscarora—a statistically significant difference. (Nevertheless, 28% of the Ojibwa sample fell within the limits assigned by Wallace to the Ojibwa modal class.)

One of the interesting features of the Wallace study is the revelation that in each case only a minority of the sample tested fell within the modal range defined by Wallace for that society. Commenting on these results, Bert Kaplan says they "seem to call for a new variety of theory that could explain how only a minority of individuals in a society, *rather than a majority*, comes to respond positively to the cultural pressure toward uniformity of personality." [75]

Another attempt to deal with the concept of the modal personality in a fairly rigorous manner is Kaplan's own investigation of four cultures in the American Southwest: Zuni, Navaho, Mormon, and Spanish-American.[76]

---

72 See Kaplan, "Personality and Social Structures," pp. 326–28.

73 Aberle, "The Influence of Linguistics," p. 26–27.

74 See Anthony F. Wallace, *The Modal Personality Structure of the Tuscarora Indians, as Revealed by the Rorschach Test*, Bureau of American Ethnology Bulletin no. 150 (1952).

75 Kaplan, "Personality and Social Structure," p. 336.

76 Bert Kaplan, "A Study of Rorschach Responses in Four Cultures," *Papers of the*

Using projective tests, Kaplan found that while the Rorschach protocols differed from group to group, there was also considerable internal variation within each group, and that the protocol overlap between the groups was significantly large.

What the Kaplan, Wallace, and other studies suggest is

> that personality variability within societies is very large. This heterogeneity indicates that the very simple model which has been utilized in the culture and personality field of a modal type around which all but a few deviants tend to cluster may be an incorrect one and that simplistic [*sic*] theories which are closer to the actual empirical findings will have to be developed. The past decade in the culture and personality field may in one sense be regarded as moving away from the simple theories of cultural determinism to more sophisticated and elaborate as well as less confident theories about the nature and extent of personality diversity in different societies and of homogeneity within societies. The suggestion of Inkeles and Levinson that societies may have multiple modes rather than a single one is a movement in this direction.[77]

One of the most interesting and suggestive treatments of the modal personality concept was proposed by the distinguished psychoanalyst Eric Fromm in his work on the German "social character" and the capitalist "market personality." [78] Fromm's formulations are significant not because his techniques for delineating modal personality were particularly rigorous: they were not. In point of fact, they were highly impressionistic. We believe the work is nonetheless important because of the conceptual framework he employed and for the way he attempts to relate the institutional arrangements of a society, its socialization patterns, and its personality structure in a dynamic gestalt. Thus, unlike the aforementioned studies of Kaplan and Wallace, Fromm wants to go beyond the simple delineation of a modal personality: he wants to *explain*.

In Fromm's theoretical schema the sociocultural institutions of a society are neither created by nor simply derived from personality factors. These institutions must be seen, Fromm maintains, as historically derived and at least semiautonomous. In turn, Fromm views personality and socialization as largely dependent variables which are more often the product of institutional pressures than the breeder of institutional structures. In short, while Fromm places greater causal emphasis on institutional than on personality factors, his approach is essentially dialectical. Taking a page from Marx, Fromm emphasizes especially the economic character of a society. Thus, the society's institutional arrangements, together with its concomitant socialization patterns, will tend to produce a personality type peculiar to that society. Applying the dialectic principle to his analysis, Fromm suggests that the institutions of a society, together with its dominant personality type or "social character," play a dynamic role in maintaining the structure of the culture or in setting up pressure for cultural change. In Fromm's view the

Peabody Museum of Archaeology and Ethnology (Harvard University: 1954), vol. 42, no. 2.

[77] Ibid., p. 337.

[78] See Erich Fromm, *Escape From Freedom* (New York: Farrar and Rinehart, 1941) and *The Sane Society* (New York: Holt, Rinehart and Winston, 1955).

institutions of a society have certain psychic or personal meanings for its members, and different cultural arrangements will have different meanings and, hence, different implications.

Finally, Fromm's construct involves a general theory of human personality which posits certain basic needs that are panhuman. When a culture thwarts or fails to satisfy the basic needs of its members, some human response will be forthcoming. And if the frustration or deprivation is severe enough, this response may take the form of a special movement directed toward a restructuring of the culture so as to bring it more into harmony with the basic needs of its participants.

At first glance, Fromm's position on the emergence of restructuring social movements would seem to challenge Kaplan's observations on the Soviet Union, for in his discussion Kaplan tells us that despite all the empirical evidence of noncongruence between personality and institutions in Soviet culture, no social movements for restructuring seem to have arisen. On the other hand, even if Fromm did not question the validity of the evidence cited by Kaplan or his conclusions about noncongruence in the Soviet Union, he might answer that the noncongruence can only be transitory and that the strains it gives rise to will eventually produce pressures for internal institutional changes; the net result will be a closer fit between Soviet institutions and the personality needs of Soviet man.

If this hypothetical rejoinder we have attributed to Fromm is not unreasonable—and we believe it is logically consistent with his theoretical position —it still leaves his schema burdened with a number of problems. Apart from the temporal uncertainties—i.e., "eventually" may be a long time (how long does it take the society—any society—to achieve a proper fit between institutions and personality?)—there are, as Inkeles has pointed out, some logical and practical difficulties of verification in Fromm's formulation:

> Given any reasonable list of human needs, no author should have great difficulty in showing that in any historical situation he might select, one or more of these needs was not adequately met. To demonstrate any necessary connection between the deprivation of the need and the emergence of a social movement, he would have to show that in all other situations in which the movement did not arise the need had to be fulfilled. Failing that improbable demonstration, he would at least have to predict the emergence of specific movements under conditions in which the deprivation is known to be developing. This too is a difficult task, partly because of the lack of adequate measures of psychosocial deprivation. Those that we do have are expensive and difficult to use on so large a scale as a whole society. In addition, prediction is difficult because we cannot easily find a sufficient number of cases involving the same deprivation, in order to test its general role in stimulating social movements. All this is quite apart from the problems which stem from the role of independent political, economic, or psychological forces, which may suppress the development of a social movement despite marked deprivations. Further difficulties inhere in the fact that deprivation of the same need may lead in different times and cultures, to quite diverse responses, not all of them easily recognizable as "social movements." [79]

---

[79] Inkeles, "Personality and Social Structure," p. 259.

The anthropologist Anthony Wallace has also attempted to frame a personality theory for explaining the emergence of social movements—in this case, a particular kind that he calls "revitalization movements" or "a conscious, organized effort by members of a society to construct a more satisfying culture" [80] (e.g., ghost dance, cargo cults, Handsome Lake movement). In its logical structure Wallace's theory is somewhat similar to Fromm's. However, Wallace appears to take his inspiration not from Freud but from stress psychology and theories of cognitive dissonance.

Wallace begins by positing what he calls "the principle of maximal organization;" that is, he assumes a specific, basic, and universal human need to order and organize experiences in some meaningful fashion. The psychic mechanism involved in this ordering process is what Wallace calls the "mazeway." The mazeway seems to be a kind of cognitive map by means of which individuals look at the world and are provided with a guide for finding their way about in their social and natural universe.

Under conditions of rapid culture change or intensive culture contact, Wallace tells us, the traditional institutional structure of a society tends to break down. At the psychological level there is a concomitant breakdown of the mazeway. Under the dramatically altered circumstances the old mazeway can no longer provide an adequate guide to social reality. The cognitive dissonance produced by this breakdown of the mazeway is a stressful situation for the individuals in the society, and they will strive to reorder their experiences into some more meaningful whole. This drive to reorder experiences will translate itself, at the cultural level, into a revitalization movement the purpose of which is to make sense out of what has become to the members of the society a disjointed and senseless world. The end result of successful revitalization is a resynthesis of the mazeway.

In evaluating Wallace's revitalization theory it is important to keep clearly in mind the distinction between the kind of information his schema is capable of conveying and the kind it cannot convey. His theory, for example, cannot tell us anything about the specific organizational form a particular movement may take or about its specific goals (e.g., why the arrival of "cargo" in one case and the return of the ancestral dead in another?), or whether the movements do in fact yield a more satisfying culture or one which may be even less satisfying than the culture that existed prior to the launching of the movement. Information of this kind, it seems to us, can be provided better by explanations rooted in or derived from a sociocultural framework.

What Wallace's theory does tell us is something about the psychological functions of such movements as well as the *general* psychological conditions which may serve to trigger the movements. (Note the formal resemblance of Wallace's theory to the ideological-psychological explanation of religious beliefs advanced by Spiro and discussed in the preceding section.)

Mazeway breakdown and resynthesis may be a *necessary* rather than a *sufficient* condition for the occurrence of a revitalization movement. It can-

---

[80] Anthony F. Wallace, *Culture and Personality* (New York: Random House, 1961), p. 125; chap. 4. See also Wallace's *Religion: An Anthropological View* (New York: Random House, 1966), pp. 30, 157–66.

not be a *sufficient* condition because, as we well know, not all situations of intensive culture contact have produced revitalization movements. In order to *confirm* the theory one would have to show that, wherever revitalization movements have occurred, they have been preceded by mazeway disintegration, and that *through the instrumentality of the movement* a resynthesis of the mazeway has taken place. Presumably, in those cases where the necessary sociocultural conditions conducive to the emergence of the movement are present, and where no movement takes place, we shall have to look for other possible explanations. Is it, perhaps, that the situation has not been stressful enough to produce mazeway breakdown? Could it be that other sociopolitical factors have intruded themselves and stifled, sidetracked, or been substituted for such movements? Or is it possible that there may be a variety of potential responses to a breakdown in the mazeway such as, perhaps, internecine warfare, mass migration, or complete withdrawal into the past?

The key problem in Wallace's theory, however, is finding evidence for mazeway breakdown and resynthesis *independent* of the fact that a revitalization movement has taken place. For if we cannot do this, then the explanation clearly becomes ad hoc—that is, it "accounts for" (postulates an empirically unverified link to the revitalization movement) but does not "explain" the phenomenon (show by means of independent evidence how the movement and the mazeway breakdown are linked).

Wallace's theory might be compared formally with a theory which explained human behavior by postulating the existence within each of us of a homunculus—the logical equivalent of Wallace's mazeway. Any observed behavior might then be explained by attributing the appropriate characteristics to each person's homunculus. The homunculus theory is, of course, a specious theory, since we have no independent evidence pointing to the existence of homunculi.

Where psychological theories of cultural phenomena contain reference to such essentially hidden, nonobservable entities and processes as, for example, mazeway, the unconscious, logicoesthetic integration, ego, etc., one is bound to encounter serious methodological problems in the validation of such theories. For unless one can marshal empirical evidence in support of the existence of such postulated entities—evidence which is independent of the behavior from which the entities are constructed in the first place—one's explanations will remain ad hoc and tautological in nature.

Wallace's work, it should be noted, represents a kind of bridge between what he himself has called the "old" and the "new" culture-personality studies. We turn now to some of the newer emphases that have emerged within this theoretical camp in the last decade or so. Two of these seem to us especially noteworthy. The first represents a shift away from a heavy reliance on Freudian psychology, with its emphasis on the affective and irrational side of personality, to a theoretical framework that stresses the cognitive aspects of human personality. The second represents a renewed interest—apparently stimulated by the recent work in ethology or animal behavior—in the relationship between the psychological nature of man and various universal features of culture.

Cognition. While the stimulus for a growing interest in cognitive anthropology has come in part from linguistics, it is clear that this interest has also, and to a significant degree, followed from the more general concern with psychological anthropology and, more broadly, the interest in mind itself. Consequently, we find it appropriate to deal with certain aspects of cognition in the present section on personality and to reserve treatment of cognition and formal analysis as a program for ethnographic description for Chapter 4.

The essential aim of cognitive anthropology is to get at the conceptual apparatus by which a people classifies, orders, and interprets its social and natural universe. The cognitionists also see the study of native models and cognitions as a device or methodology for yielding an ethnographic research product which is more true to *native* reality. They claim that such accounts are likely to be more reliable and replicable than accounts which derive from the individual investigator's accumulated cognitions as an anthropologist and a product of a culture other than the one he is examining.

We are concerned here with the cognitivists' view of culture and with some of the major theoretical assumptions which underlie their methodology and provide its rationale. Since certain of their assumptions are matters of some contention in anthropology, it seems clear to us that they ought to be considered in any discussion that deals with personality variables and their impact on culture.

First, like the earlier researchers in modal personality, the cognitive theoreticians are more concerned with group cognition than they are with the phenomena of individual cognition. Thus, Roy D'Andrade and A. Kimball Romney define the difference between the interests of the cognitive anthropologist and the cognitive psychologist in this way:

> We believe that the anthropologist focuses upon the study of learned codes shared by groups of individuals, while the psychologist focuses upon the intellective processes of the individuals. . . . The relationship between the codes an individual learns and the intellective processes of the individual is apparently quite complex. Such processes as categorization and inferences, for example, appear to be built into codes, providing the individual with a ready-made set of categories and inferences for use. However, to allow the individual to use these cognitive maps which are built into codes also demands the exercise of other complex intellective processes.[81]

In an introductory essay to a relatively recent collection of readings in cognitive anthropology, Stephen Tyler sees the focus of the field in a slightly different way:

---

[81] Roy G. D'Andrade and A. Kimball Romney, "Summary of Participants' Discussion," in *American Anthropologist* 66, no. 3, pt. 2 (Transcultural Studies in Cognition, 1964): 230–31.

Cognitive anthropology constitutes a new theoretical orientation. It focuses on *discovering* how different peoples organize and use their cultures. This is not so much a search for some generalized unit of behavioral analysis as it is an attempt to understand the *organizing principles underlying* behavior. It is assumed that each people has a unique system for perceiving and organizing material phenomena—things, events, behavior, and emotions. The object of study is not these material phenomena themselves, but the way they are organized in the minds of men.[82]

Thus, the cognitive anthropologists begin by assuming that each society has a cognitive code or set of cognitive codes (or principles) which cover all cultural domains and characterize the society. They then go on to inquire into the nature of these codes. But we wonder whether it is realistic to assume that all members of a society—or even the members of its various subgroups—can be characterized in terms of a uniform and distinctive cognitive code. Like the existence of a modal personality, the existence of a uniform cognitive code is a claim that ought to be open to empirical demonstration. If we conceive of these codes or principles as essentially psychic phenomena ("in the minds of men") which may vary from individual to individual, we may reasonably expect the investigators to make use of psychological instruments and statistical sampling techniques in order to get at the psychological complexities. Yet, with a very few notable exceptions (e.g., Romney and D'Andrade [83]), most cognitive anthropologists have not utilized these techniques for getting at a culture's cognitive codes, an omission that prompted Marvin Harris to characterize much of their work as "social psychology shorn of its statistical base." [84]

In a discussion of the psychic unity of human groups, Anthony Wallace, himself a distinguished cognitive theoretician, asks whether cognitive sharing is a functional prerequisite of society—and answers that it is not:

> Evidently, groups, as well as individuals, can integrate their behavior into reliable systems by means of equivalence structures, without extensive motivational or cognitive sharing. The equivalence structure model would be congenial to that tradition in social anthropology which interests itself in the relations between organized groups. Thus, reciprocal interactions between the representatives of geographically separate groups as alien as American Indian tribes and colonial or state governments have proceeded for centuries, with only minimal sharing of motives or understanding, on a basis of carefully patterned equivalences. Similar observation might be made of relations between castes, social classes, professional groups, kin groups, factions, parties, and so forth. In no case is it *necessary* that a basic personality or a basic cognitive framework be shared, but it is necessary that behaviors be mutually predictable and equivalent.[85]

---

[82] Stephen Tyler, "Introduction," in *Cognitive Anthropology*, ed. S. A. Tyler (New York: Holt, Rinehart and Winston, 1969), p. 3.

[83] See A. K. Romney and R. G. D'Andrade, "Cognitive Aspects of English Kin Terms," in *American Anthropologist* 66, no. 3, pt. 2 (Transcultural Studies in Cognition, 1964): 146–70.

[84] Harris, *The Rise of Anthropological Theory*, p. 585.

[85] Wallace, *Culture and Personality*, pp. 40–41.

Wallace also proposes that

> human societies may characteristically *require* the non-sharing of certain cognitive maps among participants in a variety of institutional arrangements. Many a social sub-system simply will not "work" if all participants share common knowledge of the system. It would seem, therefore, that cognitive *non-uniformity* may be a functional desideratum of society. . . . For cognitive non-uniformity subserves two important functions: (1) it permits a more complex system to arise than most, or any, of its participants can comprehend; (2) it liberates the participants in a system from the heavy burden of knowing each other's motivations.[86]

If one finds this argument persuasive—and in the main we do—then, at the very least, it clearly raises questions about the assumption that each domain of a culture can be characterized in terms of a uniform cognitive code.

Wallace is not the only theoretician to call attention to the cognitive variability that may exist in any culture or any domain of a culture. Thus, Tyler writes:

> It is highly unlikely that the members of a culture ever see their culture as *this kind* of unitary phenomenon. Each individual member may have a unique, unitary model of his culture, but is not necessarily cognizant of all the unique unitary models held by other members of his culture. He will be aware of and use some, but it is only the anthropologist who completely transcends these particular models and constructs a single, unitary model. This cognitive organization exists solely in the mind of the anthropologist. Yet, to the extent that it will generate conceptual models used by the people of a particular culture, it is a model of their cognitive systems.[87]

The first thing that strikes us about this statement is that the perceptual uniqueness that Tyler, in the quotation earlier, attributed to the group ("each people has a unique system for perceiving and organizing material phenomena") he here extends to the individual. Not only does the group share some kind of hypothetical cognitive code or codes, but each individual within the group has his own idiosyncratic collection of cognitive codes— all of which may be so.

If we understand Tyler correctly, he is suggesting that the investigator must begin by eliciting the cognitive code (for a single cultural domain) or codes (for more than one domain) of each individual or, perhaps at the very least, a broad but representative sample of all individuals in the group. He must do this, first, in order to exhaust or encompass all or most of the cognitive variability that may exist within the group. Having completed this task, he moves on by some as-yet unspecified process of induction, abstraction, and/or synthesis to derive or construct a super or "single unitary model" which now "exists solely in the mind of the anthropologist." Finally,

---

[86] Ibid., pp. 39–40.
[87] Tyler, "Introduction," p. 5.

this hypothetical construct (built out of other hypothetical code constructs) in the mind of the beholder becomes "a model of [the people's] cognitive system" which now has the (unexplained) power or capacity to generate "conceptual models used by the people."

When we turn to some of the empirical work of cognitive anthropologists, the relationship between the "unitary model" and the models actually employed by different individuals remains unclear. Nor is it easy to understand how the unitary model might be capable of generating individual models. Charles O. Frake, for example, has constructed and analyzed the folk categories or taxonomic system of human disease used by the Subanun (a people living on Mindanao in the Philippines) for diagnosing various human illnesses.[88] Frake writes: "Diagnosis—the decision of what 'name' to apply to an instance of 'being sick'—is a pivotal cognitive step in the selection of culturally appropriate responses to illness by the Subanun." [89]

The Subanun appear to have 186 named human disease categories; Frake's analysis focuses primarily on a skin disease called *nuka* or "eruption" and its variants. At the most general classificatory level, *nuka* contrasts with "wounds." But *nuka* itself may be subcategorized further into "inflammation," "sore," or "ringworm." Sores are further broken down into "distal ulcer" or "proximal ulcer," which, in turn, may either be "deep" or "shallow." Frake writes:

> Conceptually the disease world, like the plant world, exhaustively divides into a set of mutually exclusive categories. Ideally every illness either fits into one category or is describable as a conjunction of several categories. Subanun may debate, or not know [sic], the placement of a particular case, but to their minds that reflects a deficiency in their individual knowledge, not a deficiency in the classificatory system.[90]

If it is true that disagreements about identifying a particular malady do indeed arise from time to time, this could mean, as Frake seems to imply, that the distinguishing symptoms may sometimes be so subtle as to engender conflict about identification. Thus, differences in knowledge or diagnostic skills would be significant factors in placing the affliction in the proper classificatory box. On the other hand, such disagreement could also mean that the categories *within the taxonomic system itself* are so flexible or vague as to represent something less precise than Frake implies.

But—to return, and relate all of this, to Tyler's programmatic statement—what remains obscure in Frake's discussion is the relationship between his taxonomic system—apparently a composite drawn from an unspecified number of informants—and the conceptual models of disease used by any single individual or group of individuals in Subanun society. Quite clearly, if Subanun "may debate, or not know, the placement of a particular case . . ."

---

[88] See Charles O. Frake, "The Diagnosis of Disease among the Subanun of Mindinao," *American Anthropologist* 63 (1961): 113–32.

[89] Ibid., 131.

[90] Ibid.

the system may not be shared by *all* the Subanun. The important questions remaining, then, are: Is the classificatory system constructed by Frake anything more than a heuristic device—i.e., does it have any cognitive reality outside Frake's own mind? and, secondly, How can Frake's scheme be made to generate the individual conceptual models used by one or another Subanun?

Language and Cognitive Codes. A further assumption underlying much of the work in cognitive anthropology is that cognitive categories are to a large degree encoded in the linguistic structures and distinctions used by a people.[91] Thus, it is believed that investigating the linguistic designations and classifications contained in such cultural domains as disease, colors, kinship, botany, etc., will provide us with an unambiguous route into the cognitive categories employed by the members of a society in ordering and perhaps even in thinking about these domains. Yet, as numerous writers have pointed out, language may be a far from reliable guide to the cognitive thought patterns of the users of that language. For, in the first place, as Harris notes, there is a great deal of functional and ineradicable ambiguity built into all ordinary speech, as well as into more specialized forms of communication such as poetry, art, literary criticism, and the like.[92]

Harris goes on to challenge much of the work on cognition for treating these ambiguities as though they were marginal and not relevant to the analyses. This gives their work what Robbins Burling has called a "spurious precision." Burling refers to the "indeterminancy" of the classifications supposedly contained in ordinary linguistic usage. Thus, he is critical of cognitive anthropology for its "unjustified certainty":

> It is my feeling that the analyses of terms into hierarchical taxonomies that have lately been discussed have rather glossed over the problems of indeterminacy. . . . I am not at all certain, for instance, that "flower" and "bush" are really coordinate to "tree." Perhaps on the basis of size English speakers distinguish "trees" from "bushes," and "bushes" from "plants" (homonymous but not synonymous with "plants" used as a general cover term for the entire set), and then on the basis of use, divide "plants" into "flowers," "vegetables," and "weeds." What about "cedars?" Are they "needled trees?" Not really, of course, but they are not "leafy trees" either. Should "balsam," "hemlock" and "spruce" be classed together as "short needled trees" (Christmas trees) as opposed to "pines?" Or should they all have equivalent taxonomic status? What is

---

[91] See, however, B. Berlin, D. E. Breedlove, and P. H. Raven, "Covert Categories and Folk Taxonomies," *American Anthropologist* 70 (1968): 290–99. The authors point out that not all the folk categories employed by a people need be encoded in language. In this connection they quote Roger Keesing: "If we insist that the descriptive units of an ethnography be lexically labelled, we are likely to arrive at a very limited sort of description: an ethnography of how people talk about what they do, not what they do or expect to do. . . . There is ample evidence that expectations and distinctions need not be directly mapped in language."

Berlin, Breedlove, and Raven then comment: "In questioning the utility of restricting ethnographic description to labelled categories, Keesing has pointed the way toward a reexamination of *one of the most fundamental assumptions of ethnoscience* [emphasis added]" (290).

[92] Harris, *The Rise of Anthropological Theory*, p. 583.

the essential "cognitive" difference between hemlock and spruce? Is it gross size, type of needle, form of bark, or what? I do not know how to answer these questions, but they are the types of questions which must be answered before any single semantic analysis can claim to represent the cognitive organization of the people, or even claim to be much more than an exercise of the analyst's imagination.[93]

Ever since the early writings of Edward Sapir and, more especially, the more precise studies of Benjamin Whorf, anthropologists have been intrigued by the parallels and the possible relationship between the structure of language and the structure of cognitive thought.[94] But, despite their interest and their efforts, they have not yet succeeded in expressing the relationship in a nontautological form—in a form that would allow the issue to be examined empirically. In this sense, then, the relationship remains elusive— and that there is a relationship at all continues to be an article of faith rather than an empirically verifiable fact. Nevertheless, many cognitive anthropologists continue to work with a kind of Whorfian view of the relationship between language and cognition, i.e., with the assumption that language somehow embodies thought.

On the other hand, there are linguists and anthropologists who hold a somewhat different view of language, who believe that language is essentially a social instrument. In their view, language is a form of social behavior that is

> meant to influence the listener. Its organization is the product of social intercourse. The interpretation of the linguistic categories does not require us to assume that a similar organization exists within our thoughts. On the contrary, we are often aware of the discrepancy between meaning and thought. . . . Language obeys its own rules, and it would not be safe to infer anything about our minds from these linguistic rules only. Language cannot be considered the embodiment of thought.[95]

If language be seen as a social instrument, then learning to use this instrument does not necessarily commit us to the impossible task of internalizing all of its categories, distinctions, and metaphysical assumptions. Thus, the cognitive categories that an individual has internalized—or has "failed" to internalize—cannot be determined on linguistic grounds alone. Nor can linguistic usage tell us anything about the categories he is *capable* of using. As a matter of fact, anthropologists, scientists, and even poets and the members of minority subcultures like the hippies are almost continually

---

[93] Robbins Burling, "Cognition and Componential Analysis: God's Truth or Hocus-Pocus?," *American Anthropologist* 66 (1964): 25–26.

[94] See Joshua A. Fishman, "A Systematization of the Whorfian Hypothesis," in *Approaches, Contexts and Problems of Social Psychology*, ed. Edward E. Sampson (Englewood Cliffs, N.J.: Prentice-Hall, 1964), pp. 27–43; and Ian D. Currie, "The Sapir-Whorf Hypothesis: A Problem in the Sociology of Knowledge," *Berkeley Journal of Sociology* II (1966): 14–31.

[95] Eric Buyssens, "Thinking and Speaking From the Linguistic Standpoint," in *Thinking and Speaking*, ed. Géza Révész (Amsterdam: North-Holland Publishing Company, 1954), pp. 153, 164.

involved with the formulation of "new" verbal categories and distinctions that are designed for "new" purposes and may, therefore, be very different from the distinctions and purposes given them by some kind of consensus in the parent culture. In other words, neologisms, jargon, and similar linguistic fabrications provide evidence that while the categories contained in a particular language may influence one's thought processes, they do not entirely constrain or stultify them. The noun (thing) orientation of English, as Whorf has pointed out, may have led us at one time to think of, say, combustion as a *thing* (the phlogistin theory) rather than as a process; but eventually, we did come around to thinking of it as a process.

Moreover, it should be noted, the use of language as a social instrument will often vary with the social context.[96] For example, in discussing shrubs and trees with a botanist we would be likely to make certain cognitive distinctions that we would not make in talking with a nonprofessional adult. And in talking about the same things with a child we would probably make—or avoid making—still other distinctions. Which of these, then, is our "real" cognitive code? And, as the earlier quotations from Burling and Wallace suggest, we *do* generally manage to communicate or get along in many cultural domains despite the fact that our verbal distinctions may be imprecise, vague, or ambiguous.

Finally, most cognitive anthropologists assume that knowledge of a culture's cognitive categories will help us to understand (explain?) why people behave as they do in different social situations, and, by extension, why the society's institutional arrangements are what they are. In other words, if we accept the analytic assumptions of these cognitionists, we come back to the blueprint theory of society. But this time the blueprint is phrased in terms of cognitive categories and rules rather than in terms of values, norms, and ideas.

Despite our expressed reservations about some of the cognitivists' claims, we believe that cultural descriptions and/or explanations phrased in cognitive terms—like those expressed in norms—do have a certain value and importance. Such descriptions, for example, can tell us how people *ought* to behave, can tell us what is *appropriate* in this or that social situation, even while they cannot insure that the individual members of the society *will* behave "appropriately" or as they "ought" to behave. Tyler writes:

> There is no necessity to assume that the cognitive order is either systematically a derivative of or a predicator of substantive actions. Just as the grammar of a language provides no information on what an individual speaker will say on any given occasion, so too a cognitive description of a culture does not pretend to predict the actual behavior of any individual. The formal analysis of culture, like grammar, is concerned only with what is expected and appropriate.[97]

Thus, if grammatical rules and cognitive descriptions cannot tell us any-

---

[96] Stephen Tyler writes: "I know of no formal analysis that has dealt adequately with the problem of variation." "Context and Variation in Koya Kinship Terminology," in *Cognitive Anthropology*, ed. Tyler, p. 488.

[97] Tyler, "Introduction," p. 13.

thing about the content of a people's speech and action, they can at least tell us something about the structure within which those people say or do things. On the other hand, the relationship between cognitive rules and nonverbal behavior may be even more tenuous than the relationship between grammar and speech, since all behavior is not cognitive behavior. A great deal of human behavior may be simply habitual—i.e., it may follow well-worn institutional or psychic grooves. As Muriel Hammer notes:

> If my informant sorts a series of items in such a way that all the yellow objects (triangular and circular) are in one group, and all the blue objects (triangular and square) are in another, and he tells me he is sorting on the basis of shape, he may, of course, be joking, lying or stupid, or he may be rationalizing (poorly) a set of behaviors whose abstract logical principles he never learned, does not consciously use, and does not really know. The example above may be too simple to be believable, but anyone who has ever tried to give road map directions to a place he gets to with ease, or explain the construction of plural nouns to a child, or the basis of recognizing as Elizabethan a particular piece of music he has not heard before will realize that people can often "sort" reliably without having information on their sorting principles. Far worse, they may readily give information on principles they are simply not using. Verplanck summarizes relevant experimental work on this question, indicating that subjects' statements of the rules they were using and the sortings they actually made, could be experimentally controlled *essentially independent of each other.* If I want to know how he will talk about his rules for sorting, I need to study that; but if I want to know how he will sort, I had better not study his stated rules.[98]

If there is no neat correspondence between behavior and cognitive rules (because all of our behavior is not cognitive in nature), the correspondences may be further impaired because much of our behavior is simply adaptive. And while adaptation may involve behaving in terms of the cognitive rules of the society, it may also involve manipulating or completely disregarding the rules. The situations with which one has to cope—especially new situations—are not simply a matter of how these situations are cognitively viewed and defined by the individual facing them. All situations also have a logic of their own which may be independent of the observer's or participant's conceptualization of them. Thus, people will generally adapt to "the logic of the situation" regardless of the cognitive rules they may originally have brought to it. And we might add here that this is probably one of the important ways in which cognitions get modified or changed.

The Psychobiological Constant. Anthropologists have always recognized the general relationship between man as a biological animal and the nature of his culture. As White has put it, if man did not have stereoscopic vision; if he had rutting seasons; if he gave birth to his young in litters; if he were

---

[98] Muriel Hammer, "Some Comments on Formal Analysis of Grammatical and Semantic Systems," in *Theory in Anthropology,* ed. Robert A. Manners and David Kaplan (Chicago, Ill.: Aldine, 1968), p. 529.

ten feet or ten inches tall; etc.—then in certain dramatic respects his culture would be different. But since he does have stereoscopic vision, no rutting season, etc., etc., there are certain general and recurring features of culture, often rooted in or at least in part limited by man's psychobiological nature, which manifest themselves in the midst of all the striking cultural diversity of mankind. A number of anthropologists have even attempted to compile lists of universal cultural characteristics. One of the earliest of these was Clark Wissler's delineation of what he called the "universal culture pattern." More recently Malinowski and Kluckhohn have drawn up similar schema, Malinowski focusing on institutional universals and Kluckhohn examining "universal values." Presumably such cultural universals reflect in some sense the uniform psychobiological nature of man. But the search for cultural universals has invariably yielded generalizations of a very broad, and sometimes not particularly illuminating nature—such as, all cultures prefer health to illness; or, all cultures make some institutional provision for feeding their members; or, all cultures have devices for maintaining internal order.

But to say, for example, that every culture makes some institutional provision for feeding its members does not help us to understand the wide variations in the way this is done. Much of anthropology, therefore, has been concerned with documenting the enormous *differences* that occur within the "universal culture pattern" and, by implication, with demonstrating the species' "incredible" maleability. When most anthropologists have tried to explain specific institutions and specific cultural differences, they have tended to treat man's biological makeup as a constant. Since it is impossible to explain a variable by a constant, they have felt justified in disregarding the biological factor. The reasons for this approach were ideological as well as scientific. On the "straight-scientific" side, there is no convincing evidence for significant psychobiological change within the species in historic times; nor is there persuasive evidence for such differences among contemporary populations of the world. The ideological-*cum*-scientific side has to do with the sensitivity of most anthropologists to the race issue. Because there is no evidence for innate differences in racial endowment, they tend to view biological explanations of cultural variations as racist, open or disguised; and from here it is only a short but logical "ideological step" to shunning research in the area of biological determinants of cultural differences.

In recent years, however, there has been a revived anthropological interest—generally minus any racial implications or overtones—in the biological basis of all human behavior and culture. In a discussion of the "old" and "new" culture-personality theories, Anthony Wallace notes that some of the "new" theorists have challenged the assumption that biological factors can be considered a constant in explanations of behavioral differences. He writes:

> The observations of ethologists, the recent discoveries in biological psychiatry, and the increasing attention to physiological process in the new physical anthropology have conspired to make highly questionable the assumption that biological factors in behavior are for all practical purposes constants. Biological determinants of behavior—working *via*

disease, nutrition, exposure to sunlight, etc. as well as *via* constitutional factors—are now to be regarded as significant variables for both the group and the individual.[99]

Since Wallace is not more specific, it is impossible to know, for example, which "recent discoveries" in biological psychiatry he has in mind, or precisely which biological determinants are to be considered significant variables in explaining group and individual behavior. For while such phenomena as disease, nutrition, and exposure to sunlight may indeed have an impact upon culture, it is clear that the importance of their impact is largely a function of cultural determinants rather than of biological ones.

Other investigators, taking a different tack, do not question the existence of a biological constant; rather, they have reasserted its crucial importance, insisting that the balance which has swung so far toward *nurture* must now be redirected to indicate the significance of man's primate and mammalian heritage and *nature*. These writers seem to be saying that when we look at variations in cultural performance, we find that often these are simply variations on certain common cultural themes and that these themes (e.g., territoriality, aggression, gregariousness, male-bonding, sexual antagonisms, etc.), in turn, reflect the psychobiological nature of man. Thus, they maintain that the biological constant (because or although it *is* a constant!) can never be disregarded.

Curiously enough, this newly awakened interest in the nature of man and the renewed emphasis on the biological basis of culture has come not so much from any new revelations about the psychobiological nature of man himself. Rather, it seems to have been inspired by the growing corpus of research in infrahuman animal behavior that has been accumulating over the past few decades. After all, we are reminded, man's anatomical structure and his physiology testify to his mammalian and primate background. It is reasonable, therefore, these researchers argue, to draw conclusions about the psychobiological nature of man by inference from observations of mammalian and primate social behavior.

It is precisely here that the rub comes in. A comparison between certain limited aspects of primate social behavior, for example, and a reconstructed picture of early human society (based on ethnographies of contemporary hunters and gatherers) does suggest certain continuities. But the same comparison also reveals striking discontinuities. This raises certain crucial questions concerning the legitimacy of drawing inferences about the nature of man from the behavior of infrahuman animals. For example, if we identify a particular behavioral trait in some mammalian society which seems to resemble a trait found in man, can we assume that we are really talking about the same phenomenon? And, further, can we assume that the causative factors operating in each case are the same? We note, for example, that certain birds and mammals forage or hunt in a given territory and often appear to defend it against encroachment by outsiders of their own or another species. We then note that human hunting-and-gathering societies

---

[99] Anthony Wallace, "The New Culture-And-Personality," in *Anthropology and Human Behavior*, ed. Thomas Gladwin and William C. Sturtevant (Washington, D.C.: Anthropological Society of Washington, 1962), p. 8.

also occupy a given territory and may also resist encroachment by other groups of hunters and gatherers. Or we observe that societies are organized into territorial states and often go to great lengths to defend the political integrity of their borders. By applying the same label (e.g., "territorial imperative") to all these phenomena, are we not obscuring what may be important differences among them, both in terms of their nature as well as the causation operating in each case?

As another example, consider the concept of aggression, about which so much has been written lately. We observe that two male deer will engage in combat over a mate or in competition for food. We label this behavior "aggressive" and its determinants are clear. Now take an Ifugao of the Philippines, who shows his manhood by taking a head from some unfortunate member of a neighboring tribe. This may also be called aggressive behavior. But how much of this behavior is biologically determined, and how much of it is learned as being culturally appropriate? To carry the argument one step further: modern warfare is also called aggressive behavior. But when a soldier sits in a Pentagon office shuffling papers, is he acting aggressively? Or when President Nixon calmly orders several hundred bombers to drop thousands of tons of explosives on Cambodia or Laos, is he also acting aggressively? To what extent are these latter behaviors similar to those of the deer or of the head-hunting Ifugao? And to what extent are the determinants of these several behaviors the same or even similar? Until and unless such extremely sticky conceptual difficulties are clarified, any inferences from animal to human behavior, however suggestive, must remain inconclusive and highly debatable.[100]

Within recent years the biological-roots-of-human-behavior theme has reached a wide and receptive public audience through the popular, semipopular, and often vivid works of such writers as the ethologist Konrad Lorenz (*On Aggression*), the zoologist Desmond Morris (*The Naked Ape* and *The Human Zoo*), and the Hollywood scenarist and amateur anthropologist Robert Ardrey (*African Genesis*, *The Territorial Imperative*, and *The Social Contract*). While these works have come in for a great deal of criticism from scholars and journalists alike—both for their conceptual fuzziness (e.g., what is aggression?) and for the tendency of their authors to make facile leaps from animal behavior to human behavior [101]—they have had a strong public impact. And, if we are to judge from a comment by

---

100 The ethologist J. P. Scott has remarked in this connection: "There are two conclusions that can be reached from our current information regarding agonistic behavior in other animals. One is that we cannot justify the existence of human warfare on the basis of a general evolutionary tendency, because there is no evidence that such a tendency exists. Rather, agonistic behavior has evolved in a great variety of ways, related in each case to the social organization typical of the species. The second conclusion is that if we are to understand human behavior from the biological viewpoint, we must study human beings as human beings and not try to derive all our information from distantly related, animals" ["Biological Basis of Human Warfare: An Interdisciplinary Problem," in *Interdisciplinary Relationships in the Social Sciences*, ed. M. Sherif and C. W. Sherif (Chicago: Aldine, 1969), pp. 128–29].

101 See, for example, the collection of critical articles and reviews on Lorenz and Ardrey in *Man and Aggression*, ed. M. F. Ashley Montagu (New York: Oxford University Press, 1968). Also Hilary Callan, *Ethology and Society: Towards an Anthropological View* (Oxford: Clarendon Press, 1970).

Cyrus Sulzberger, Editor of the *New York Times* (October 14, 1968), it may be anthropology rather than ethology, zoology, or Hollywood that is associated in the mind of the public with these latest and startling "discoveries" about the nature and behavior of the human animal. Sulzberger writes: "Modern anthropology teaches that nationalism and imperialism are deeply rooted in our animal pasts, and, perhaps like our own, the foreign policy of the Kremlin may sometimes derive from remote instincts first noted among wolves, horned owls or lions patrolling their preserves for sustenance."

A small but increasing number of anthropologists has also joined in the search for the animal roots of human behavior.[102] Although they have generally been more circumspect in their extrapolations from animal to human behavior than have the aforementioned writers, the logic of their arguments and their conclusions are often pretty much on a par with those of Lorenz, Morris, Ardrey, and company.

Robin Fox, for example, in an essay entitled "The Cultural Animal," [103] asserts that anthropologists have been "suffering from ethnographic dazzle" [104]—that is, they have allowed the vast array of often trivial differences among cultures to fog their vision, making it difficult to discern the universal similarities beneath these differences:

> All human cultures have some kind of courtship ceremonies, and when you look at them they look very much alike despite the different cultural trappings. If all you want to explain is why in America girls wear their dates' fraternity pins while in Fiji they put hibiscus flowers behind their ears, then that is fine. But (a) it doesn't seem worth explaining, and (b) there probably is no "explanation" in any scientific sense—it is just what they do. These are simply ways of getting the same courting job done, and the interesting thing to me is the universality of various similar symbolic devices.[105]

In contrast to the more general anthropological view of man as a highly malleable animal whose behavior varies with the cultural setting, Fox tells us that

> once one gets behind the surface manifestations, the uniformity of human behavior and of human social arrangements is remarkable. . . . Much of our behavior and in particular our social arrangements can be seen as a variation on common primate and gregarious mammalian themes.[106]

Here the key words "a variation" are made to carry an inexcusable and logically indefensible load. It is one thing to say, for example, that the variations that distinguish one earthworm from another are not nearly so

---

[102] For example, Lionel Tiger and Robin Fox, "The Zoological Perspective in Social Science," *Man* 1 (1966): 75–81; Derek Freeman, "Social Anthropology and the Scientific Study of Human Behavior," *Man* 1 (1966): 330–42; and Lionel Tiger, *Men in Groups* (New York: Random House, 1969).

[103] Robin Fox, "The Cultural Animal," *Social Science Information* 9 (1970): 7–25.

[104] Ibid., 12.

[105] Ibid., 11.

[106] Ibid., 12, 22.

typologically significant as their similarities. But it is quite another thing, again for example, to assert that locating, wounding, and stalking a giraffe for two or three days in the Kalahari Desert is just "a variation" on buying a frozen rib roast in the nearest supermarket. In these terms, the argument has about the same logical force as asserting that because all animals must eat to live, there is no difference between a robin and a chimpanzee; or that because the circulatory system of all living animals requires oxygen for its maintenance, there is therefore no difference between a manatee and a man.

What is at issue here are radically different models of man. Anthropologists have traditionally worked from the point of view that man is a cultural animal who has some residue of primate and other mammalian traits. Whatever the biological capacities that underlie cultural systems, they are *general* capacities. What Fox (and some other ethologically and biologically oriented anthropologists) seem to be claiming is that this residue of primate and mammalian traits is much larger and more significant than the traditional anthropological view implies. Moreover, they suggest that man is programmed, genetically committed to certain actions and responses, many of which leave little or no room for altering or improving the human condition, in any but the most minimal details. As Fox remarks:

> What I am trying to say is that the human organism is like a computer which is set up or "wired" in a particular way. . . . Our secular societal ideology . . . says: when in trouble, change the program because we can write any program we want to. What we should say is: when in trouble, find out what is in the wiring, because only then will we know what programs we can safely write. . . . We are not simply the *producers* of institutions like the family, science, language, religion, warfare, kinship systems and exogamy; we are the *product* of them. Hence it is scarcely surprising that we continually reproduce that which produced us. We were selected to do precisely this, and in the absence of tradition our mythical tribe would do it all over again in the same way. It is not only the *capacity* for culture that lies in the brain, it is the *forms* of culture, the universal grammar of language and behavior.[107]

How do we decide which of these differing emphases and models makes the most sense? Should we accept Fox's notion that the "wiring" is not only a *given* but that it is highly "constrictive" in determining the cultural responses open to man? Or should we adhere to the more traditional anthropological view that, on the one hand, accepts the existence of a biological wiring but, on the other, assumes that the wiring may be accommodated to a great variety of cultural inputs and that the organisms' responses (because they are *culturally conditioned responses*) will, in turn, determine the impact and the effects of future inputs?

Certain facts are essential to any appraisal of these contrasting views. Thus, for example, social arrangements in infrahuman animal populations are largely species-specific—that is, they tend to be "uniform" throughout

---

[107] Ibid., 16, 17, 21.

the species.[108] This suggests that such patterns are overwhelmingly a reflection of the biological structure of the species in question. But, as the ethnographic literature and common experience clearly show, social arrangements in *Homo sapiens* vary from population to population. And these variations, as we indicated earlier, may be of far greater import than whether—as in Fox's earlier example—girls wear their dates' fraternity pins in one culture and a hibiscus flower in another. There can be no gainsaying the assertion that of all animal species man displays by far the greatest plasticity of behavior. The limits of this intraspecific plasticity are, of course, an important issue and one that merits continued investigation. It is precisely with regard to the issue of plasticity vs. biological wiring that the views of the more traditional (the ethnographically dazzled) anthropologists and of the new biological determinists diverge.

If we are skeptical of Fox's model of man, it is because the model appears to be heuristically limited: it seems incapable of eliciting answers either to questions Fox himself raises or to those questions which we, along with many other anthropologists, believe are significant. For example, if all members of *Homo sapiens* are linguistically programmed in much the same way ("despite the enormous variety of 'surface grammar' . . . all [grammars] are doing the same job and are constrained to do it in a limited number of ways" [109]) we would want to ask, with George Steiner:

> Why this fantastic diversity of human tongues, making it difficult for communities, often geographically proximate and racially or culturally similar, to communicate? How can such exceeding variety have arisen if, as transformational grammar postulates and biology hints, the underlying grid, the neuro-physiological grooves, are common to all men and, indeed occasion their humanity? Why, as carriers of the same essential molecular information, do we not speak the same language or a small number of languages corresponding, say, to the small number of genuinely identifiable ethnic types? . . .

---

108 Uniformity and its obverse, variability, are concepts that are often difficult to pin down. Reading the works of a number of ethologists sometimes intensifies the confusion. Thus, for example, T. E. Rowell observes that "It is unlikely that we shall find variety of social organization in other primates to approach that of man . . . However, it should not be surprising to find the same *sort* of variability in the similar social organizations of related species" (emphasis in original). A little later on Rowell concludes his essay with the observation: "Only for one species, man, is the range of variability in social organization fairly well known, but it is suggested that *variability of the same order might reasonably be expected in other primates*" (emphasis added). "Variability in the Social Organization of Primates," in *Primate Ethology*, ed. Desmond Morris (Chicago: Aldine, 1967), pp. 232–33.

Now while a good deal of variability (or uniformity) may indeed exist in the eye of the beholder, we cannot possibly understand how the range of variability among *any* infra-human primates can match the variability in the social organization of Homo sapiens, with anything from the nuclear family to the factory; from age-grading to the modern military machine of a country like the United States; from the matrilineal clan to the Supreme Presidium of the Soviet Union or the United States Congress. Such comparisons might be good for a small chuckle, but they would make a mockery of scientific typologizing.

109 Fox, "The Cultural Animal," p. 14.

How "universal," in fact, are their invariants? And if linguistic universals are a simple, determined biological datum, why the immense number and consequent mutual incomprehensibility of local transformations? [110]

Or take supernatural beliefs. All cultures have a set or sets of beliefs and practices that relate man to the supernatural—or, more loosely, they have religion. According to Fox, this religion has become a part of the "wiring" of *Homo sapiens*. If this is so, how may we explain the fact that in Western industrialized societies there has been a steady erosion of supernatural beliefs over the past several hundred years? If the response is that other *kinds* of religious beliefs have sprung up, then one can only wonder whether the respondent is simply playing with words.

Finally, when we compare the mechanized, urbanized, electronically enmeshed cultural arrangements of certain modern Western societies with the hunting-and-gathering complex of, say, the Australian aborigines, are we talking about institutional and behavior patterns which are *at bottom* similar in form and which lie "in the brain"? What can such a claim possibly mean?

Nevertheless, and despite the foregoing reservations, we do not deny the legitimacy and the possible fruitfulness of exploring the biological basis of culture and of man's behavior. In reacting against the racial explanations of a bygone era, anthropologists may have overstated the case for the human animal's inherent malleability. But if we are ever to arrive at a more precise definition of the limits of that malleability, it seems to us a sounder procedure to look *directly* at man rather than to see him reflected through the overwhelmingly cultureless and distorted mirror of infrahuman social behavior. Even so, as the entire history of social science affirms, trying to separate what is nature from what is nurture in man is a more formidable task than many of the ethologically oriented anthropologists and nonanthropologists would often have us believe.

We conclude this discussion on the biological roots or sources of human cultural behavior and institutions with a somewhat lengthy but most illuminating quotation from S. A. Barnett:

> Just as property holding and social status in man differ fundamentally from territory and systems of dominance, respectively, so does war differ from conflict within other species. Once again, the rules of war vary with time and place. Moreover, although there nearly always are rules, they do not prevent (as do the "aggressive" signals of other species) severe injury and death. The absence of fixed, species-characteristic signals and responses obliges man to adopt, with conscious intelligence, agreements to limit or abolish conflict, if he is to survive. This has been achieved with notable success *within* many large communities, even though it has not yet been achieved for our whole species.
>
> The objections, then, to simple analogies between human aggressive and other social behavior on the one hand, and apparently similar behavior

---

[110] George Steiner, "The Language Animal," *Encounter* (August 1969), 11.

in other species, on the other, are two. First, they may lead to gross misinterpretations of animal behavior. They may lead us to expect and even to think we have seen violence in other species, when in fact no such violence exists. Secondly, one may be led to think of human behavior as fixed, in the sense that that of other species is stereotyped and difficult to alter. Some writers are tempted to describe property holding or war in man as if they were what were once called "instincts." The implication is that the behavior cannot readily be changed.

What use, then, is it to compare other species with ourselves? There is no great problem when, say, the effect of a drug or a vitamin is closely similar in a laboratory animal and in man. Less obviously, the contemplation of animal behavior might, by analogy, suggest useful hypotheses about our own behavior, though whether it often does so, is doubtful. But discussions of aggression and other social behavior usually seek conclusions of wider generality than do comparisons of the effects of drugs, and of greater precision than can be derived from analogical reasoning. Explicitly or not, they often contain the question: how can we learn to control our own behavior? The answers are unlikely to be found in the behavior of other species. Their physiology, especially when we know it better, may tell us much about ourselves. But, when we look for wisdom in our dealings with each other, the Delphic exhortation still holds: know thyself.[111]

In this section we have taken a look at the personality subsystem, and, more specifically, at some of the theories formulated by those anthropologists who stress the variables of this subsystem in their explanations of cultural phenomena. We want to call attention to the fact that the form and even much of the content of personality theories are similar to those of the ideological theories discussed in the preceding section. Thus, anthropologists who are partial to explanations phrased in terms of personality will probably find ideological explanations congenial, and vice-versa.

Furthermore, many of the same kinds of ambiguities and problems that we referred to in the case of ideological explanations also turn up in personality explanations. The reasons are not hard to discover: both types of explanation focus on "inner processes" and employ explanatory devices that are essentially nonobservable. It is also true, of course, that no one has ever observed a social structure, a class, a caste, or a redistributive network; but we seem to have greater success in assigning empirical referents to these concepts, since they are not "hidden" in the mind in the same way as are the referents for values, covert themes, basic needs, and cognitive maps.

Our summary appraisal of ideological explanations would also hold for personality. Thus, while we have expressed some skepticism about the personality theories reviewed, we do not reject the possible causal impact of personality factors on cultural systems. For if there are panhuman basic needs—and if we can find some consensus on what these are—and if it can be convincingly shown that personality traits tend to cluster around certain modes and produce different personality types in different cultures, then

---

[111] S. A. Barnett, *Instinct and Intelligence: Behavior of Animals and Man* (Englewood Cliffs, N.J.: Prentice-Hall, 1967), pp. 64–65.

it might be granted that these factors sometimes play a significant role in maintaining cultural systems as well as in promoting or inhibiting change.

Obviously, the causal impact of personality factors is a sometime thing. More often, culture histories demonstrate the reverse—i.e., when rapid and major culture change has occurred, personality "type" may be transformed almost overnight. The transformation of the "meek, docile, and peaceful" hunting-and-gathering Shoshone into the horse-riding "fierce, warlike" Comanche of the Plains within a generation or so is a good example of the more usual—or, at least, the more readily documentable—cause-and-effect sequence. Indisputable cases of the reverse sequence (in which personality facilitates or obstructs culture change) are a little harder to document. Thus, theories which attribute culture change, or the lack of it, to great men, national pride, or a people's "logico-aesthetic integration" are rarely, if ever, in our opinion, so clearcut or demonstrable as the kind we have just cited for the Shoshone-Comanche.

Concluding Remarks

Although we have treated the subsystems of anthropological theory separately and have suggested that each subsystem may be identified more or less with a school or schools of anthropology, we have also noted that, in practice, cultural anthropologists of any persuasion usually employ variables from two or more subsystems when they turn either to analysis or explanation. In short, while anthropologists may be variously interested in techno-economics, or social structure, or ideology, or personality, when it comes to explaining problems of cultural functioning, maintenance, or change, they generally find that they cannot to offer monocausal explanations (i.e., demonstrate that causality is categorically determined by the variables of one particular subsystem). Or if they do, their explanations, more often than not, are likely to prove unsatisfactory.

Max Weber's "The Protestant Ethic and The Spirit of Capitalism" (1930), which is often cited as a classic treatment of ideological causation or determinism, is a case in point. Weber was, of course, fully aware of the techno-economic influences and social-structural factors involved in the growth of capitalism, but he was interested as well in exploring the "special peculiarity of Occidental rationalism" and its contributions to the rise of capitalism. Thus, he tells us:

> Now the peculiar modern Western form of capitalism has been at first sight strongly influenced by the development of technical possibilities. Its rationality is today essentially dependent on the calculability of the most important technical factors. . . . But the *technical* utilization of scientific knowledge . . . was certainly encouraged by economic considerations, which were extremely favorable to it in the Occident. But this encouragement was derived from the peculiarities of the social structure of the Occident. . . . Every . . . attempt at explanation must, recognizing the fundamental importance of the economic factor, above all take account of the economic conditions. But at the same time the op-

posite correlation must not be left out of consideration. For though the development of economic rationalism is partly dependent on rational technique and law, it is at the same time determined by the ability and disposition of men to adopt certain types of practical rational conduct. When these types have been obstructed by spiritual obstacles, the development of rational economic conduct has also met serious inner resistance. . . . We are dealing with the connection of the spirit of modern economic life with the rational ethics of ascetic Protestantism. . . .[112]

And finally, with reference to monocausality, Weber concludes his work with the following words:

> But it is, of course, not my aim to substitute for a one-sided materialistic an equally one-sided spiritualistic causal interpretation of culture and of history. Each is equally possible, but each, if it does not serve as the preparation, but as the conclusion of an investigation, accomplishes equally little in the interest of historical truth.[113]

But multicausal explanations may turn out to be unsatisfactory, too. They make things hard to pigeonhole. They are not neat. They are invariably less orderly than explanations that give exclusive causal weight to the elements of a single subsystem. Besides, it often happens that multicausalism becomes, in fact, a retreat from explanation, a confession of despair, the final refuge for those who find the birth, life, and death of human institutions and the intricacies of human behavior much too complex to understand. For them the system, like the astronomer's universe, is always expanding and the effective variables are always infinite.

Where does this leave us? We have tried to make it clear that we recognize the variable causal impact of each of the subsystems under differing circumstances. At the same time we believe that most of the time the technoeconomic components are "more causal" than the others—that "normally" and in the "long run" they are likely to have a greater impact on the personality, social-structural, and ideological subsystems of a society than the other way around. For when we examine the variety of explanations and theoretical propositions produced by anthropologists, it seems to us that technoeconomic variables most often comprise the one set of factors that it would be impossible to ignore without vitiating the quality of the explanation.

Yet technoeconomic arrangements neither arise nor are changed in a cultural vacuum. And as for that celebrated "long run" to which social scientists (ourselves included) continually allude—in that "long run," Maynard Keynes has reminded us, we will all be dead. In the less-than-long run, we have also pointed out, there are cultural circumstances, historically certifiable, in which it might be correct, in our opinion, to assign an equal or

[112] Max Weber, *The Protestant Ethic and the Spirit of Capitalism* (New York: Scribners, 1930), pp. 24–27.
[113] Ibid., 183.

perhaps even greater causal significance to factors in one or more of the other subsystems (i.e., to label them independent variables).

Unfortunately, we can offer no general formula, holding for all times and places, for determining when a particular subsystem has or may have a prepotent determinative causal impact. To those who seek *a* universal theory of culture this might seem a distressing admission. But the failure to achieve total theoretical omniscience need not drive us back to a historical particularism or to a multicausal view in which all variables are of equal significance and everything that occurs makes a difference. We can seek to formulate theories of somewhat less than global scope which apply to certain ranges of cultural circumstances or to certain structural types.

So while we would adopt a position which does not assign primary causal impact to a single subsystem under *all* circumstances we would, following what seems to us to have been a fruitful tradition in the social sciences, opt for a kind of limited technoeconomic determinism tempered by ideology, tempered by social structure, and, sometimes even tempered by personality.

Four Formal Analysis

According to the logic underlying the organization of this book, the two theoretical schemata which form the topic of this chapter might have been included in the sections dealing with ideology or personality in the preceding chapter. For to the extent that structuralism and the new ethnography (the latter including those approaches variously referred to as ethnosemantics, ethnoscience, componential analysis, etc.) focus on cultural codes, conceptual principles, symbolic systems, and the like, the theories involved in these approaches might be considered ideological in nature. And to the extent that the theoreticians of these approaches seek the source of their codes, principles, and systems in mental processes, their theories might be grouped with those discussed under personality. In the case of Lévi-Straussian structuralism, nothing less than the logical properties of the human mind itself are the focus of inquiry and the source of "explanation." And in the case of the new ethnography, the conceptual principles, the cognitive rules, and the categories by which people in different societies order their experiences are said to explain their behavior and sociocultural arrangements. However, since the principles, rules, and categories of the new ethnographers are ultimately psychological in nature, these ethnographers, like Lévi-Strauss, must end up seeking their explanations in the human mind. And this is an ancient anthropological enterprise. For, as we have already remarked, the anthropologist's interest in mental processes (and certainly his interest in idea-systems) is as old as anthropology itself. Thus, in the area of cognition, for example, Durkheim and Lévy-Bruhl, in their concern with "collective representations," were in effect dealing with phenomena that could in all probability be articulated under the label of "cognitive categories" by the new ethnographers. And if it be conceded that the novelty of the new ethnography does not consist in its efforts to understand mental processes but perhaps, among other things, in the application of linguistic models to culture, then here, too, one may question its newness. For, as David Aberle points out,[1] a number of the earlier culture-personality writers, especially Sapir and Benedict, leaned heavily upon the linguistic analogy in their work.

What gives structuralism and the new ethnography their distinctively avant-garde appearance—and the main reason they warrant a separate chapter—is that to a large extent the methodology, terminology, and conceptual framework employed is drawn not only from structural linguistics but from the most recent developements in "high science": computer technology, communications theory, cybernetics, game theory, systems analysis, and symbolic logic.

Above all, however, the reigning model is language; and to both Lévi-Strauss and the new ethnographers culture is seen essentially as language-writ-large. But it is the formal-structural, quasi-mathematical features of language that have most captured the imagination of these theoreticians. It is these features which they have attempted to transfer to culture. It may be said, then, that these theoreticians do not see culture as being made up of institutions, events, processes, and behaviors. For them, cultural phenomena dissolve into formal codes, logical relationships, binary oppositions, contrastive sets, and skewing rules. For example, Lévi-Strauss writes:

> Language can be said to be a *condition* of culture, and this in two different ways: First, it is a condition of culture in a diachronic way, because it is mostly through the language that we learn about our own culture—we are taught by our parents, we are scolded, we are congratulated, with language. But also, from a much more theoretical point of view, language can be said to be a condition of culture because the material out of which language is built is of the same type as the material out of which the whole culture is built: logical relations, oppositions, correlations, and the like. Language, from this point of view, may appear as laying a kind of foundation for the more complex structures which correspond to the different aspects of culture.[2]

And, in a similar vein, Charles O. Frake, one of the leading spokesmen for the new ethnography, sees the central aim of ethnography, and indeed of all anthropology, to discern

---

[1] See David F. Aberle, "The Influence of Linguistics on Early Culture and Personality Theory," in *Essays in the Science of Culture*, ed. Gertrude E. Dole and Robert L. Carneiro (New York: Thomas Y. Crowell, 1960), pp. 1–29.

[2] Claude Lévi-Strauss, "Linguistics and Anthropology," in *Structural Anthropology* (New York: Basic Books, 1963), pp. 68–69.

how people construe their world of experience from the way they talk about it. Specifically these [methodological suggestions] concern the analysis of terminological systems in a way which reveals the conceptual principles that generate them. . . .

The analysis of a culture's terminological systems will not, of course, exhaustively reveal the cognitive world of its members, but it will certainly tap a central portion of it. Culturally significant cognitive features must be communicable between persons in one of the standard symbolic systems of the culture. A major share of these features will undoubtedly be codable in a society's most flexible and productive communication device, its language. . . . As Goodenough advocates in a classic paper, culture *"does not consist of things, people, behavior, or emotions," but the forms or organization of these things in the minds of people* [emphasis added].[3]

If these theoreticians work with a model of culture which sees cultural phenomena as being, at bottom, essentially codes, logical relationships, and oppositions, it must follow that the model of man that they subsume is one in which the emotional and irrational side of his nature is either completely elided or, at the very least, deemphasized. Their basic premise is that man is basically a cognitive animal, a logical machine "programmed" (by whom? by what?) to elaborate intricate and wondrous codes and symbolic systems (to what end?). The goal of a theoretical anthropology, then, is seen as the construction of formal models which will help us to unravel and to understand the intricacies of these codes and lead us, it is hoped, ultimately to the logical workings of the human mind itself. It is all very heady stuff. The ideas are not new, but the methodological and terminological matrix in which they are cast and presented are very *au courant*, to say the least.

Models
As Heuristic Devices

Since the notion of *models*, especially formal models, figures so prominently in the work of the structuralists and new ethnographers, we feel it is essential to preface our examination of structuralism and the new ethnography with some general remarks on the meaning and use of models in anthropology.

It is difficult to glean any clear idea of what a model is from the anthropological literature, for anthropologists use the term in a variety of ways. From our point of view, we believe it is best to define, or at least to think of, a model as an analogy or a metaphor. Many social scientists, however, are highly suspicious of reasoning by analogy or through the use of models. The suspicion is not altogether unwarranted. For sometimes, "false" analogies have been used to persuade the unwary, and claims for the explanatory power of models have often been extravagant or unjustifiable. But as long as one

---

[3] Charles O. Frake, "The Ethnographic Study of Cognitive Systems," in *Anthropology and Human Behavior*, ed. T. Gladwin and W. C. Sturtevant (Washington, D.C.: Anthropological Society of Washington, 1962), pp. 74, 75, 85.

remembers what a model can and cannot do, the use of models as analogues can be an important conceptual aid in analysis and explanation in anthropology. In any event, all scientific disciplines, "hard" and "soft" alike, employ models, analogies, and metaphors.

It is sometimes maintained that the most important attribute of a model is its logical and predictive rigor. While we do not wish to downgrade these properties, an overemphasis on rigor and precision, especially in the social sciences, may serve to constrict a discipline rather than liberate it. It may lead one to pursue unrealistic research goals or to become preoccupied with trivial problems. The most useful feature of a model, we believe, is not its precision but its heuristic possibilities. Like all analogic reasoning, a model may serve as a device for suggesting ways in which knowledge gained in one area of inquiry can help to illuminate some other area of inquiry. Thus, the organic analogy or model of culture suggests that in certain respects cultural systems will exhibit relationships and processes similar to those encountered in organic systems. Whether this particular model is useful—that is, whether the expectations it creates are warranted—will depend, of course, on the empirical investigation of specific cultural systems. Only in this way can we determine whether there are indeed any similarities between the behavior of cultural systems and the behavior of organic systems.

In the use of models there are, however, several significant cautions that ought to be borne in mind. First, a model is always an approximation. The relationship between the model and any empirical phenomenon is always *partial*. Thus, with the organic analogy: a cultural system may behave like an organic system in some respects but not in others. Secondly, the relationship between a model and empirical phenomena is always *isomorphic*—i.e., it is a relationship in similarity of structure rather than an identity. To say, for example, that certain processes which go on in cultural systems are similar to those that go on in organic systems is not to assert that cultural systems *are* organic systems. Investigators who have employed linguistic models of cultures seem often to have forgotten the partial and isomorphic character of all analogues. The results are sometimes strikingly inappropriate. It is one thing to say that some cultural phenomena bear a structural resemblance to (are isomorphic with) linguistic phenomena in certain respects. It is quite another thing to assert that culture *is* a logical grammar, or a code, or a set of formal-structural rules for generating appropriate acts.

Although there are many kinds of models in use, those designated "formal" are probably among the most widely used in the sciences.[4] Put simply and succinctly, a *formal model* is a set of precisely defined elements plus the logical rules for combining and manipulating them. Since we are only concerned in a formal model with the purely logical relationships existing among the elements, the whole system can be commonly cast in a symbolic form.

Formal models are the stock-in-trade of the mathematician and the logician. A good example of such a model is Euclidean geometry, which is made up of a set of carefully specified basic axioms and all the postulates

---

[4] For a discussion of different kinds of models, see Abraham Kaplan, *The Conduct of Inquiry* (San Francisco: Chandler, 1964), chap. 7.

and theorems that can be derived from these basic axioms by the rules of formal logic. There is nothing in the Euclidean construction that is not already logically contained in its basic axioms. Thus, the entire system is one vast tautology. For our purposes, a noteworthy aspect of the Euclidean formal system is that it does not refer to any empirical phenomena whatsoever. It is sometimes easy to forget that theorems such as, "The shortest distance between two points is a straight line," or, "The three angles of a triangle add up to 180°," are not empirical propositions at all. They are formal statements which follow tautologically from the basic axioms or assumptions of the system. They are not even universally valid as *formal* statements. In other geometries which start from different basic axioms, the shortest distance between two points is *not* a straight line and the three angles of a triangle add up to more than 180°. Thus, to assess the validity of a formal proposition, one first has to know the formal system of which it is a part. Moreover, the criteria for evaluating a formal system (such as Euclidean geometry) are always formal or logical criteria, not empirical ones. Formal models, like formal arguments, may be judged valid or invalid. The question of their truth or falsity is not relevant. Only empirical propositions can be true or false.

From everything we have said about the analogic and metaphoric character of models in general, and as should be evident from the above example, no formal model (and indeed no model) is capable by itself of explaining empirical phenomena. *Theories explain, models do not.* Of course, a formal model can be converted into a theory by assigning a specific empirical content to the various symbols of the model. Then, the elements of the model would become empirical entities and the relationships among these entities would become empirical relationships rather than purely formal ones. For example, we might empiricize the Euclidean model by, among other things, defining "points" in terms of specific spatial locations, e.g., Chicago, New York, etc. We would find that when we are dealing with relatively short distances, the Euclidean model works fairly well, but that as we begin to approach problems involving terrestrial curvature or astronomical distances, the Euclidean system is no longer adequate and some other geometric model must be employed.

Consider an example from economics, the social science which has so far made the widest use of formal models. The branch of economics known as microeconomics leans heavily upon certain basic assumptions and the formal propositions derived from these assumptions. For example, one premise of microeconomists is that the collective wants of man are unlimited relative to the means for satisfying them. Another major premise states that people's economic behavior will be rational—i.e., that ethical, magical, or religious considerations will not enter into their *economic* calculations. Finally, it is assumed that all persons operate with a preference scale to which they can attach specific values. From these assumptions certain conclusions follow. Thus, all individuals (buyers, sellers, consumers, entrepreneurs) will engage in a decision-making process which allocates scarce resources to alternative ends in such a way that the total values of their preference scales are maximized. But we sometimes forget that these propositions are purely formal in nature and that they rest always on the contingent proposition of "all other things being equal." If we want to use this model of "economic man" to "explain" concrete economic behavior, we must give it an empirical content. We must know, for example, whether human wants *are* indeed unlimited, either in an individual or collective sense. We must also know whether empirical economic agents *do* act in terms of a fixed preference scale to which they can assign specific values. For if their preferences change over time and/or if they are unable to assign values to their scale preferences, then quite clearly this model is inadequate. If one does not know when one's total values are maximized, then obviously one cannot work toward this point. To be sure, economists have wrestled with these problems, but whether they have succeeded in resolving them is another matter. When empirical studies have revealed, for example, that entrepreneurs do *not* always act so as to maximize profits—in part, of course, because they do not always know when profits are being maximized—some economists have tried to save the maximization postulate by arguing that entrepreneurs are maximizing prestige, status, satisfaction, utility, or what have you. But this removes the maximization principle from all possible refutation—it becomes compatible with all possible behaviors.

If we remember to keep in mind the limitations of formal models when applied to empirical situations, such models—even though they cannot *explain* empirical phenomena—may be important heuristic devices in helping us to *arrive* at explanations. The formalization of an empirical system may serve to simplify a very complicated set of empirical relationships and processes. Such simplification-through-formalization may have a number of advantages: it may enable us to comprehend the workings of a culture more easily than if we had to try to cope with that culture's "complex" empirical reality; certain problems may become clarified; gaps in our knowledge may be more easily located; and, finally, we may be able to discern certain potentially important relationships among the elements of the system that we might otherwise have missed. For example, Evans-Pritchard's analysis of Nuer society (see pp. 80–81, *supra*) is framed largely in terms of a formalized model of their segmentary lineage organization. The whole society can be diagrammed in terms of increasingly more inclusive segments of opposition.[5] Not only is our understanding of the workings of Nuer society enhanced thereby, but the model is applicable to other societies as well. Or, to take an example from a practice now widely applied in anthropological research, the formal analysis of a system of kinship terms often reveals certain aspects of kin classification that might otherwise have escaped us. Nevertheless, while such an analysis may improve the analyst's understanding of a system of kinship terminology, there is no certainty that it will reveal anything about the "native's" conceptual principles for classifying kin.

At best, a formal analysis can only reveal certain formal relationships which might or might not be empirically relevant. But if we want to do more than engage in purely logical exercises—that is, if we want to frame explanations of empirical phenomena—then we must have some way of

---

[5] See Marshall D. Sahlins, *Tribesmen* (Englewood Cliffs, N.J.: Prentice-Hall, 1968), pp. 50–51. See also Sahlins' "The Segmentary Lineage: An Organization of Predatory Expansion," *American Anthropologist* (1961), 322–45.

making the transition from the formally possible to the empirically probable. Some structuralists and new ethnographers, as we suggested earlier, often seem to overlook the fact that there is a logical gap between making statements about the formal properties of codes and making empirical statements about what is actually going on inside the human mind. Or if they do perceive it as a gap at all, they tend to interpret it as narrow enough to be bridged with relative ease. We are reminded here of a book written some years ago entitled *The Mysterious Universe* by the eminent British astrophysicist Sir James Jeans, in which he suggests that the universe must have been created by a "Great Mathematician," since so much of its apparent structure could be formulated in mathematical terms. Whether Sir James was being playful or serious is irrelevant here. What we would like to point out is that a similar kind of reasoning is often employed by some of the more exuberant of the new ethnographers. That certain cultural domains lend themselves to formal and quasi-mathematical analyses suggests to them that the logical principles with which they are working must in some way reflect the logical principles created and utilized by the "natives."

Anthony Wallace, one of the new ethnographers who has recognized the gap between the formal properties of the code and mental processes, has phrased it as the problem of getting from "structural reality" to "psychological reality." The problem of making this transition, however, is a formidable one. Robbins Burling, for example, has shown that it is hypothetically possible, using a cultural domain consisting of only four items, to produce as many as 124 formal models or analyses of this domain. Furthermore, Burling writes, "clearly with five or more items the possibilities would rapidly become astronomical. . . . Homonomy, empty spaces, non-binary distinctions, parallel components, and redundant solutions all add considerable complexity to the possibilities for analysis of a set of terms. In principle, the number of possible analyses becomes infinite." [6] Thus, Burling is highly skeptical that the formal analysis of linguistic codes will ever lead us to the empirical psychological processes said to generate these codes:

> Students who claim that componential analysis or comparable methods of semantic analysis can provide a means for "discovering how people construe their world" must explain how to eliminate the great majority of logical possibilities and narrow the choice to the one or few that are "psychologically real." I will not be convinced that there are not dozens or hundreds of possible analyses of Subanun disease terms [see pp. 146–47] until Frake presents us with the entire system fully analyzed and faces squarely the problem of how he chooses his particular analysis. In the meantime, I will doubt whether any single analysis tells us much about people's cognitive structure, even if it enables us to use terms as a native does.[7]

It is a curious fact, as we noted in the last chapter, that Wallace himself has expressed a viewpoint which seems to raise serious doubts about the

---

[6] Robbins Burling, "Cognition and Componential Analysis: God's Truth or Hocus-Pocus?," *American Anthropologist* 66 (1964): 23–24.

[7] Ibid., 26.

possibility of discovering "psychological reality" through the formal analysis of linguistic codes. He writes:

> Now, just as the ethnographer may invent a taxonomic model which will predict satisfactorily how a speaker will refer to his kinsmen but which does not describe how the speaker reckons kinfolk, so it is possible that two members of the same society may produce similar or complementary behaviors without sharing the same cognitive model.[8]

Wallace's proffered solution to the "gap" problem revealed in this statement is to suggest that a metacalculus (or Stephen Tyler's "unitary" model referred to in Chapter 3) be constructed which will embrace the "diverse calculi of particular individuals or subgroups cooperating to maintain stable systems of relationships."[9] But as Muriel Hammer notes: "Such a calculus cannot be presumed to have any 'psychological reality' for anyone except, perhaps, the ethnographer."[10]

Finally, we wish to emphasize that, while formal analyses and formal models have distinctive heuristic advantages, they also carry with them certain potential liabilities in addition to those already mentioned. Thus, an excessive reliance upon formal models may produce an overemphasis on the importance of symbols, logical form, and rigor at the expense of either content or significance. We may, in other words, become so overly concerned with methodology that we allow the methodologies to select the problems rather than allowing the problems to determine the methodologies. Thus, we run the risk of becoming more precise and rigorous about a narrow range of problems, while the empirical importance of these problems bears little relationship to any ongoing theoretical tradition in the discipline. An added danger is that we may become so enamored of the logical and even the aesthetic neatness of the formal models that we trim our data to fit the models. The result is likely to be an oversimplification and, indeed, a falsification of empirical reality. Finally, as Eugene J. Meehan notes: "catastrophic results" may follow when "those who use formal models . . . forget that models are not theories."[11]

Structuralism

The concepts of *structure* and *social structure* are used so pervasively in anthropology and in the social sciences in general that it is important at the outset to indicate the distinction between these terms and the theory of "structuralism" as this is associated with Lévi-Strauss and his followers. All science (hard, soft, physical, biological, social) is concerned with structure— that is, with the way in which parts of a given system relate to each other.

---

8 Anthony Wallace, "Culture and Cognition," *Science* 135 (1962): 356.

9 Ibid., 356.

10 Muriel Hammer, "Some Comments on Formal Analysis of Grammatical and Semantic Systems," *American Anthropologist* 68 (1966): 370.

11 Eugene J. Meehan, *Contemporary Political Thought: A Critical Study* (Homewood, Ill.: Dorsey, 1967), p. 294.

With reference to our own discipline, the British social anthropologists—acknowledging their debt to Durkheim—have for a long time devoted much of their effort to dealing with problems of social structure. American anthropologists, especially within the last few decades, have also turned heavily toward the study and analysis of structural issues in their work.

But there is an important difference between the kinds of structure and structural problems that have occupied the attention of most anthropologists and the structural issues that have been elaborated by Lévi-Strauss into a special theory of his own. Edmund Leach defines the difference by observing that, for the social anthropologist,

> *social structure* is something which "exists" at much the same level of objectivity as the articulation of the human skeleton or the functional-physiological interdependence of the different organs of the human anatomy. In contrast, Lévi-Strauss . . . is concerned with nothing less than the structure of the human mind, meaning by "structure" not an articulation which can be directly observed but rather a logical ordering, a set of mathematical equations which can be demonstrated as functionally equivalent (as in a model) to the phenomenon under discussion.[12]

No other theoretical position discussed in this book is as closely identified with the work of a single man as is "structuralism" with the writings of Claude Lévi-Strauss. Leach refers to him as "the founder of 'structuralism,' on a par with Sartre, the founder of existentialism." [13] The analogy is apt. For while existentialist philosophy is much older than Sartre, it is Sartre's unique approach to existentialism that marks him off from earlier users of the term. Similarly with Lévi-Strauss's structuralism and the structuralists who preceded him. Thus, it does not seem at all inappropriate to say metaphorically that Lévi-Strauss *is* structuralism.

This is not to say that even his special version of structuralist theory was invented by Lévi-Strauss all in one piece. The debt owed to the work of structural linguistics, for example, is obvious and especially significant. Moreover, one can find in the work of Lévi-Strauss unmistakable evidence of influences from a number of the earlier French sociologists and anthropologists—Durkheim, Lévy-Bruhl, and especially Mauss. Yet, at the same time, it can be said that with Lévi-Strauss certain intellectual trends, especially in French social science and social philosophy, have reached a new level.

Nor do we wish to imply that no one beside Lévi-Strauss has contributed to contemporary structuralist thought and theory. In the main, however, the writings of these other structuralists, at least in anthropology, seem largely to be commentaries on, footnotes to, or elaborations of, ideas first put forth by Lévi-Strauss. Not only is he the charismatic leader of contemporary structuralism, but he seems clearly to be the final arbiter of what constitutes

---

[12] Edmund Leach, "Claude Lévi-Strauss—Anthropologist and Philosopher," in *Theory in Anthropology*, ed. Robert A. Manners and David Kaplan (Chicago: Aldine, 1968), p. 542.

[13] Ibid., p. 541.

"genuine" and what "spurious" structuralist theory. To talk of structuralism, therefore, is to talk of French structuralism, and to talk of French structuralism is to talk of Lévi-Strauss's theoretical schema.

In order better to understand the rationale behind Lévi-Strauss's theoretical speculations, one must keep in mind the perspective and methodology of structural linguistics. Any language is essentially an arbitrarily constructed symbolic system. Considered as a system of sounds, the constituent units of a language are its *phonemes*—significant classes of sound elements definable, not in terms of the properties common to the class, but rather in terms of the features by which the classes contrast with each other. Phonemes by themselves are, of course, meaningless. What is more, the phonemes utilized by any particular language are purely arbitrary. It is only when phonemes are combined into larger linguistic units (morphemes, words, phrases, sentences, etc.) according to morphological and grammatical rules which vary arbitrarily from language to language that meaning emerges and with it communication.

Most native speakers of a language are totally unaware of the phonological and grammatical rules which lie "behind" overtly expressed speech patterns. Yet they are able to use their language as an instrument of communication effectively and efficiently. Thus, if these rules can be said to have any existence in reality outside the mind of the linguist, they must, it is argued, be subconscious in nature. The job of the linguist, then, is to formulate and make explicit what lies hidden from view and buried in the unconscious—that is, to look beyond the surface manifestations of linguistic expression to the underlying structural principles which are said to generate these linguistic expressions. To know the structural principles is to explain the language. It should be noted, of course, that while some linguists are concerned primarily with demonstrating that basic structural principles vary from language to language, others have sought the structural ur-principles which underlie all languages. It is from these latter linguists that Lévi-Strauss appears to have drawn his major inspiration.

To Lévi-Strauss culture is essentially a symbolic system or a configuration of symbolic systems. Moreover, to understand any particular set of cultural symbols one must first see them in relation to the total system of which they are a part. When Lévi-Strauss speaks of cultural phenomena as being symbolic in nature, however, he is not concerned with the empirical referents or meanings of symbols. Rather, he is concerned with the formal patterns, with the way symbolic elements *logically* relate to one another to form an overall system. In an early, seminal paper entitled "Structural Analysis in Linguistics and in Anthropology," Lévi-Strauss expresses this viewpoint with regard to kinship systems:

> But what confers upon kinship its socio-cultural character is not what it retains from nature, but, rather, the essential way in which it diverges from nature. A kinship system does not consist in the objective ties of descent or consanguinity between individuals. It exists only in human consciousness; it is an arbitrary system of representations, not the spontaneous development of a real situation. . . . The essence of human

kinship is to require the establishment of relations among what Radcliffe-Brown calls "elementary families." Thus it is not the families (isolated terms) which are truly "elementary," but, rather, the relations between these terms. . . .

Because they are symbolic systems, kinship systems offer the anthropologist a rich field, where his efforts can almost (and we emphasize the "almost") converge with those of the most highly developed of the social sciences, namely, linguistics. But to achieve this convergence, from which it is hoped a better understanding of man will result, we must never lose sight of the fact that in both anthropological and linguistic research, we are dealing strictly with symbolism. And although it may be legitimate or even inevitable to fall back on naturalistic interpretation in order to understand the emergence of symbolic thinking, once the latter is given, the nature of the explanation must change as radically as the newly appeared phenomenon differs from those which have preceded and prepared it. Hence, any concession to naturalism might jeopardize the immense progress already made in linguistics, which is also beginning to characterize the study of family structure, and might drive the sociology of the family toward a sterile empiricism, devoid of inspiration.[14]

As another example, consider myth.[15] To most of the nineteenth-century anthropologists mythology was a kind of pseudohistory or pseudoscience whose main purpose for the people involved was to explain the facts of the natural and cultural world. Since Malinowski, however, the majority of anthropologists have tended to treat myths in terms of their social functions, i.e., as a "charter" sanctioning sociocultural arrangements. But Lévi-Strauss is not so much concerned with the social context of myth; nor does he view myth as a device for explaining the world—although he does emphasize the intellectual significance of myth.

The analysis of myth, according to Lévi-Strauss, should proceed much like the analysis of language: the elements of myth, like those of language, have no meaning in themselves, but acquire meaning only when they are combined into a structure. Myths contain a kind of coded message, and the job of the analyst is to decipher the code and reveal the message.

The structure of myth, argues Lévi-Strauss, is dialectical; that is, certain oppositions or contradictions are posed—man:woman, endogamy:exogamy, elder:younger, earth:heaven, etc.—and then somehow mediated or resolved. (The process, of course, resembles very closely Hegel's thesis, antithesis and synthesis.) Myth, viewed in terms of its functions, serves to depict certain contradictions in life and then to resolve these contradictions. Or, as Leach illustrates the dialectic,

---

[14] Claude Lévi-Strauss, "Structural Analysis in Linguistics and in Anthropology," in *Structural Anthropology*, pp. 50–51.

[15] See Claude Lévi-Strauss, "The Structural Study of Myth," in *Structural Anthropology*, pp. 206–31. See also Lévi-Strauss, *The Raw and the Cooked: Introduction to the Science of Mythology*, vol. 1, trans. John and Noreen Weightman (New York: Harper and Row, 1969); *Mythologiques II: Du miel aux cendres* (Paris: Librairie Plon, 1966); and *Mythologiques III: L'origine des manieres de table* (Paris: Librairie Plon, 1968).

The concept of life entails the concept of death. A living thing is that which is not dead; a dead thing is that which is not alive. But religion endeavors to separate these two intrinsically interdependent concepts so that we have myths which account for the *origin* of death or which represent death "as the gateway to eternal life." Lévi-Strauss has argued that when we are considering the universalist aspects of primitive mythology we shall repeatedly discover that the hidden message is concerned with the resolution of unwelcome contradictions of this sort.[16]

Myth, of course, does have a narrative content, but that, according to Lévi-Strauss and those who follow him, is not its main significance, for myth transcends narrative. What is significant is the purely formal pattern of myths, the logical relationships among the elements contained in the myths. Considered on a global scale, the apparent variations in myths are seen as logical transformations of a set of enduring structural relationships. The discovery of this basic, underlying structural core, then, is Lévi-Strauss's major concern in the analysis of myth. For ultimately, this structural core will reveal to us the structure of human thought itself and the binary logic upon which it rests. In this regard, Leach draws an analogy between the structure of myth and the structure of music and drama:

> What we hear is a tune, a melody; but the experience of music is not just a collection of tunes. What the musically sensitive person responds to is the structure of the music as a totality, the complexities of counterpoint and of harmony and the relations between a theme and its variations. Likewise, in drama, what distinguishes a powerful, emotionally significant, play from a triviality is not a quality of the story but a quality of the inner structure to which we can respond even when we cannot consciously recognize what it is. Lévi-Strauss' thesis is that inner structure of myth systems are everywhere much the same. . . .[17]

Or to take another example, totemism: in a number of primitive societies one finds beliefs positing a sort of kinship relationship between each of various social groupings (clans, sibs, gens) of the society and particular plants, animals, or objects found in the environment. The members of the bear clan, for example, consider themselves descended from bear and will adopt a ritualistic attitude toward the species. At least, this has been the classical approach to totemic beliefs in anthropology. Lévi-Strauss finds it inadequate. Some years ago, however, Radcliffe-Brown suggested that such totemic beliefs function to personalize nature and to bring into the kinship system, in a metaphoric way, certain animal species that may be critical to the survival of a society. In this way, the environment is rendered more familiar and understandable, enabling the native to relate to it and to cope with it more effectively.

Lévi-Strauss's view of totemism has developed in part from certain of

---

[16] Edmund Leach, *Claude Lévi-Strauss* (New York: Viking, 1970), pp. 57–58.
[17] Leach, "Claude Lévi-Strauss—Anthropologist and Philosopher," in *Theory in Anthropology*, p. 547.

Radcliffe-Brown's notions. He argues that totemic beliefs are a sophisticated conceptual device which enable the native to classify and order the social units of his culture—and, metaphorically, to relate these units to each other and to a similar kind of ordering in the natural world. In other words, totemism is essentially a duel system of classification, a way of imposing logical order on the natural and cultural worlds of the "savage" through the employment of a unitary set of conceptual principles. The result is that a set of natural entities is superimposed upon a set of cultural entities.

In ordering the world of animal species, for example, the savage, Lévi-Strauss proposes, employs classificatory principles that reflect those sensible qualities by which each species is distinguished from all others. The contrastive features which serve to discriminate among animal species are, by analogy, believed to be on the same logical level as those which discriminate among the totemic clans of the society. Thus, for every term or verbal category that appears in the classification of the natural world there is a logically corresponding term in the classification of the social world. In this way the facts of social life, the function and roles of different clans—their hunting rights and obligations, their spatial position vis-à-vis one another, their hierarchical and exogamous relationships, etc.—are symbolically represented or "coded" by a set of principles derived from a classification of the totemic objects of the environment. To give an example—according to Chickasaw mythology:

> The Raccoon people were said to live on fish and wild fruit, those of the Puma lived in the mountains, avoided water of which they were very frightened and lived principally on game. The Wild Cat clan slept in the daytime and hunted at night, for they had keen eyes; they were indifferent to women. Members of the Bird clan were up before day-break: "They were like real birds in that they would not bother anybody. . . . The people of this clan have different sorts of minds, just as there are different species of birds." They were said to live well, to be polygamous, disinclined to work, and prolific.
>
> The people of the Red Fox clan were professional thieves, loving independence and living in the heart of forests. The "wandering Iksa" were nomadic and improvident but nevertheless enjoyed robust health "for they did not do anything to run themselves down." They moved slowly, thinking that they were going to live forever. The men and women paid little attention to their dress or appearance. They were beggars and lazy. The inhabitants of "the bending-post-oak" house group lived in the woods. They were of a changeable disposition, not very energetic, given to dancing, always anxious and full of care. They were early risers and clumsy. The High Corncrib house group people were respected in spite of their arrogance: they were food gardeners, very industrious but poor hunters, they bartered their maize for game. They were said to be truthful and stubborn, and skilled at forecasting the weather. As for the Redskunk house group: they lived in dugouts underground.[18]

---

[18] Claude Lévi-Strauss, *The Savage Mind* (Chicago: University of Chicago Press, 1962) pp. 118–19. See also Levi-Strauss' *Totemism* (Boston: Beacon Press, 1962).

Thus, when a native says he is a member of the Raccoon clan and his neighbor is a member of the Wild Cat clan; and that each of these clans is separately descended from these animals, his statement is not to be taken literally, as a biological theory of paternity. Rather he is employing a metaphor to characterize the differences and relationships between the two clans, to emphasize that these differences and relationships are similar to those that obtain in nature between the species. Totemism, then, is a kind of primitive science, an imaginative and aesthetic ordering of the world in terms of the perceived, sensible aspects of things.

"Considered term by term," Clifford Geertz remarks of Lévi-Strauss that:

> totemic beliefs are simply arbitrary. "History" has cast them up and "history" may ultimately destroy them, alter their role, or replace them with others. But seen as an ordered set they become coherent, for they are able then to represent symbolically another set similarly ordered: allied, exogamous patrilineal clans. And the point is general. The relationship between a symbolic structure and its referent, the basis of its *meaning,* is fundamentally "logical," a coincidence of form—not affective, not historical, not functional. Savage thought is frozen reason and anthropology is, like music and mathematics, "one of the true vocations." [19]

Once one has grasped the essentially formal nature of cultural systems, claim the structuralists, all manner of logical relationships among cultural phenomena become discernible. A structure which appears on one level with respect to a particular content may reappear at another level with respect to an entirely different content. For example, on one level we may find certain food prohibitions based upon beliefs concerning a reincarnated ancestor in the form of a plant or animal. These prohibitions can be transposed to the level of language as a prohibition against using any of the homophones of the deceased ancestor. Or a structure which appears in one tribe may reappear as a transformed structure in a neighboring tribe. Also, in certain societies a man may, before he dies, indicate the animal form in which he will be reincarnated. This animal then becomes the object of a food prohibition for all of his descendants. The content—i.e., the particular food that may be tabooed or the particular reincarnation beliefs—may, and often do, vary enormously from society to society.[20] But the structure of these customs, the forms from which they derive or are generated, are limited by the very nature of the human mind. Transformations may produce structural and content variations among these customs. But since the "mind," which is the source of all custom—however such custom may have been modified or transformed by the particular culture—works in the same way for all human beings, the observed differences in content are "irrelevant"; or at least it does not really matter whether they are the same or not. For if they are dissimilar, that very

---

[19] Clifford Geertz, "The Cerebral Savage: On the Work of Lévi-Strauss," in *Theory in Anthropology*, p. 555.

[20] See Robert L. Zimmerman, "Lévi-Strauss and the Primitive," *Commentary* 45 (1968): 57.

dissimilarity merely represents a superficial content variation produced by the "transforming" capacity of the human mind. This mind operates unconsciously out of its limited repertoire of forms as it produces the vast and visible array of different customs. But if we want to "understand" the way that mind works, we can only do so through an examination of the systems it creates: kinship systems, myths, totemic beliefs, or the more prosaic and marginal aspects of culture such as hair styles, tattoo designs, cookery, or designs on Australian bullroarers.

The aim of structural inquiry, then, is to explain the world of experience and to grasp the basic rationality underlying this phenomenal world. And this is achieved by deciphering the often cryptic and coded messages revealed as end-products of transformation. This "rationality"—the basic explanatory structural principles—consists of logical categories and relationships constructed out of the tendency of the human mind to perceive the universe in terms of a "coincidence of form"—or, more usually, according to Lévi-Strauss, in terms of binary discriminations and oppositions, e.g., high and low, male and female, right and left, good and evil, war and peace, hot and cold, light and dark, etc.

Thus formal models, according to Lévi-Strauss, can "explain" cultural phenomena, because cultural systems are at bottom essentially formal systems.[21] Then, by an intriguing reversal of the usual process, Lévi-Strauss becomes the ultimate logician of culture. For if the logician starts out with a set of basic axioms and derives formally valid propositions from these axioms by applying to them a set of precisely defined rules of transformation, Lévi-Strauss starts out with derived cultural phenomena and works his way back from these to the basic cultural axioms. Then it turns out that these basic axioms ("binary relationships") underlie all aspects of a single culture, and at the same time may be found at the base of *all* cultures. Thus, the postulated basic axioms both reflect and testify to the universal workings of the human mind. And Lévi-Strauss's theory may, in some sense, be seen as a reaffirmation that all mankind exhibits a fundamental psychic unity.

On one level it appears that *despite* the striking similarity between this basic postulate of nineteenth-century evolutionism and contemporary Lévi-Straussian structuralism, there is an important conceptual distinction. For example, to the nineteenth-century theorists psychic unity meant that, *regardless of time and place*, when the human mind is confronted by a similar set of physical and cultural circumstances it will react, resolve, or cope

---

21 Lévi-Strauss has been most emphatic in asserting that structuralism is not formalism. He insists, on the contrary, that the structuralist method challenges the distinction between form and content: "*Form* is defined by opposition to a *content* which is foreign to it; but *structure* has no distinct content. It *is* the content itself apprehended in a logical organization, conceived as a property of the real" [quoted by Michael Lane, "Introduction," in *Structuralism: A Reader*, ed. Michael Lane (London: Jonathan Cape, 1970), p. 31].

Most anthropologists, however, have failed to see the distinction. For example, see K. O. L. Burridge, "Lévi-Strauss and Myth," in *The Structural Study of Myth and Totemism*, ed. Edmund Leach, ASA Monograph no. 5. (London: Tavistock, 1967), where he says: "the distinction which Lévi-Strauss is making seems to be one between form and content" (p. 98).

in essentially the same way; whereas Lévi-Strauss seems to be saying that, regardless of time, place, or circumstances, the logical properties of the human mind are such that it will work in fundamentally the same way.

But the difference may be more apparent than real. For at bottom Lévi-Strauss would undoubtedly agree with his nineteenth-century progenitors that the *content* of reaction, resolution, or coping will differ under the differing circumstances that may prevail in the total environment. But to him—and certainly not to the nineteenth-century writers—the content of the response is relatively unimportant; it is only the mental process or the formal logical patterns of response that count. The human mind is ineluctably programmed. Whether that mind is embedded in an industrial-atomic-capitalistic cultural matrix or a Paleolithic hunting-and-gathering central Australian desert ambience, it will *work* the same way. Thus, the difference between Lévi-Strauss and the nineteenth-century anthropologists is not at all a difference with regard to the essential functioning of the human mind, but only a difference with regard to the observable and tangible consequences produced by that mind at work under particular environmental circumstances. Lévi-Strauss is apparently not interested in the institutional and artifactual distinctions that characterize different human groups. Nineteenth-century anthropologists— and most contemporary anthropologists as well—are interested in the way "circumstances" affect this "single" mind.

Hence, if one accepts Lévi-Strauss's premise, it is not difficult to reconcile his point of view with any theory of cultural change—*even* with one that involves profound institutional transformations. The observable variations in cultural content and form which anthropologists have spent so much time documenting are to Lévi-Strauss merely secondary and derived minor variations on a set of basic, persisting, unchanging structural themes or principles. For him, then, the more things change the more they remain the same. With Lévi-Strauss we seem to have returned to Plato and the parable of the cave.[22]

Much in Stephen Toulmin and June Goodfield's characterization of the Platonic world-view has its parallels in the Lévi-Straussian world-view:

> Almost everything in philosophy became subordinated to . . . explaining the "transitory flux" of experience in terms of the "unchanging

---

[22] Lévi-Strauss is full of surprises. For example, one finds the following passage in *The Savage Mind* (p. 117): "It is of course only for purposes of exposition and because they form the subject of this book that I am apparently giving priority to ideology and superstructures. I do not at all mean to suggest that ideological transformations give rise to social ones. Only the reverse is in fact true. Men's conception of the relations between nature and culture is a function of modifications of their own social relations. But, since my aim here is to outline a theory of superstructures, reasons of method require that they should be singled out for attention and that major phenomena which have no place in this programme should seem to be left in brackets or given second place. We are however merely studying the shadows on the wall of the Cave without forgetting that it is only the attention we give them which lends them a semblance of reality."

If we take this passage seriously, then we shall have to admit that our interpretations of Lévi-Strauss's thought is all wrong. But, then, the interpretations of most other commentators and exegetes would be just as wrong. For the passage does not seem to fit in with what *appears to be* the central argument of *The Savage Mind* or of Lévi-Strauss's other major works.

realities" that lay behind it. Once the axiom was accepted, that all temporal changes observed by the senses were merely permutations and combinations of "eternal principles," the historical sequence of events (which formed a part of the "flux") lost all fundamental significance. It became interesting only to the extent that it offered clues to the nature of the enduring realities. So questions about historical change ceased to have any relevance to the central problems of philosophy, and philosophers concerned themselves instead with matters of *general principle*—the geometric layout of the heavens, the mathematical forms associated with the different material elements, or the fundamental axioms of morals and politics. More and more, they became obsessed with the idea of a change-less universal order, or "cosmos": the eternal and unending scheme of Nature—society included—whose basic principles it was their particular task to discover.[23]

It is obvious from the enormous amount of commentary and the variety of exegeses that have accumulated over the past several years that the corpus of Lévi-Strauss's writing is neither easily summarized nor understood.[24] His ideas are often highly abstract and elusive, and the style of presentation is itself frequently abstruse. In part, the difficulties may be a product, as Leach indicates, of translation:

> Lévi-Strauss chooses and arranges his words with scrupulous care so that in the original the result often has a poetic quality in that a sentence may contain a variety of *harmonic ambiguities* over and above what appears to be said on the surface. This faces his translators with a difficult if not impossible task. Paradoxically, some of the really difficult passages seem quite straightforward in English simply *because the built-in opacity cannot be reproduced in translation.* Philosophers who attempt in this way to talk about the unsayable are almost bound to be misunderstood [emphases added].[25]

But as Leach suggests, translation itself cannot be held entirely accountable for the various meanings, interpretations, inferences, and constructions that have been attached to Lévi-Strauss's work. For even the most sophisticated expositors and proponents of structuralism have discovered that at times they disagree among themselves as to what he means. And, even more importantly, they have found, much to their chagrin, that on occasion their interpreta-

---

[23] Stephen Toulmin and June Goodfield. *The Discovery of Time* (New York: Harper Torchbooks, 1966), p. 40.

[24] See for example, Edmund Leach's volume in The Modern Masters series, *Claude Lévi-Strauss;* and *Claude Lévi-Strauss: The Anthropologist as Hero,* ed. E. Nelson and Tanya Hayes (Cambridge, Mass.: M.I.T. Press, 1970).

[25] Leach, "Claude Lévi-Strauss—Anthropologist and Philosopher," p. 550. Marvin Harris comments on another, even more ironic aspect of Levi-Strauss's opacity. In preparing the second edition of his famous *Elementary Structures of Kinship,* Harris observes, Lévi-Strauss "confesses that once he has finished a book it becomes a strange body to him, no longer capable of engaging his interest and that 'it is only with difficulty sometimes, that I come to understand it' " [*The Rise of Anthropological Theory* (New York: Thomas Y. Crowell, 1968), pp. 511–12]. We are reminded here of the well-known rejoinder usually attributed to Robert Browning when he was asked about the meaning of a passage in one of his poems "God and I both knew what it meant once; now God alone knows."

tions of Lévi-Strauss's meaning have been rejected by the master himself. But if the subtleties of Lévi-Strauss's thought are often difficult to grasp, even by his most ardent supporters, the logical structure and empirical implications of his theoretical schema are clear enough. It is with these aspects of his work that we are mainly concerned.

Lévi-Strauss's writings can be evaluated on a number of different levels and in a variety of different contexts: as literary or poetic anthropology, as speculative philosophy, or as a series of logic "games." We believe, however, that his work ought to be assessed on the grounds that he himself apparently wishes it to be judged—namely, as scientific theory which purports to explain empirical cultural phenomena. Considered in *this* context, his theoretical structure raises some troublesome questions.

First of all, it must be emphasized that neither Lévi-Strauss nor anyone else has direct access to a culture's "deep structure." Thus, his "elementary structures," "structural principles," and "structure of the mind," are *inferences* from empirical data. They are, in other words, hypothetical or theoretical constructs, pure and simple. To be certain, all sciences employ such inferred entities as explanatory devices. And provided these constructs are utilized to link two sets of observable phenomena, and are therefore open to possible refutation, they present no logical difficulties. Lévi-Straussian structural principles, however, can be utilized, if one is ingenious enough and employs the appropriate transformations, to account for virtually *all* possible variations in cultural performance. To many adherents of structuralism, it is precisely this all-encompassing nature of Lévi-Straussian theory that is most appealing and is taken as a measure of its explanatory power. But a theory that is capable of explaining everything should be suspect. What sort of evidence could one conceivably adduce, for example, to show that the basic axioms of culture are *not* logical relationships constructed out of "binary oppositions"? Until a question like this (and it should be recalled that the concept of "binary opposition" provides the foundation for much of Lévi-Strauss's theoretical superstructure) can be posed and answered, it is difficult to see how Lévi-Strauss's theoretical speculations can ever be confirmed or disconfirmed. In point of fact, the kind of depth interpretation in which Lévi-Strauss is engaged resembles closely the procedures of psychoanalysis. And what Meehan has written of the Freudian logic of explanation might apply with the same force to the Lévi-Straussian logic of explanation:

> In an explanation the conceptual framework serves as a linking mechanism; events are related and explained *through* the conceptual framework. Freud consistently explained phenomena by relating them to theoretical terms which did not provide linkages with other observables. In some cases the theoretical structure served as one terminus of a two-part linkage; when the structure did serve as a connecting device, a connection was made not to other observable events but to other theoretical constructs. Freud's theoretical system, in other words, has no inputs—there are only outputs and sources. The powerful scientific technique of relating inputs to outputs and thus specifying the internal structure of an unknown system is not used in Freud's work. Instead, he was forced to infer inner structure solely from performance. Instead of relational propositions linking inputs and outputs, Freud produced propositions

that link outputs to hypothetical constructs. The hypothetical constructs do not *connect* the phenomena, they *account* for them.[26]

A further difficulty in Lévi-Strauss's theoretical schema relates to the logical transformations by which he gets from the basic structural principles to variations in cultural performance. These transformations tend to be highly idosyncratic and difficult, if not always impossible, for other anthropologists to replicate. But even if we assume that transformation procedures could be spelled out more precisely, we would still be faced with the difficulties of relating Lévi-Strauss's formal models to the kinds of empirical materials and issues with which anthropologists usually deal. For example, in a rather remarkable section of *The Savage Mind*, Lévi-Strauss demonstrates how the Indian caste system can be derived by a logical transformation from the totemic system of the Australian aborigines.[27] One has the overpowering sensation after reading this discussion that one has just witnessed—as Leach commented with respect to some other features of Lévi-Strauss's work—a "verbal sleight of hand." Does Lévi-Strauss *really* mean that the natives created the Indian caste system by employing the same—or at least a similar —logical analysis to the analysis he employed? It is hard to know. For it is not clear where Lévi-Strauss's reasoning leaves off and native reasoning begins, or what relationship this reasoning bears to the empirical world.

Nothing that we have said about Lévi-Strauss should, of course, be construed as impugning the remarkable ingenuity and erudition displayed in the pages of his writings. Nor would we deny the numerous insights and suggestive passages scattered throughout his work. Nevertheless, it seems to us that the enthusiastic reception his work has received, both within and outside anthropology, owe more to aesthetic considerations and the psychological satisfaction that may be drawn from his writings than they do to the scientific merit of the theories themselves. If we may hazard a prediction, we would say that the ultimate impact of Lévi-Strauss will *not* come from his theoretical stance or mode of explanation. Two thousand years of Western intellectual history indicates that the kind of ultrarationalism that characterizes Lévi-Strauss's work is not very fruitful—at least as a way of ordering and explaining empirical reality. Rather, we believe that his influence will make itself felt though the impact of his ideas on other investigators who have been jarred by Lévi-Strauss's insights into casting his observations, intuitions, and constructions into a less idiosyncratic form and employing them as research leads.

Or, as Edmund Leach, sympathetic interpreter and an admirer of much of Lévi-Strauss's work, has said: "The genuinely valuable part of Lévi-Strauss's contribution, in my view, is not the formalistic search for binary oppositions and their multiple permutations and combinations but rather the truly poetic range of associations which he brings to bear in the course of his analysis. . . ." [28]

---

26 Meehan, *Contemporary Political Thought*, pp. 238–39.
27 See Lévi-Strauss, *The Savage Mind*, chap. 4.
28 Leach, *Claude Lévi-Strauss*, p. 127.

The New Ethnography

Within recent years there has emerged, among American anthropologists in particular, a growing interest in various formal approaches to the analysis of ethnographic materials—ethnoscience, ethnosemantics, componential analysis, and the like. William Sturtevant, one of the expositors of this recent trend, has applied the collective label "the new ethnography" to these formal approaches, thus emphasizing their character as a methodological program for conducting ethnographic field research. But methodologies do not develop in a conceptual vacuum. Behind most methodologies is a theory, either implicit or explicit, which provides the rationale for the methodological approach. In the case of the new ethnography the theoretical rationale rests on a set of assumptions concerning the relationship among language, cognitive rules, principles and codes, on the one hand, and patterns of behavior and sociocultural arrangements, on the other. Having discussed these theoretical assumptions in the section on the personality subsystem in the preceding chapter, we feel no need to review them here. Therefore, we shall deal with the new ethnography as a program of ethnographic research, with brief asides to the theoretical assumptions which undergird its methodology.

The ostensible aim of the new ethnography is to make ethnographic description more accurate and replicable than it has presumably been in the past. To achieve these goals, it is argued, the ethnographer must attempt to reproduce cultural reality as it is perceived, ordered, and lived by the members of a society. This means that a description of a given culture should be couched in terms of "native" conceptual principles, cognitive rules, codes, and categories, rather than in terms of the conceptual categories the ethnographer brings to his researches from his training as an anthropologist. An ideal ethnography, therefore, ought to include all of the rules, principles, and categories that the native himself must know in order to understand and act appropriately in the various social situations that confront him in his day-to-day existence. Only in this way, it is believed, can the distorting effects of the ethnographer's theoretical predilections and cultural biases be neutralized and a description which mirrors the "true" cultural reality be more closely approximated.

The first question that one might raise in connection with this procedure is: What theoretical aim lies behind one's attempt to reproduce cultural reality from the native's viewpoint? As we indicated in the first chapter, the idea that ethnographic description, or any description, can or ought to reproduce reality is an entirely chimerical notion. Descriptions, even of the simplest set of events, are inevitably selective and partial, and unless we know the purpose of the description, it is difficult to evaluate it.

Now, there are issues, problems, and questions of concern to anthropologists in which a description in terms of native categories may not only be helpful but indispensable. But whatever these issues and questions may be, they certainly do not begin to exhaust the aims of anthropology. If one sees ethnography as an adjunct to a theoretical anthropology—that is, as a kind of laboratory in which theories are formulated, tested, modified, or revised—then a description couched in terms that go beyond native categories is essential. The reason for this is not difficult to see. Native categories, principles, and codes are by their very nature highly context-bound and relative to a particular cultural setting; while theories refer to *classes* of phenomena, *kinds* of situations, and cultural *types* which transcend a particular cultural setting.

In an article published in 1956, Ward Goodenough, one of the leading theoreticians of the new ethnography, recognized the problem of relating an ethnography which relies on native categories to a more broadly conceived theoretical anthropology. At that time Goodenough tried to resolve the problem by suggesting a separation between the anthropologist as descriptive ethnographer and the anthropologist as comparative ethnologist. While he has since modified this earlier position somewhat (see below), the original article has had a strong and continuing impact on anthropological thought. We believe, therefore, that the analysis he offered in 1956 is still pertinent as representing the thinking of many of the new ethnographers. In 1956 Goodenough remarked:

> What we do as ethnographers is, and must be kept, independent of what we do as comparative ethnologists. An ethnographer is constructing a theory that will make intelligible what goes on in a particular social universe. A comparativist is trying to find principles common to many different universes. His data are not the direct observations of an ethnographer, but the laws governing the particular universe as the ethnographer formulates them. It is by noting how these laws vary from one universe to another and under what conditions, that the comparativist arrives at a statement of laws governing the events in their respective social universes. Although they operate at different levels of abstraction, both ethnographer and comparativist are engaged in theory construction. Each must, therefore, develop concepts appropriate to his own level of abstraction, and in the case of the ethnographer to his particular universe. When we move from one level to the other we must shift our conceptual frameworks in accordance with systematic transformation procedures.[29]

We find this formulation unacceptable on several counts. First, in any scientific discipline there is a constant interplay between the theoretical concepts and principles of the discipline and its empirical findings. But Goodenough has here imposed such a sharp conceptual distinction between these two intrinsically interacting aspects of a discipline that it is hard to see how they could function with the complementarity that scientific logic demands. Second (if we understand Goodenough correctly), what he seems to be saying is that every ethnographic description of a particular culture contains

---

[29] Ward H. Goodenough, "Residence Rules," *Southwestern Journal of Anthropology* 12 (1956): 37. Elsewhere, Goodenough has said: "Ethnographic description, then, requires methods of processing observed phenomena such that we can *inductively* construct a theory of how our informants have organized the same phenomena [emphasis added]" (quoted by W. C. Sturtevant "Studies in Ethnoscience," *American Anthropologist*, 66, no. 3, part 2 [1964] [*Transcultural Studies in Cognition*, ed. A. Kimball Romney and R. G. D'Andrade]: 100.

a theory of that culture. It is then left to the comparative theoretician to generalize from these context-bound theories to a larger universe of cultures. This looks to us like saying there is one law of falling apples, another law of falling acorns, still another law of falling stones, etc., from which we generalize to a law of falling bodies. But clearly, the inductive recommendations offered by Goodenough in this selection stand logical procedures on their head. It is the law of falling *bodies*, of course, which helps to explain falling apples, acorns, and the rest. And we find it difficult to imagine an ethnographer framing a theory of a particular culture which does not draw upon the general theories that are a part of his discipline. It would be a curious discipline—not to mention an idiosyncratic kind of science—where the concepts used to explain a particular phenomenon (culture) were vastly different from the concepts used to explain the class of phenomena (cultures) of which that phenomenon is a member.

In the paper under consideration Goodenough asserts that when we move from one level of abstraction (a particular culture) to another (a class of cultures), we "must shift our conceptual frameworks in accordance with systematic transformation procedures." But he does not specify what these "transformation procedures" are. At the very least, however, they would have to involve a process of *de*contextualizing the descriptive materials (since these are framed in native terms and categories) as one moved inductively from the ethnographic description of culture X to a theory of culture X to a more general theory of the class of cultures of which culture X is an instance. Yet the act of decontextualizing must destroy the very fabric of Goodenough's theoretical structure. For if each empirical case reflects specific native categories of thought, each is idiosyncratic. It is difficult for us to see how one may expect to apply a general theory to any specific empirical case when the concepts involved in both are different—on the one hand the native's, on the other the anthropologists's. Under these circumstances, the use of general or comparative theory to illuminate the particular is futile and the entire enterprise of general theory formulation becomes empirically vacuous.

Because he chooses here to maintain the distinction between ethnographic description in terms of *native* categories and comparative ethnology in terms of the *theoretical* categories of the anthropologist, Goodenough's position is completely artificial and untenable. Yet his discussion (insofar as it summarized his position as well as that of many of the new ethnographers) does serve to clarify the issues—although certainly not in the way he intends. We reject the notion that anthropologists work with two fundamentally different kinds of theory, one produced by descriptive ethnographers and the other by comparative ethnologists. To apply the term *theory* to a set of statements that is so closely tied to a particular historical instance that it has no comparative implications is, we believe, to use the term in a Pickwickian sense. Theory is always comparative—and this holds for physical, chemical, and biological as well as anthropological theory. When Goodenough argues, therefore, that there is a broad conceptual gap between *an ethnographic description framed wholly in native terms and categories* and the formulation or testing of comparative propositions, he is, in effect, emphasizing the limitations of such *descriptions* for the development of a theoretical anthropology.

In the more recent and more comprehensive statement to which we referred in the preceding discussion, Goodenough appears to have altered somewhat the theoretical stance he assumed in his 1956 paper on residence rules, and, in doing so, seems to come a little closer to the position we have been arguing here. Thus, he writes:

> emic description [i.e., descriptions couched in native concepts and categories] requires etics [i.e., the anthropologist's concepts and categories], and by trying to do emic descriptions we add to our etic conceptual resources for subsequent description. It is through etic concepts that we do comparison. And by systematizing our etic concepts we contribute to the development of a general science of culture. Therefore, I agree heartily with [Marvin] Harris about the fundamental importance of etics. But unlike him I see etics as bogging down in useless hairsplitting and overpreoccupation with recording hardware, unless it is accompanied by a concern for emics. For Harris, concern with emic description competes with the development of etics; for me, it contributes most directly to it.[30]

Although we have some difficulty understanding how "useless hairsplitting and overpreoccupation with recording hardware" apply more cogently to etic than to emic research and analysis, we believe Goodenough is saying, overall, that often the source of the etic categories and concepts are, and indeed should be, the native's concepts and categories. In some sense, then, the foregoing statement (if we interpret it accurately) represents a shift away from Goodenough's earlier sharp dichotomization between emic and etic—i.e., now there *are* no emics without etics; and, we would add, no ethnographic research of any kind except as it is filtered through the ingrained etic screen of the observer. Finally, the point we wish to stress is that when the anthropologist draws on "native concepts and categories," he readapts them for his own theoretical purposes (compare the quotation from J. Pitt-Rivers, pp. 22–23, *supra*), and in the process he "eticizes" these "concepts and categories." Thus, ultimately, all of the concepts utilized by anthropologists in communicating with other anthropologists or with the public at large are and must be etic. A true and completely emic account of a culture would be incomprehensible except perhaps to some of the members of that culture.

Emic and Etic Approaches to Cultural Phenomena

One of the principle aims of the new ethnography is to attempt to eliminate, or at least to neutralize, the potentially distorting biases of the ethnographer. The premise is simple: if one records only the native's view of his culture and not the ethnographer's perceptions and interpretations of

---

[30] See Ward H. Goodenough, *Description and Comparison in Cultural Anthropology* (Chicago: Aldine, 1970), p. 112. In this book Goodenough is responding in part to some of the criticisms levelled at him by Marvin Harris (*The Rise of Anthropological Theory*, chap. 20). For other responses to the kinds of objections to aspects of the new ethnography raised by Harris, see also: Brent Berlin, "A Universalistic-Evolutionary Approach to Ethnographic Semantics," in *Current Directions in Anthropology*, ed. Ann Fischer (Bulletin of the American Anthropological Association, Vol. 3, No. 3, Part 2 [1970], pp. 3–18; and Paul Kay, "Some Theoretical Implications of Ethnographic Semantics," Ibid., pp. 19–31.

what the culture is all about, one gets at "the real thing" as it is perceived, lived, and understood by the members of the particular society. But the attempt to eliminate completely the conditioning, the preconceptions, and the biases of the ethnographer is about on a par with trying to invent a perpetual-motion machine. We would do better to expend our efforts in other directions. No one has direct access to anyone else's mind. Thus, cognitive principles, rules, and codes are in the final analysis only inferences drawn by the ethnographer—they are his conceptions of what the informant's conception might be. But since these inferences must be cast in a form that makes sense not only to the ethnographer but to his colleagues as well, it means that the ethnographer has to employ categories of thought drawn from anthropology and not exclusively from the native informant. We are all inevitably comparativists. At most, Goodenough's recommendations (especially in the 1956 article on residence rules), if they are followed, might yield suppressed comparisons. They can never eliminate the process itself. For we can only begin to understand a culture in terms of its differences from and similarities to other cultures we have experienced or read about. To think otherwise is to delude ourselves. Thus, it seems to us that the way to make ethnographic reporting more replicable is not by trying to eliminate the role of the ethnographer but by trying to make his theoretical predilections, his cultural biases, and his active role as explicit as possible.

Finally, when the new ethnographers assert that the goal of ethnographic description is to recreate cultural reality "from the native viewpoint," one might well ask, "which native"? Here, it seems to us, the new ethnographers have gone astray because they have tended generally to apply the methods of linguistic analysis to ethnographic inquiry. A linguist investigating the phonemes of standard American English, for example, does not have to work with a random sample of inhabitants of the United States. Dialects aside, one, two, or three informants will probably suffice, since all native speakers make the same kinds of phonemic distinctions—that is, they all share the language. But all of the individuals who make up a particular culture do not share or participate in their culture in the same way. (See David Aberle for a relevant view of "participation." [31] Although Aberle emphasizes interaction and interdependence rather than cognition, the point he makes is similar to that made by Wallace in the discussion cited earlier, pp. 144–45, *supra*). This means that the "cultural reality" may be different for the chief and commoner, the adult and child, the rich and poor, the handsome and ugly, etc. But it obviously does not mean that the participants are incapable of acting cooperatively, complementarily, or with adequate appreciation of their roles in the cultural system. Aberle not only tells us that the simpler societies manifest differences in the nature and patterns of "participation," but he goes beyond this to remind us that increasing complexity *demands* differential participation. It seems reasonable to conclude, therefore, that from the cognitive viewpoint as well as the interactive, there is no one "cultural reality," but there may be a host of differing "cultural realities."

By and large the new ethnographers have not employed the kind of sta-

---

[31] See Aberle, "The Influence of Linguistics," pp. 14–15.

tistical sampling procedures that would seem to be required by the "participational" and cognitive distinctions just discussed. They have tended to assume that a few or a handful of informants somehow encapsulate the conceptual principles and cognitive categories of the culture. But, as we have emphasized, this is an unwarranted assumption.

Although the new ethnographers have produced a great many programmatic statements, they have not yet given us a full-scale description of a single society utilizing the methodology of the new ethnography. The investigations that have been carried out have tended to focus on specialized and restricted cultural domains like disease categories, color categories, firewood, numeral classifiers, and kin terms. Perhaps the main reason that no one has produced a description of a single culture using the formal techniques of the new ethnography is that such a study, according to Sturtevant, would run into "many thousands of pages." But to us, formidable as it may appear, Sturtevant's figure is much too low, and his estimate of the feasibility of such an enterprise is overly optimistic. For if one considers all the possible variations in conceptual principles, cognitive rules, and categories which may guide persons who occupy different positions in a social structure—especially if one considers these in the context of a complex cultural system like that of, say, modern Japan or the United States—then a "new ethnographic" description might require at least several lifetimes to carry out and run into many tens of thousands of pages. But a conceptual scheme or research program that encourages us to pursue what are essentially impracticable research procedures and unobtainable research goals has, *ipso facto*, certain serious defects.

On the positive side, the new ethnographers have reminded us not to abandon or forget a basic anthropological premise—namely, that all peoples do not order and classify their social and natural universes in precisely the same way. They have further sensitized us to the fact that the kinds of conceptual distinctions we make or fail to make in the cognitive schema of our discipline or, more generally, in our own culture, may not be duplicated in other cultures. The point is an important one, but it can be overstressed to the detriment of anthropology's growth as a scientific discipline. We ought not to be lead from these understandings into a world of Whorfian relativity. After all, our ability even to talk about the cognitive categories of other peoples demonstrates that the "world-views" of different societies are not *wholly* incommensurable with our own or with each other.

Finally, we reiterate a point made in the first chapter of this book: native cognitive categories are designed to get people around in their culture. For the most part they are, like the language a people use, accepted and used unreflectively. The cognitive categories of the anthropologist as anthropologist, on the other hand, are designed for another purpose: they are not intended to *reproduce* "cultural reality" but to render it understandable in a comparative frame. Moreover, the categories used by the anthropologist are subject to constant revision and self-critical appraisal in a way that is normally not true of the cognitive categories used in one's day-to-day activities. Thus, the purpose for which the research and description are undertaken will determine whether an ethnographic account is couched in "native categories" (emic terms), in the "anthropologist's categories" (etic terms), or, as is overwhelmingly the case, in some combination of the two.

Thus, if there are certain benefits to be derived from the pursuit of the new ethnography, they will not follow either from the attempt to "get inside the native's head" or from the equally implausible attempt to do a "complete study of a single culture" uncontaminated by the anthropologist's intellectual or ideological intervention. Sturtevant, apparently realizing that some of the goals envisioned by the new ethnography may be unrealistic, concludes that "emphases in ethnography will continue to be guided by ethnological, comparative, interests. Some domains will receive more attention than others."[32]

In concluding this chapter we should like to reemphasize some of our earlier observations on the limitations of linguistic models as applied to cultural studies. Our emphasis is determined by the fact that both Lévi-Strauss and the new ethnographers rely heavily on the linguistic analogy. Conceptually, they view culture as a logical grammar, as a code, or as a set of structural rules for generating culturally appropriate behavior.

When employed with proper caution, the linguistic model can be fruitful and suggestive in dealing with certain kinds of problems. But if one forgets the partial and isomorphic nature of the linguistic analogy, the questions that it raises may appear in a form that make resolutions or "answers" difficult to obtain. And, from the point of view of the discipline as a whole, the isomorphic nature of the analogy may even block off many of the questions that most anthropologists would like to ask.

For example, linguists may be concerned with the morphological and grammatical rules that characterize, say, spoken Japanese and spoken Indonesian. However, *why* the structural rules of these two languages differ from one another is not ordinarily a question that occupies the attention of the linguists. Yet it is precisely this kind of question that may be posed by an anthropologist probing nonlinguistic aspects of these cultures; e.g., what are the differences between the socioeconomic structures of modern Japan and modern Indonesia, and what are the specific factors (technoeconomic, socialstructural, ideological, or psychological) that might explain these differences?

The point can be made more generally. If we ultimately view cultures as codes or cognitive rules and categories, we encounter the same kinds of explanatory difficulties that we noted when culture is seen essentially as a system of norms and values—that is, the most fundamental aspect of the culture, the code itself, remains unexplained, unexplainable, a mystery.

What, for example, makes the cultural code of the Japanese differ from that of the Indonesians? Climate? Toilet-training? Race? The vagaries of historical accident? Or is it something peculiar and special about the collective mental structure of the people, however derived? The question we are raising here, of course, is the problem of accommodating the "code" view of culture to a theory of culture change. We believe it may be difficult if not impossible to reconstruct the code and conceptual principles of most cultures as they functioned in the past. And even where we do have partial or relatively "complete" access to such data, how may we explain changes in the codes without reverting to the metaphysics of some kind of Platonic rationalism? We should point out, of course, that for Lévi-Strauss this particular problem

---

[32] Sturtevant, "Studies in Ethnoscience," 123.

does not arise simply because he *has*, in effect, adopted a variant of Plato's theory of innate ideas. Lévi-Strauss's elementary structures are formal—therefore, fixed, enduring, and unchanging.

But the new ethnographers do not work from the same set of theoretical assumptions as Lévi-Strauss. Hence, they must confront the problem of change if they intend—as they seem to—that their program should apply to something more than the formal analysis of narrow and esoteric domains like, for example, how to order a beer in the Philippines.

Despite the strictures we have pointed to throughout this chapter, we are not urging anthropologists to abandon linguistic models in their cultural studies. But those who employ such models ought always to bear in mind that the linguistic analogy—like any model—has certain limitations. In some ways it may be suggestive; in others it may act as an impediment in dealing with questions and issues that have always been a central concern to anthropology.

Five Epilogue:
Some Old Themes
and New Directions

Anthropology in Crisis

There are certain periods in the history of all scientific disciplines when new data and new questions arise which cannot be handled or explained by the application of traditional ideas and concepts. Physics, for example, passed through such a crisis in its development at the turn of the twentieth-century when the Newtonian world-view underwent significant modification at the hands of Einstein and others. And, to take an example from biology, the Darwinian theory of natural selection required more than half a century of tortured growth plus the explosive impact of Mendelian genetics in order to become today's synthetic theory of biological evolution.

Anthropology now seems to be going through a similar period of crisis. It would be optimistic, if not presumptuous, to assume that the magnitude of any possible breakthrough, if it comes, will compare in impact or importance with the examples just cited. Nevertheless, it is quite clear that anthropology is undergoing a crisis which has been occasioned in the first place by the

This chapter appeared in *The Southwestern Journal of Anthropology*, 27 (1971): 19–60.

virtual disappearance of the primitive world—a world that has in the past provided the anthropologist with his only natural laboratory and most of his data. Partly as a corollary of this development and partly for other reasons, there has been a growing demand (from inside as well as outside the profession) that anthropology become more "relevant" and more activist—that it should begin to play an important role in *promoting* social change. Under the impact of these pressures anthropologists have been forced to ask: Where do we go from here? In this chapter we offer some ideas about where we think anthropology might be going. To do this, however, we must first examine where anthropology has been.

The Traditional View

From its inception, anthropology has—at least in principle—considered all cultures at all times and in all places to be its legitimate province. In practice, however, anthropologists have generally concerned themselves with non-Western cultures, and especially with the small-scale and exotic among these.[1] There are several reasons for this concentration. In the first place, by the middle of the nineteenth century political science, economics, and even sociology were emerging as fields of study which dealt primarily with the institutions of Western society. While many social scientists of this period may have been acquainted with the data that came from remote and exotic areas, they apparently did not see much purpose in either abandoning their concern with the institutions of their own culture or conducting first-hand research among "primitive peoples."

In short, none of the "established" social sciences saw any reason to desert the relative comforts of research and speculation at home for the discomforts of the field. They did not, as Jarvie comments picturesquely in another context, seem too eager "to come down off the verandah and muck in with the fieldwork programme."[2] Interestingly enough, however, even most of those who did identify themselves as anthropologists in the early years of the discipline were not field anthropologists. It is alleged, for example, that "Sir James Frazer, when asked if he had ever seen one of the primitive people about whose customs he had written so many volumes, tersely replied, 'God forbid.'"[3] Tylor traveled to some of the remote "uncivilized" regions of Mexico and the American Southwest, but he never conducted any systematic field work in those areas. Among the pioneers of anthropology, Morgan was virtually alone in his willingness to expose himself, at least briefly, to some of the lesser discomforts of field research. It may be said that while anthropologists before Franz Boas were intellectually committed to the study of

---

[1] It was not the "discovery" of China or even the early trade with India that led to the emergence of modern anthropology. It was the nonliterate cultures of Africa, the New World, and the Pacific and Indian Oceans that seemed to demand and concomitantly to lend themselves to the holistic studies that are the hallmark of anthropology.

[2] I. C. Jarvie, *The Revolution in Anthropology* (New York: Humanities Press, 1964), p. 13.

[3] John Beattie, *Other Cultures* (New York: Free Press, 1964), p. 7.

primitive cultures, they were on the whole temperamentally unsuited to or ideologically unconvinced of the need for conducting such study on the ground. For the most part they were bound to the museums, libraries, and the postal service even while their intellectual commitment to understanding exotic cultures remained firm. For the primitive world offered a vast comparative laboratory in which one might learn something about the *nature* of man—about his potentialities and his limitations, about where he had been and where he might be going. And, related to this was the belief that the study of small-scale exotic societies would reveal certain basic social processes with greater clarity and definition than comparable studies in the more complex societies of the Western world, because the "savage" cultures were less encumbered by the baggage and trappings of civilized life. Thus, it was argued that the study of cultures distant and vastly different from one's own enabled one to gain a perspective and objectivity with respect to one's own culture that could not be achieved in any other way.

Finally, we would emphasize one factor that has contributed to the delineation and growth of anthropology as a specialized social-science discipline. We refer to the emphasis on field work and participant observation that began, around the turn of the century, to emerge as the major anthropological device for data gathering. Before this, most anthropologists, as we implied above, had relied almost exclusively on the accounts of travelers, traders, missionaries, and colonial administrators for their ethnographic materials. But in the early decades of the twentieth century the anthropologist began increasingly to gather his own materials. Indeed, field research became the defining cachet of the anthropologist.

Now, while participant observation is both a practicable and desirable data-gathering technique for use in a small-scale situation such as that of a primitive band, tribe, or village, it is much less feasible as a technique for the study of more complex social groupings. Sometimes the tail wagged the dog. And anthropologists found themselves selecting situations and problems for investigation that *could* be handled by what they considered the most important technique or method in the research arsenal of their discipline. This is an important issue to which we shall return later.

In studying the simpler, small-scale societies, anthropologists operated with certain methodological assumptions. They assumed, for example, that these societies could be treated as more-or-less self-contained isolates and that such an approach would not distort one's understanding of how the societies functioned. In other words, the anthropologist was generally unself-conscious about the physical and social boundaries of his field research entity, making no distinction between these and his "unit of analysis." Nor did he bother particularly to distinguish "system" from "environment." He would usually select a linguistic, geographic, or cultural unit that was somewhat manageable (manageable in terms of field research that could be carried on by a single anthropologist), identify it as culture X, and proceed to analyze this arbitrarily defined unit as though it were a "system."

Of course, the system treated by the anthropologist as his unit of *analysis* was rarely coterminous with the unit of *observation*. Thus, while some anthropologists employed a kind of sampling technique in their studies, settling themselves for varying lengths of time in different segments or in different villages or hamlets of a given society, no anthropologist could study a whole society, a whole tribe, a chiefdom, or even a congeries of bands or nomadic herding groups.[4] Inevitably, then, the fieldworker's conclusions about the whole society were extrapolated from his study of one or more segments of that society.

In sum, the usual, if not the exclusive, research pattern adopted was for the investigator to settle in a village, hamlet, or other comparable segment of the society in which he was interested. He carried on his researches and later assembled his data in the form of a report on the culture—or certain aspects of the culture—of such-and-such a tribe, people, chiefdom, or society. In point of fact, his observations and the contingent account prepared by him had been based not on the study of all of the sometimes widely dispersed segments of society (Navajo, Eskimo, Crow, Tiv, Bushman, etc.), but only on that group or those groups among whom he had conducted his work. It was generally assumed that the part studied stood for the whole; that if you had seen one or a selected few segments of tribe X, you had seen them all; and that whatever you were able to report for the microcosm within which you had lived would hold as well for the rest of the society. In truly segmented so-cieties (that is, where each village or segment is largely a carbon copy of the others and where no hierarchical ranking of the segments prevails) the ac-count and the analysis of the single or sample segments could often indeed stand for all of the remaining segments. Such a study may have revealed, as well, the interlocking and interdependency mechanisms that wove these sep-arate units into a tribal or societal whole. But there are many preliterate social groupings studied by anthropologists where the whole is greater—or at least different—than the sum of its parts, where the social system consists of complementary village, hamlet, or other units, and not of matching or seg-mented equivalents.

Malinowski, for example, discusses "the culture of the Trobriand Is-landers" largely on the basis of his intensive study of a particular village within the Kiriwina district.[5] But, as the residence of the paramount chief, this village seems to have had a special character that distinguished it from other Trobriand Island villages. Thus, whatever Malinowski's assumptions about the microcosmic nature of his village may have been, the picture of Trobriand life that emerges in his numerous accounts is based primarily on his study of *that* village in *that* district. Consequently, as Powell tells us, the sense of a strong hierarchical political structure and a relatively power-ful chief conveyed by Malinowski's accounts does not apply with the same force to many of the Trobriand villages that lay outside the direct control

---

[4] Even the small hunting band or nomadic herding group that might be the object of study was never completely and permanently isolated from other similar groups. Periodically they would come together for ritual, mate-seeking, economic, or other purposes. And in this temporary but patterned manner they constituted a social unit different in form and function from that of each of the individual segments that made it up. The anthropologist could not study all of the segments at first hand even if he could sample them and study their collective activities on those occasions when they came together.

[5] See, for example, Bronislaw Malinowski, *Argonauts of the Western Pacific* (New York: Dutton, 1922); also *Coral Gardens and Their Magic* (London: Allan & Unwin: 1935) 2 vols.

of the paramount chief nor to Trobriand life "as a whole." [6] To the extent that Malinowski generalized from this village to all of Trobriand culture, his presentation and his analysis are somewhat skewed.

What Malinowski did (and many others as well have done) results from a widespread and, until fairly recently, unexamined anthropological assumption about the nature of the social structure of many of the simpler societies. The errors to which it has often led owe their origin, as we have already suggested, to a research methodology which grew up with the discipline itself.

Ordinarily, the field anthropologist reached the scene of his researches long after the objects of his study had been exposed to the influences of the explorer, trader, foreign missionary, and colonial administrator. Thus, by the time he arrived, much of the "primitive world" had become involved in the acculturation process initiated by the explorations of the late fifteenth century. This is not to say that culture contact, diffusion, and acculturation began with the era of exploration. The historical and archaeological records clearly demonstrate that change through contact has been going on since there have been human societies. What makes modern processes of acculturation unique, however, is that they have emanated overwhelmingly from a single cultural source—industrialized Western society—and have left few if any cultures untouched as they have reached into all parts of the globe. It can be said, therefore, that all of mankind has now become a part of true world history.

Until quite recently the tempo and impact of these modern acculturative forces emanating from Western societies were variable. Some cultures, like those of the American Plains Indians which stood in the way of our westward expansion, were shattered and transformed with a dramatic and often heartbreaking rapidity. However, many other cultures, located in relatively remote or inaccessible parts of the world, continued to retain important features of their traditional lifeways and social structures despite influences reaching them from Western society.

In many respects, these variations in degrees of acculturation or deculturation are reflected in the slightly different emphases of British anthropology (functionalism) vis-à-vis American (historical reconstruction) during the first decades of the twentieth century. With very few exceptions, the Americans carried on their researches among aborigines whose cultures had been radically transformed by the intrusive whites. On the other hand, British anthropologists, working mostly in Africa or Oceania, studied groups whose cultures, though clearly affected, had not for the most part been obliterated or so drastically altered by the modern contact as those of most American Indians. Thus, the British could more readily assume that "life-as-it-is-lived-now" is much like "life-as-it-was-lived-then," while the American anthropologist was compelled to reconstruct or recreate life-as-it-was-lived-then through the use of oral histories, legends, and so on—or what some British anthropologists referred to disparagingly as "conjectural history." In any case, both groups believed one of the principal aims of field work was to preserve a record of the aboriginal—or early-modified aboriginal—way of life before all

---

[6] See H. A. Powell, "Competitive Leadership in Trobriand Political Organization," *Journal of the Royal Anthropological Institute* 90 (1960): 118–45.

traces should be lost forever under the massive impact of acculturational forces.

Given this view of the anthropological mission, it is no wonder that anthropologists tended to treat each of the groups with which they worked as an isolate, as a virtually self-sufficient and bounded social system, generally no larger than several bands, villages, or a tribe. In short, they studied primitive societies as though they were independently functioning entities rather than increasingly dependent and subordinate parts of much larger economic, political, and social systems.

It should be emphasized that we are attempting here only to identify what seems to have been a dominant theme or viewpoint in anthropological research until fairly recent times. We are not indicating that anthropologists were unaware of the numerous acculturative influences that had impinged on the societies of the primitive world. Even a quick look at some of the early classics of American anthropology, such as Mooney's analysis of the Ghost Dance, Wissler's studies of the impact of the horse upon Plains culture, or even Morgan's early monograph on the Iroquois, should be enough to remind us that anthropologists were not that naïve.[6A] But it was not until the 1930s that the discipline as a whole began to devote attention to the problems of acculturation. Nevertheless, and despite an increasing sophistication about the processes—or at least the consequences—of culture contact, the anthropologist's unit of research *and* analysis remained the small-scale system: the village, tribe, reservation, community. Most anthropologists were still involved, for example, with trying to demonstrate the enormous variety of cultural arrangements in the world and the striking malleability of "human nature"; also they were fighting the battle to prove that "primitive culture" did not mean "primitive mentality." In short, they were trying continually to drive home the meaning and lesson of cultural relativity. And in pursuit of this aim they were led to adopt a methodological position which viewed primitive societies as independently functioning systems. We believe it is fair to say that, with certain notable exceptions, this viewpoint was dominant in anthropology up to fairly recent times.

Criticisms
of the Traditional View

Within the last few decades a number of anthropologists have raised important questions about the implications of treating the traditional units of anthropological research as though they were relatively autonomous and functionally independent entities. Some of them have based their criticism primarily on methodological issues. They have suggested that, whereas autonomy and intragroup functional independence may have been useful methodological assumptions when there existed a greater degree of cultural isolation,

---

[6A] See: James Mooney, *The Ghost Dance Religion and the Sioux Outbreak of 1890* (Washington: Bureau of American Ethnology, 1896); Clark Wissler, "The Influence of the Horse in the Development of Plains Culture," *American Anthropologist* 16 (1940): 1–25; Lewis Henry Morgan, *League of the Ho-de-no-sau-nee, or Iroquois* (Rochester: Sage and Brother, 1851).

in modern times autonomy and isolation are palpable myths, and that to continue to treat tribes and other social groupings as if they were in fact bounded and independent systems is methodologically indefensible. We shall return to this issue shortly.

Another group of intramural critics have asserted that the very methodological assumptions upon which the traditional approach rests are neither dispassionate nor neutral. They charge that these assumptions reflect an underlying ideological bias, a bias built into the discipline itself. Thus, in addition to pointing out the purely methodological shortcomings of the traditional approach, they have added a sociology-of-knowledge kind of critique, much more sweeping and damning in its nature and implications.

This latter group argue that since anthropology is tied historically to the imperialist expansion of the West, the field anthropologist was generally linked, either officially or unofficially, to one or another of the Western powers. Whether the links were formal or not, the anthropologist usually conducted his work in an internal or external colonial setting. (Some early community studies like James West's *Plainville*, Lloyd Warner's Yankee City series, and the Lynds' researches in Middletown may be cited as exceptions.) 6B In treating the societies of the primitive world as though they were "pristine" functioning units, in focusing on such "safe" topics as marriage, the family, kinship, or the techniques of basket weaving, the anthropologist became, these critics state, a tool of the exploiting interests. Whether or not he was aware of the contributions made by his action or inaction in this exploitative enterprise is essentially irrelevant. For while he may have felt and often expressed sympathy for the plight of the people he was studying, this sympathy, these critics assert, was rarely if ever translated into an analysis of the larger political and economic system which was responsible for the observably unhappy circumstances. The anthropologist was in effect disregarding the involvement of the colonialized people in worldwide imperialist networks; he was in effect ignoring the exploitation to which they were being subjected. His failure to play an active role on behalf of the oppressed or even to analyze the sociopolitical nature of imperialism could therefore be interpreted as indifference to the disintegrative consequences of the contact and exploitation on the peoples and their cultures.

The thesis stated above has been expressed in a variety of ways. Some critics have been more sweeping in their assault on the work of anthropologists than others. But however they may differ in emphasis or intensity, their critiques add up to an indictment of anthropology for its conservative bias.[7]

6B See: James West, *Plainville, U.S.A.* (New York: Columbia University Press, 1945); W. Lloyd Warner and Paul S. Lunt, *The Social Life of A Modern Community* (New Haven: Yale University Press, 1941); W. Lloyd Warner and Leo Srole, *The Social System of American Ethnic Groups* (New Haven: Yale University Press, 1945); W. Lloyd Warner and J.O. Low, *The Social System of the Modern Factory* (New Haven: Yale University Press, 1947); Robert Lynd and Helen Lynd, *Middletown* (New York: Harcourt-Brace, 1929); Robert Lynd and Helen Lynd, *Middletown in Transition* (New York: Harcourt-Brace, 1937).

[7] Perhaps the best known expression of this view is contained in a symposium on the social responsibility of anthropology in *Current Anthropology* 9 (1968): Gerald D. Berreman, "Is Anthropology Alive? Social Responsibility in Social Anthropology," 391–96;

In other words, the common thread of criticism that runs through the several arguments is that anthropologists betrayed both the humanistic and scientific potential of the discipline. On the humanistic level they failed as a group to take a stand against the social injustices revealed to them by their researches. And as social scientists they were deficient because they failed to analyze some of the most politically significant events of our time. In combination, then, the discipline has been guilty of "ignoring" the social, political, and economic inequities of the status quo, especially in the colonial situation.

Now, evaluating this position presents a number of difficulties. In the first place, the nature of the charges leveled against anthropology is not always clear. For example, are anthropologists being accused primarily (given their ideological background) of deliberately choosing to study issues and problems that are not really important, relevant, and significant ones? Or is it that their analyses of the problems which they do select for study are (again because of their ideological background) biased, inaccurate, and distorted? Or is it some combination of these? Moreover, the critical thesis is difficult to evaluate because it rests ultimately on the imputation of collective motives over time to virtually an entire profession—motives of which the accused themselves may be entirely unaware.

While many of these arguments have appeared in strong polemical form, we should not allow the polemics to obscure the essentially valid observations that are contained in the thesis of the critics. Anthropology did develop and carry on its researches alongside the imperialist powers and under the aegis of their local representatives. While many anthropologists were indeed critical of some of the consequences of colonialism (internal as well as external) for the peoples of the primitive world, the major critiques of the imperialist system were *not* produced by anthropologists. Whatever their personal feelings may have been, they apparently did not regard criticism of the imperialist enterprise as their principal mission.

Also, it can hardly be doubted that working in a colonial context imposed certain restraints upon the anthropologist. Usually, he was permitted to carry on his investigations of a particular society only at the sufferance of some officialdom or other. Hence, if certain proposed researches threatened to probe issues or problems considered sensitive by the colonial administration—assuming anthropologists were interested in pursuing these researches—it is unlikely that they would have been undertaken. Finally, the field work of many anthropologists, especially those working in overseas colonies, was often financed by various agencies of the colonial administration. Thus, these an-

---

Gutorm Gjessing, "The Social Responsibility of the Social Scientist," 397–402; and Kathleen Gough, "New Proposals for Anthropologists," 403–7. See also the accompanying comments on the above papers by various social scientists, and the authors' rejoinders.

In more general terms, the last few years have witnessed the publication of a number of books and articles dealing with the social responsibility of social scientists and the relationship between ideology and social science knowledge. See, for example, Gideon Sjoberg (ed.), *Ethics, Politics and Social Research* (Cambridge, Mass.: Schenkman, 1967); Irving Louis Horowitz, *Professing Sociology* (Chicago: Aldine, 1968); and Ralph L. Beals, *Politics of Social Research: An Inquiry into the Ethics and Responsibilities of Social Research* (Chicago: Aldine, 1969).

thropologists appear to have had at least some kind of obligation to deal with problems that were of interest to the colonial administrators, in addition to those issues that may have been of greater academic interest.

What do the foregoing observations suggest about the dominant methodological and intellectual position of anthropology during the course of its development? It seems to us that at the very most they may allow us to infer that the problems selected for study by anthropologists and the analytic framework within which they handled these problems were influenced by the political, economic, and ideological milieu in which they worked. It does not mean, however, that their analyses of the problems which they selected for investigation are necessarily wrong or inaccurate. Of course, they may be. But if they are that would have to be demonstrated on other grounds than the simple assertion that the ideology which inspired the analyses is objectionable. It is one of the easiest, if not one of the most rational, of critical procedures to dismiss a body of work as being ideologically tainted. Every piece of anthropological analysis ever written can be interpreted, if one wishes to do so, as motivated by some ideology or other. For if we have learned anything from the sociology-of-knowledge approach, it is that all thinking, in and out of the social sciences (including, of course, the thinking of the critics under discussion), is likely to be influenced by the political, economic, social, and ideological milieu of the times.[8] But this does not mean that anthropology is nothing

---

[8] Philosophers of science have made a useful distinction between the *generation* of ideas and theories and their *evaluation*. Hans Reichenbach has referred to the first of these as the "context of discovery" and the second as the "context of justification" (*Experience and Prediction* [Chicago: University of Chicago Press, 1938], pp. 6–7). (See also our discussion of this theme in Chapter 1.) One may be concerned with the social and psychological sources of a scholar's ideas (the context of discovery), and that is, of course, a completely valid scholarly interest. But this kind of research can tell us little or nothing about the scientific validity and explanatory fruitfulness of those ideas. These features must be demonstrated logically and empirically (the context of justification). (For a good discussion of these and related issues in a social science context, see Benjamin Walter, "The Sociology of Knowledge and the Problem of Objectivity," in *Sociological Theory: Inquiries and Paradigms*, ed. Llewellyn Gross [New York: Harper and Row, 1967], pp. 335–57.)

In the context of discovery, then, one will be concerned primarily with the ideological milieu in which a certain research is carried on and in which particular ideas and concepts arose. One need not be concerned with the validity of the ideas and concepts themselves. One would hope, then, that those contemporary anthropologists who *are* interested in the ideological context would extend toward their intellectual predecessors the same kind of relativistic understanding as they do toward the peoples among whom they do their field work. Thus, it seems to us that it is somewhat unfair to indict the anthropology of 1890, or 1910, or 1925, or 1940 for slighting issues and problems which, in the 1970s, have become "the burning issues of our time." Such an indictment clearly lacks anthropological perspective.

Naturally, many of the critics of whom we speak are indicting a fair percentage of the anthropologists of today as well as those of the past. However, it seems to us slightly misleading to deal with present-day anthropology as though it were a relatively changeless extension or continuation of what anthropologists were doing in 1940 and earlier. The discipline as a whole—and this is certainly true of American anthropology—has never been homogeneous with regard to its interests and approaches. Thus, in the last few decades a number of anthropologists have indicated their concern with issues and problems which, in many respects, parallel those of today's critics. It may be, then, that the real complaint of

more than a collection of ideologies. Nor does it mean that there are no non-ideological standards and criteria for judging whether some analyses are more useful, fruitful, or "truer" than others.

Since one of the major assumptions of this body of critics is that the issues and problems studied by anthropologists are largely, if not wholly, determined by influences from the wider society, there seems to be little or no determinative role left for the internal development of the discipline itself. It is true, of course, that anthropology, like all of the social sciences, responds to the cultural currents of the times. Yet the discipline also possesses a body of intellectual traditions which has, to some degree, a historical development of its own. Thus, when an anthropologist selects a particular problem for investigation, we cannot know with certainty whether he is responding unconsciously to ideological pressures, whether he is reacting to the intellectual traditions and historically given problems of his discipline, or whether we are dealing with some combination of both.

Finally, let us be as clear as we can about the source of our unease with regard to the thesis we have been discussing. When critics charge anthropologists with neglect of significant issues, problems, and variables, they are referring to issues, problems, and variables which they, the critics, consider significant. In short, they have ideological positions about the importance or relevance of these items. Now, with reference to the selection of issues and problems for study and analysis, the influence of ideology is virtually inescapable. As far as variables are concerned, however, whether these are important or relevant to the understanding of a particular problem is not a matter that can be decided on ideological grounds alone. The significance of such variables can, in principle, be decided on logical and empirical grounds. Even with regard to issues and problems, it is important to remember that they too may "rise above" ideology. Certainly there are many issues and problems which would be considered significant by anthropological ideologues of varied coloration. In these cases, significance might be determined by the perception that the particular issues and problems need study because knowledge about them may further our understanding of cultural institutions, how they work, persist, or are subject to change.

Kathleen Gough, certainly one of the most articulate spokesmen among those who charge anthropology with a degree of social irresponsibility, has herself indicated that "the debate need not be primarily ideological . . . but could become at least partly empirical." [9] How much of the decision about

---

these critics is that the changes have not been widespread enough, that they are too often slow in coming, and that they do not reflect a proper degree of political commitment.

[9] Kathleen Gough, "Replies," *Current Anthropology* 9 (1968): 429. Elsewhere in a critique of the objectivity and ethical neutrality stance of anthropology, Gough writes: "Moreover, values do enter anthropological research at many points, whether or not this is recognized. They enter into the selection of problems, the choice of variables, and thus the interpretation of data" ("World Revolution and the Science of Man," in *The Dissenting Academy,* ed. Theodore Roszak [New York: Pantheon, 1968], p. 149). That values and biases are inevitably implicated in the "context of discovery" is, as we have already noted, beyond dispute. Nor can one quarrel with the claim that they may also intrude themselves into the interpretation and explanation of data. The crucial question, however, is whether we can detect in such interpretations the difference between "fact" and "value" masquerading as fact. For only then can we hope to correct for distorted and biased interpretations.

significance, cruciality, etc. of the issues, problems, and variables is to be left to ideology and how much should be decided on other grounds is not clear. In the final analysis, however, if we wish to develop a science of culture which can be applied to social problems (a view and a commitment with which, we are certain, Gough would be in complete accord), then commitment is not enough. Anatol Rapoport's comments about C. Wright Mills are pertinent in this connection:

> Much as I applaud Mills' insistence that imagination and commitment ought to be recognized as indispensable components of the sociologist's [anthropologist's] toolbox, I cannot minimize the importance of other tools whose very use is incomprehensible except to a specialist. The acquisition of relevant knowledge is not only a matter of being attuned, motivated, sensitive, and emancipated, it is also a matter of being sophisticated in evaluating the reliability of what one observes and deduces.

> Science, with its attitude of detachment, is the only mode of cognition we know which can make showdowns between incompatible views productive and which can reveal the degree of incompatibility between views. Hence logical analysis, extension of concepts, tests of hypotheses, and the rest cannot be avoided if we wish the clashes between serious thinkers to generate light as well as heat.[10]

This brings us back to "the source of our unease." It is the tendency of the critics to cast their critiques often in a narrowly ideological framework. Under such circumstances, it becomes difficult if not impossible to work toward a logical and empirical resolution of the issues. If we followed their lead, then, what passes for anthropological knowledge would be nothing more than a pack of ideologies from which one might pick and choose according to one's aesthetic tastes, political beliefs, or other value biases. To any one interested in a science of culture (or indeed in the creation and dissemination of any

---

Although the task of separating "fact" from "values" may indeed be difficult, it is not, we believe, impossible. For as Gough herself points out: "I suggest that an anthropologist who is explicit about his own values is likely to frame his problems more sharply and to see more clearly the lines between values and data more than one who has not examined his values" "World Revolution," p. 149).

To return to a point already discussed in Chapter 1, we believe that the mistake made by Gough and many of the other critics as well is that they have tried to locate objectivity where it has never existed—namely, in the minds of individual anthropologists. We agree that all anthropologists, like all people, are biased. If anthropology is to claim any objectivity whatsoever, then, that objectivity can only emerge from the collective work of anthropologists—involving the interplay of many different biases—over time. Or, as Charles Frankel has observed: "There are two principal reasons why scientific ideas are objective, and neither has anything to do with the personal merits or social status of individual scientists. The first is that these ideas are the products of a co-operative process in which the individual has to submit his results to the test of public observations which others can perform. The second is that these ideas are the results of a process in which no ideas or assumptions are regarded as sacrosanct, and all inherited ideas are subject to the continuing correction of experience" (*The Case for Modern Man* [New York: Harper, 1955], pp. 138–39).

[10] Quoted in Eugene J. Meehan, *Contemporary Political Thought: A Critical Study* (Homewood, Ill.: Dorsey, 1967), p. 93.

✓ reliable knowledge) this kind of epistemological relativism is unthinkable. For if political predilections, aesthetic leanings, and value biases were to determine the truth or falsity of anthropological analysis and explanation—or what constitutes "good" or "bad" anthropology—the potential of anthropological knowledge for contributing either to explanation or application would be seriously undermined.

Lee Rainwater, a sociologist dealing with the aims and tasks of sociology, has suggested that the ultimate value of the sociologist's contribution depends upon his freedom from "co-optation" of any kind and from any ideological quarter. We believe his views are pertinent to the tasks of all social scientists:

> Sociology is extremely fashionable these days—with undergraduates, with the mass media, and with government. But, its popularity comes not so much from an understanding of what sociological knowledge has to offer, as from the belief that other branches of knowledge have failed to "solve" our problems and because sociology talks about some of the most obvious ones (race, poverty, alienation, bureaucracy, etc.) it has the solution. The autonomy of the sociologist to pursue knowledge and develop theory will be seriously threatened by this popularity—not only by the threat of co-optation by the powers that be, but also by the threat of ideological co-optation in the service of the powers against the powers that be. Sociological knowledge is potentially extremely embarrassing to all of these forces since it seldom neatly confirms the preferred world view of any of the contenders in the political process. Sociology is in a position today to make crucial contributions to changing society, but it is in that position only by virtue of several decades of empirical and theoretical work which was relatively insulated from *direct* political interference by the society at large or on the campus. Now the pressures to interfere are strong. And the more accurate sociological depiction becomes, the stronger these forces will be. Sociologists will need a strong sense of solidarity no matter how varied their own individual pursuits of sociological knowledge. If they are to weather these pressures, they will need a deep and sensitive commitment to each other's freedom of responsible inquiry, and an insistent resistance to distortion of their findings by those who perceive themselves to be adversely affected by "sociological trust." [11]

Future Trends

Convergence with the Other Social Sciences

Since the end of World War II the pace of global acculturation and change has accelerated at an astonishing rate. Many primitive or preliterate societies have completely disappeared as semi-independent entities through absorption into larger units; the old empires have been largely liquidated and dozens of new nations have come into existence; above all, the growing inter-

---

[11] Lee Rainwater, "The Sociologist as Naturalist," in *Sociological Self-Images: A Collective Portrait*, ed. I. L. Horowitz (Beverly Hills, Cal.: Sage, 1969), p. 100.

dependence of systems has tended to redefine economic and cultural boundaries. In short, the cultures of the world appear to be converging toward a single cultural type—or at most a few cultural types—with an industrial technology at their base. Concomitantly, and despite several noteworthy and dramatic political movements of a nationalist nature to the contrary, there is an increasing trend toward the interdependence of social, political, and economic units. Yet much of the empirical data as well as the basic concepts and theories of anthropology have been derived from the study of primitive and relatively autonomous social units. The disappearance and/or transformation of these units has obvious and important implications for the future of anthropology.

How have anthropologists reacted to the drastic contraction of their "laboratory"? They seem to be responding in three fairly distinct ways. One group feels the hallmark of anthropology to be its methodology of field work with participant observation. Since this methodology is especially adapted to the study of small-scale units, these anthropologists would limit the field to research among those social aggregates that lend themselves to study through participant observation. Thus, they continue to seek out the few remaining societies which even now are relatively isolated and autonomous, like those in the interior of New Guinea and parts of South America. When they turn from these more conventional entities to the study of such "complex" units as preindustrial and industrial agglomerations, they continue to focus on small-scale units: a village, an urban ward, a ghetto neighborhood, a factory work group, a hospital, etc.

Another group of anthropologists has argued against the value and the feasibility of focusing on the small-scale situation, especially in a complex society. To do so, they assert, may mean to miss the most significant relationships and structures that define and govern that society. For such relationships and structures often transcend a specific locale and do not lend themselves easily to the methodology of traditional anthropological field work. This latter group of anthropologists has pointed out that the very act of limiting the problems of anthropology to those that can be handled by the traditional methods of field work constricts the discipline unnecessarily. Such a procedure, they add, would tend to leave most of the significant and interesting issues to the other social scientists. The most fruitful feature of the anthropological method, they maintain, is not the technique of participant observation but, rather, its comparative and holistic approach. Thus, they want anthropology to move beyond the study of villages and neighborhoods to the holistic analysis of large-scale systems like nation-states.

There is, however, a wing of this group of critics which takes issue with the recommendation for holistic studies of large-scale systems. While they agree that anthropologists can no longer assume that most small-scale social units are autonomous, they believe it is unrealistic and impracticable to attempt holistic analyses of large-scale contemporary social units like the nation-state. They point out that while it is one thing to attempt a holistic study of the Zuni or even the Nuer, it is quite another to attempt to deal holistically with modern China or India, or even the eastern seaboard of the United States. They have sought, therefore, to define units of research and analysis that lie somewhere between the local village and the nation-state—

units and entities such as networks, quasi groups, hinge groups, and brokers. Entities like these, it is asserted, may be handled by most of the traditional anthropological techniques, while at the same time they may serve to illuminate the links among the local, regional, and national levels of a society.

There is a third group of anthropologists which has apparently not felt itself hampered either by the virtual disappearance of the primitive world or by the increasing interdependence of all parts of the globe. Some of this group have retreated entirely from the empirical world and taken refuge in the elaboration of new and ornate methodologies. Others, like Lévi-Strauss, seem to be trying to probe the structure of the human mind itself. For them the nature of the cultural context in which mind operates and manifests itself is not particularly important.

While the historical developments of recent years have forced anthropology to temper its holistic approach and to modify its field-work practices, the discipline has not abandoned its emphasis on comparison. And it seems quite clear to us that despite the indisputably important intellectual gains that have resulted from holism and field work, anthropology's most lasting and significant contributions to social science have come from its comparative method and findings.

There was a time when the combination of holism, extended periods of field work, and comparison made anthropology unique among the social sciences. But this is no longer true. As anthropologists have become increasingly involved in the study of more complex systems, they have found themselves turning more and more to the use of statistical and other quantitative techniques long utilized by economists, sociologists, and psychologists in their work in Western society. At the same time that anthropologists have been forced to modify their holism and their reliance on direct observation, the other social sciences have tended to move in the opposite direction: they have become more holistic, more comparative, and more and more dependent upon the techniques of direct observation in the field. This obvious and growing convergence of method reflects in turn a growing interest in a similar set of issues and problems. The transformation of the primitive world into the underdeveloped or developing world has provided a common arena of research for large numbers of social scientists. And problems of "development" and "underdevelopment" have become the concern of *all* the social sciences.

As a result of these changes, all of the social sciences are becoming less distinctive and specialized in their methodologies, more interdependent in research, analysis, and application as they move collectively toward a new kind of holism. We do not mean to imply that the individual identities of the disciplines will continue to fade until ultimately they have become faceless particles in one grand, all-encompassing *science of man*. The growing complexity of our world will certainly demand a continuing division of labor among the social sciences. Thus, problems and even methodologies distinctive of each of the various disciplines will remain. However, the inevitable pressures and the need to focus on the same kinds of research problems must be accompanied by a cross-fertilization of methodologies: the facts of a shrinking world, of a decline in cultural variety and in the automomy of social units must impel all of the social sciences to lean upon each other, to make use of the insights, techniques, and data of the others as the best way of dealing with issues and problems that are of common concern to all disciplines—indeed, to all mankind.

Another contemporary development in anthropology is the greater emphasis placed on social criticism and on the "social-engineering" or applied aspects of the discipline. Pressures for the increasing involvement of the social sciences in programs of social change appear to come from two principal sources. First, the industrialized as well as the "postindustrial" societies require increasing numbers of all kinds of technicians, including social scientists. And second, the trend toward industrialization in the developing areas as well as the movement of the already industrialized areas into the electronic era produces social dislocation and a host of social problems. Hence, there is a growing demand for the social sciences to interpret and to help frame programs for the alleviation—or, ideally, for the elimination—of the most distressing consequences of the massive social changes now taking place. For example, social scientists might be called upon to suggest ways of dealing with some of the unhappy effects of large-scale male migration from rural to urban centers in the industrializing areas. But often the anthropologist is urged not only to analyze a social problem and make recommendations for its resolution, but to play an active role, political and otherwise, in correcting the conditions which are said to have created the problem. All of this exhortation to greater involvement, concern, and, ultimately, activist participation in social change may be summed up by the growing demand in recent times for greater "relevance."

Deciding when a question or problem is "relevant," as we have learned in recent years, is not nearly as simple as it may seem. It is impossible to conceive of an issue, idea, phenomenon, or "social fact" that is without relevance to *something*. The crucial matter, however, is what the issue we are talking about is relevant *to*. Or, as Robert Merton, dealing with the matter from a slightly different perspective, points out, framing a significant and relevant question may often be the most difficult and creative part of scientific inquiry. Merton notes that Darwin, in reflecting on

> the course of his inquiries into the origin of species, . . . wrote: ". . . you would be surprised at the number of years it took me to see clearly what some of the problems were which had to be solved. . . . Looking back I think it was more difficult to see what the problems were than to solve them as far as I have succeeded in doing, and this seems to me rather curious." [12]

Merton adds:

---

[12] Robert K. Merton, "Notes on Problem-Finding in Sociology," in *Sociology Today*, ed. Robert K. Merton, Leonard Broom, and Leonard S. Cottrell, Jr. (New York: Basic Books, 1959), p. ix.

What Darwin thought strange, if not singular, present-day scientists take as thoroughly familiar and typical. As the biologist Agnes Arber says, the current difficulty in most scientific work lies in framing the questions rather than in finding the answers.[13]

Perhaps a question or problem might be said to be "relevant" when it calls forth answers that confirm, illuminate, or even significantly modify the ongoing theoretical traditions of a discipline. Merton apparently had such a notion of relevance in mind when he wrote that

> in science, the questions that matter are of a particular kind. They are questions so formulated that the answers to them will confirm, amplify, or variously revise some part of what is currently taken as knowledge in the field. In short, although every problem in a science involves a question, or series of questions, not every question qualifies as a scientific problem.[14]

But many of those who are currently urging anthropology toward a "new relevance" do not seem to have this particular concept of relevance in mind. What they appear to be advocating is that anthropology become more relevant by involving itself directly and intensively with contemporary social issues and problems—and, beyond this, that anthropologists should utilize their special knowledge to plan an active role in promoting social change in order to create a "better world."

On the face of it, one cannot quarrel with the demand for this kind of relevance. A social science which has little or nothing significant to say about contemporary social issues is not much of a social science. Also, there is no logical reason why the "pure" and "applied" aspects of a discipline must be separate—although, in actual fact, they often are. Ideally, these two aspects of the scientific endeavor should continually complement and revitalize each other. In short, the scientist, no less than the political philosopher, must be alert to the creative advantages that may result from wedding theory to practice.

However, a discipline which comes to devote the major portion of its energies to the applied and the immediate may be engaging in an ephemeral or spurious kind of relevance. Its practitioners may find that the "practical" solutions they offer are generally piecemeal, fleeting, and have little or no long-term "relevance" to the growth of theory and explanation in the discipline. They may find as well—as have many contemporary physicists who are distressed about the constricting and stultifying effects of an over-emphasis on applied work in their discipline—that the new concepts and fruitful ideas upon which the growth and vitality of any discipline depends seem not to be forthcoming. For to concentrate exclusively on the practical, on the applied, on the attempt to resolve current dilemmas may very well impede the development of any scientific discipline. Concern with applica-

---

[13] Ibid.
[14] Ibid., p. x.

tion alone encourages the investigator to lean most heavily on what is *already* known, to employ the techniques, the methods, and the data *already* at hand in order to cope with the special problem. It has a tendency to deflect the scientist from the free and imaginative speculation which forms the lifeblood of his discipline in its growth as a scientific enterprise. If practice and an overwhelming emphasis on the applied inevitably produced theoretical wisdom, then the field of social work would be the most theoretically sophisticated of the social sciences, and all automobile mechanics would be physicists.

Lee Rainwater, whom we have cited earlier, is one social scientist whose entire career has been involved with the more applied aspects of his discipline. He states the case for sociology. His remarks here, like those quoted above, apply with equal force to all of the social sciences:

> The relationship of sociology to social problems was at the heart of my initial interest; for many years I functioned as an applier of social science knowledge and research techniques to the concerns of highly varied clients, and more recently I have been concerned to develop knowledge into sociologically informed programs for undoing the damage of racial oppression and economic exploitation of the poor. Even so, I value the wide range of styles of work in the field—from the men who do not want to move out of the ivory tower to those who are willing to work actively for change by getting their hands dirty in political movements and bureaucratic organizations. A sociology which strives so hard for relevance and application that there is no play for pure curiosity must inevitably use up its intellectual capital; a sociology in which application is either rejected or considered "dirty work" better delegated to other professions like social work or planning runs the very real risk of losing touch with the reality its theories are supposed to encompass.[15]

The demand that anthropology become more relevant, not simply by analyzing social problems but by taking an active role in promoting some kinds of institutional changes, raises still other questions. Such activism would inevitably involve the anthropologist in making judgments about what "ought to be." We see no reason why anthropologists, like any other concerned citizens, should not make such judgments. Certainly a sophisticated understanding of social and cultural phenomena is relevant to the making of programmatic decisions. And a well-informed judgment is likely to be wiser than one dredged up out of ignorance. After all, if political and moral judgments about what "ought to be" are to be made in a responsible fashion, they should have some relationship to what is or is not possible in this world. Some "oughts" are clearly more feasible, practicable, or possible than others; and a discrimination among these possibilities is certainly aided by knowledge. But—and this is the important point—it seems to us that anthropology as a corpus of knowledge does not automatically lead one to adopt any specific political or moral stance.

As Robert Nisbet notes, in referring to the Supreme Court desegregation decision of 1954, the findings of social science with respect to racism and race relations did not provide the basis for the court's decision:

---

[15] Lee Rainwater, "The Sociologist as Naturalist," p. 99.

In that landmark of American law, there were some references to sociological and psychological "knowledge" about the deleterious effects of segregated schooling. But as Morroe Berger pointed out in a bold and brilliant article on the decision, such references were, first, dubious on strictly scientific grounds and, second, expendable. All that was really required for that great and long-overdue decision was the combination of moral percept and legal precedent that the decision in its best sections exemplified. Putting the matter differently, sociology does indeed study race relations and yields us much knowledge about the subject; *but* that decision not only *was* made fundamentally on the nonsociological grounds of legal precedent and ethical consideration, but could scarcely have been improved had all the resources of an *exact science* of race relations been available.[16]

Nisbet then goes on to emphasize, as we have done, that sociological (read "anthropological") knowledge is not *totally* irrelevant to the making of moral-political decisions:

Does this mean, then, that *no* relation exists between sociological knowledge and social planning? Of course not. It means only that we have no more right to expect sociology to be the immediate platform of social policy or social action than we have to expect physiology to be a sole and immediate platform for measures in public health. But I would be unhappy under any public health officer who had never studied physiology.[17]

Sometimes, anthropologists appear to believe that it is possible to derive particular moral judgments from the findings of the discipline. Thus, many anthropologists seem to have thought that the facts of cultural relativity and the variations in values from culture to culture could lead to the formulation of more-or-less precise ethical statements about what *ought* to be. Paul Schmidt has argued, however, that such optimism is unwarranted:

√ The thesis of cultural relativism is a factual hypothesis about values, not itself a value judgment. This distinction is an instance of a general distinction made in value theory between what is and what ought to be, or between factual judgments and value judgments. . . . As a descriptive hypothesis the thesis [of cultural relativism] could be and was held by the Nazis who believed it right to kill Jews and by Americans who believed it wrong. It could be held consistently by Christian, Mohammedan, Buddhist, and atheistic thinkers, each maintaining value judgments incompatible with those held by the others. Thus knowledge of and belief in cultural relativism are compatible with diverse value theories and do not . . . imply specific value judgments.[18]

The above point may be made in a slightly different way. When the American Anthropological Association declares that, according to the evi-

---

[16] Robert A. Nisbet, "Sociology as an Idea System," in Horowitz (ed.), *Sociological Self-Images*, op. cit., p. 199.

[17] Ibid.

[18] Paul Schmidt, "Some Criticisms of Cultural Relativism," in *Theory in Anthropology*, ed. R. A. Manners and D. Kaplan (Chicago: Aldine, 1968), pp. 171–72.

dence available, there appear to be no significant differences among the racial populations of the world with regard to intelligence, potential, etc., it is making a very different kind of statement from one in which it declares itself against war. In the first case the association is telling us something about the empirical state of the world (what "is"), while in the second case it is telling us something about its political, moral, and humanistic convictions (what "ought to be"). It is important to keep in mind the difference between these two kinds of declarations. For even if it *were* possible to demonstrate significant differences among racial populations of the world, most anthropologists could still maintain, on purely humanistic grounds, that they deplored all forms of racial discrimination and exploitation.

We are not suggesting that anthropolgists ought to refrain from engaging their intellectual and activist energies in practical causes. Nor do we believe that anthropologists, individually or collectively, ought not to take political and moral stands. But it does seem indisputable that the anthropologist, qua anthropologist, is no better qualified to make *value judgments* than any other well-informed citizen (even if he is better qualified to make *knowledgeable statements* about the present state of the evidence concerning, e.g., racial differences).

It seems clear, then, that the trend in the immediate future is for anthropology and the other social sciences to become more applied and activist-oriented. But we should not be surprised to find that individual anthropologists involved in these endeavors derive very different political and moral lessons and implications from the empirical findings of their discipline. For, as we have tried to emphasize, the findings of anthropology seem to be compatible with a broad range of political and moral positions.

Finally, in an effort to caution all altrustically minded and humanitarian anthropologists that they ought not to allow their good intentions and ebullience to distort their collective mission as students of the "science of culture," we close with the following kindly and perceptive admonition from Merton:

> Because war and exploitation and poverty and racial discrimination and psychological insecurity plague modern societies, social science must justify itself by providing solutions for all of these problems. Yet social scientists may be no better equipped to solve these urgent problems today than were physicians, such as Harvey or Sydenham, to identify, study, and cure coronary thrombosis in 1655. . . . The urgency or immensity of a practical social problem does not insure its immediate solution. At any given moment, men of science are close to the solutions of some problems and remote from others. It must be remembered that necessity is only the mother of invention; socially accumulated knowledge is its father. Unless the two are brought together, necessity remains infertile. She may of course conceive at some future time when she is properly mated. But the mate requires time (and sustenance) if he is to attain the size and vigor needed to meet the demands that will be made upon him.[19]

---

[19] Robert K. Merton, "On Sociological Theories of the Middle Range," in *On Theoretical Sociology* (New York: Free Press Paperback, 1967) pp. 49–50.

Before we add our own "amen" we would like to suggest a cautionary codicil. Unless Merton's "knowledge" be taken to include knowledge of strategy and tactics—the *how* as well as the *why*; and unless this kind of knowledge is wedded also to adequate power and capabilities, necessity—no matter how dire—and knowledge—no matter how keen, detailed and insightful—will not suffice to produce the alterations demanded by conscience, morality, and the most sophisticated social science analysis.